Horse and Pony Stories for Girls

Horse and Pony Stories for Girls

ILLUSTRATED BY F. D. PHILLIPS

HAMLYN
LONDON . NEW YORK . SYDNEY . TORONTO

The publishers wish to express their thanks to I. P. C. Magazines Ltd., for permission to include *Racing Rivals* and *The Ghost Horse of Hidden Valley* (previously entitled *Judy of Whispering Valley*) in this collection.

First published 1971
Third impression 1973
Published by
THE HAMLYN PUBLISHING GROUP LIMITED
LONDON . NEW YORK . SYDNEY . TORONTO
Hamlyn House, Feltham, Middlesex, England

ISBN 0 601 07454 8
Printed in Czechoslovakia by Státní tiskárna, Prague
51063/3

Contents

List of Illustrations

The Battle for Blandy Common

by Robert Bateman

Jill and I swung our ponies off the footpath and began a gentle canter across the common towards the river. It was one of those days when life seems so perfect you're almost scared of it because you know it can't last.

It didn't last. Jill was riding slightly in front, and she pulled old Codger to a halt so hard that he nearly threw her.

'Hey!' I said. 'Careful!' I looked at her in astonishment. 'You'll hurt the old chap.'

Then I saw the reason, just in time to drag my own pony, little Patsy, round to the left. Barbed wire caught my ankle, tearing my socks, and then ripped into Patsy's hind quarter as she turned.

It hurt. The pain was so fierce that I thought I was going to faint. Underneath me, poor little Patsy was bucking and whinnying.

I slid off her back. The vicious barbs had dug deep into her. I'd escaped with no more than a nasty scratching, but Patsy was going to need stitches.

Jill took in the situation at a glance. 'Stay here!' she said. 'Keep Patsy quiet – don't let her move about. I'll go and 'phone for the vet.' She was off like a shot, galloping back towards the footpath.

I tied my sock round the wound on my ankle. Then I persuaded Patsy to lie down. She never did need very much persuading to do that even at the best of times, let alone now.

I don't think I've ever been more angry in my life than I was at that moment. Poor old Patsy lay very quietly, but every now and again her hind quarter twitched with the pain of the wound. My own ankle throbbed, and I began to wonder whether the barbs of the wire were clean, or whether we'd both have septic sores.

I glared at the wooden stakes driven into the ground, and the strands of gleaming wire that ran between them.

I'd been coming on to Blandy Common ever since I was big enough to walk, and I'd been riding on it for six years – from the time when Patsy was given to me for my seventh birthday. There'd never been any barbed wire, and everybody had been allowed to go where they pleased.

I stroked poor old Patsy's nose. Her eyes opened and looked at me in a sad, puzzled way. I tried to explain to her what had happened, but though after a while a pony learns lots of the easier kinds of human words, like Whoa, Gee-up, Quiet, and Good Old Girl, there's no way of making it understand what barbed wire means – or Rights of Way, and Common Land, and Cruel Vicious Brutes.

I gave it up, and sat waiting beside Patsy for Jill to come back with the vet.

It was a long wait. The vet lived at Brampton, more than six miles away, and even though at this time of the afternoon there was a good chance he'd be at home, his old square saloon car was no fast mover. I leaned against Patsy's big shoulder, and dozed off.

Jill shook me awake. 'We're here!' she said. 'Mr Connolly's all ready to stitch up Patsy's hind quarter.'

I sat up. 'Thanks for coming, Mr Connolly! Is Patsy going to be all right?'

The vet was busy with needle and thread. Patsy lay quite still, making no fuss. She knew the feel of Mr Connolly's

Barbed wire ripped into Patsy's hind quarter as she turned.

hands from the time she'd had some weird disease and Mr Connolly had come over every day for a week and nursed her out of trouble.

'Och, she'll be right as rain come Sunday!' Mr Connolly put away his needle, and slapped Patsy gently on the uninjured side of her stern. 'Up you get, girl! Time to go home.'

Home was one of the words Patsy knew. Her ears pricked up, and she scrambled to her feet.

'She'll be lame, mind you, until those stitches heal the wound. Don't ride her for a week, but take her for a walk every day. Make her keep on her feet as much as you can. If she thinks she can get away with it, she'll keep on being an invalid.' He chuckled. 'I know your Patsy. She's a born malingerer!'

'What's a malingerer?' asked Jill.

'Somebody what doesn't want to get well because it's more convenient to stay ill. Like I'd be if I had a job digging ditches. I'd be after dodging it whenever I could.' He jerked a thumb at Patsy. 'Your pony's got the same idea.'

I had to admit he was right. If Patsy could find an excuse to be lazy, she'd jump at it. 'Mr Connolly,' I said, 'what can we do about this barbed wire?'

He stared at it, frowning. 'Who put it up?'

'I don't know. It wasn't here yesterday. And anyway, this is a common, not private land. Surely nobody's got a right to put up fences.'

He looked puzzled. 'That's right enough – if it *is* a common.'

'But it's *called* Blandy Common!'

'Och, that's true enough. But in this world, things ain't always what they seem. Over at Brampton there's a big hospital. You must know it? Aye, I thought you would. Well, it's called the Brampton Free Hospital, but when I went there as a boy to have my appendix out, my old dad got a bill as long as your arm. Free! Huh! So don't put too much faith in the name Blandy Common.' He looked down at my ankle. 'Human injuries are not my job – but you'd be wise to call in at the doctor's on your way home, and get him to put a dressing on those scratches. Barbed wire makes a nasty mess.'

He walked with us back to the road. Patsy hobbled badly, but didn't seem to be in any pain, and the stitches held firm.

'How can I find out about the Common?' I asked Mr Connolly.

He scratched his head. 'Well, I reckon it's really a job for a lawyer. But why not ask Sergeant Moult down at the police station? He's sure to know something about it.' He climbed into his battered old car. 'Call me if Patsy shows any signs of pain. But you're lucky – I don't reckon it's done her much harm.'

The last words were almost drowned in a frightful rattling noise from the engine. The whole car vibrated, and then crawled off down the road, leaving a thick cloud of oily blue smoke.

I took Mr Connolly's advice, and called in at the doctor's surgery while we were in the village. When I told him about the barbed wire he was as puzzled as the rest of us.

Then I walked Patsy home. Jill came too, because her pony lived in our stable. 'Stop and have some tea,' I said. 'Mum won't mind.'

'I'd love to. But are you sure?'

'Extra sure. And I want to talk to you about the barbed wire. We've got to do something. The Common is the only place for riding anywhere near here, and if we lose it, then what happens to our ponies?'

Jill's eyes opened very wide and round. 'But we *can't* lose the Common!' she burst out. 'It's ours! It always has been. It belongs to everybody in the village.'

'Exactly. At least that's what I've always believed. But

somebody seems to have other ideas. So let's have a quick tea and then go down to see Sergeant Moult.'

I nipped upstairs, quickly changed my socks and washed, and warned Jill not to tell Mum what had happened. Mum's a bit of a fusspot about bangs and scratches, and I could see that if the subject came up, instead of getting down to the police station we'd spend the next hour in a merry round of home medicine, with my poor old ankle getting doused in iodine and cold compresses.

When we reached the police station, we found Sergeant Moult busy in the garden digging up potatoes. He was a big, red-faced man, a bit fierce at times, but wonderfully good when there was any kind of trouble – not that trouble happened often in Blandy. Blandy's the kind of village where a cat stuck up a tree is the biggest news in a month.

'Hello!' he greeted us. 'Have you come for the cuttings of chrysanthemums I promised your mother?'

I shook my head. 'It's about the Common. Somebody's put barbed wire across it. We went right into it this afternoon on our ponies, and poor Patsy got a nasty gash.'

His eyebrows shot up. 'Barbed wire? Now that's a bit drastic, even for Mr Molyneux!'

'Mr Molyneux? Who's he?'

'The new man who's moving into The Grange.'

'But surely he has no right to put up wire on the Common?'

'Oh, that's not really a Common. All that land belongs to the Grange. It was only called the Common because old Mr Hatherley never minded who used it. This Mr Molyneux must have different ideas.' He frowned. 'Can't do anything to stop him fencing it off if he wants to. But I can stop him using barbed wire unless he puts up a warning notice. 'Tis dangerous.'

I pointed to the bulge under my sock. 'If my ankle goes septic, I'll... I'll... I'll sue him or something.'

Sergeant Moult grinned at me. 'Now don't get all upset! I'll go up and see this Mr Molyneux. I haven't met him yet, but I don't doubt he'll be reasonable. I'll tell him what's happened, and ask him to put up some ordinary wire that won't do no harm to anybody that runs into it. Either that, I'll tell him, or he's got to put up notices.'

'But what about us?' I burst out desperately. 'Where can we ride our ponies?'

He sighed. 'Ah, that's another question entirely. That's not so easy. I reckon there's precious little land around here where nobody minds you riding ponies.' He scratched his head. 'We'll have to think about that problem when we come to it, like.' He picked up his jacket from its resting place on top of a spade driven into the earth. 'Meantime, I'll go up and see this Mr Molyneux. He's bound to be there, because builders is in making alterations.' He grinned. 'I shan't be long. If you want to wait, there's a long row of potatoes there that wants lifting. Fair crying out for it, they are.'

I picked up the fork, and drove it into the ground beside the next potato plant.

We had the whole row up, and the potatoes in the barrow, by the time he came back. He leaned his bike against the gate, and chuckled. 'I came back the long way round. Thought I'd give you a chance to get that little job finished for me.'

I wiped the perspiration off my forehead. 'You and your old potatoes! I hope you've done as much for us.'

The Sergeant came inside the gate. 'Well, now, I have and I haven't. This Mr Molyneux's a funny kind of chap. I don't know quite what to make of him. First he seemed all friendly like – until I told him what I'd come for. Then his face went as hard as nails. No, he said, he was sorry but that land was his, and nobody was going to use it. He wasn't going to have picnic parties come out from Brampton and leave tins and paper and polythene bags and things all over the place.'

'But Brampton people never come out here to Blandy! I've never seen any picnic people on the Common.'

'That's what I told him, but it didn't make no difference. Seems his mind's made up. All I could get him to do was say he'd put up notices about that barbed wire.'

I looked at him glumly. 'Is there nothing else we can do?'

'I reckon not. You see, if that land had been open to the public for a long time, then a lawyer could make a case out of it.'

'How d'you mean?'

'Well, there's some kind of a law which gives you a Right of Way if you've used it for long enough, even though the land is private. But old Mr Hatherley didn't take over the Grange until about twelve years ago, and before that the land was all fenced off. I don't know much about that law, but I do know twelve years isn't enough.'

'Oh, crumbs!' said Jill. 'I can see us ending up riding our ponies round and round the village duckpond! There's nowhere else.'

'Couldn't you use the roads?' suggested the Sergeant. 'If your're careful, and keep well in to the side, it shouldn't get you in no trouble with cars.'

'You can't teach old ponies to use the roads,' I said. 'Patsy gets scared even to cross a road if there's a car in sight.'

Gloomily we walked back through the village. It was a hot evening, so we called in at Jill's house for a drink. As we passed the entrance to The Grange, next door, Jill made a face. 'I don't think I'm going to like having that man as a neighbour,' she said.

'Perhaps he won't stay long,' I said hopefully.

'Huh! Someone who isn't planning to stay in a house hardly goes to all the trouble he's taking. He's having a whacking great tower built on one end of it.'

'A tower? But why, what would he do that for?'

'Oh, he's supposed to be an astronomer. The tower's for his telescopes and things.'

We went up to Jill's bedroom. From the window we stared out at the Grange, and the tall scaffolding which stuck up at the nearest end of the building. 'That's his beastly tower!' Jill muttered angrily. 'I know exactly what's going to happen. Once that wretched thing is up, I'll get no more sun in my bedroom in the mornings. There's going to be a whacking great tall shadow right across our house and garden.'

I watched workmen carrying a load of bricks on a wheelbarrow.

And then something clicked in my brain. 'Wait here!' I said.

'Where are you going?' asked Jill, startled.

'I shan't be long.'

'Yes, but where...?'

'I'm going to pay a call on Mr Molyneux!'

Her eyes nearly started out of her head, but even if she'd tried to stop me she'd have had no luck. I had a bee in my bonnet. 'Where d'you keep your encyclopedia?' I demanded.

'My what? Oh, I know what you mean. Dad's got an old one on the bottom shelf of the big bookcase in the hall.'

'Thanks.' I raced downstairs, took out the volume I wanted, and read three paragraphs hurriedly. Then I marched out of the house, down the drive, and into the gates of the Grange.

Fifteen minutes later I was back again. My face must have been crimson with triumph, for Jill gave a huge grin as I burst into her room. 'What have you been up to?' she exclaimed.

'Come over to the window, and you'll see.'

We stood there, side by side. Nothing seemed to be happening. 'Well?' she demanded impatiently, 'I don't see anything.'

'You will,' I said, but my confidence was beginning to ebb away. Maybe Mr Molyneux was smarter than I'd thought.

But then the builders tipped their bricks out of the barrow, and walked away from the scaffolding, down the garden towards the Common.

'I still don't understand,' said Jill.

'You will,' I repeated. I hadn't any doubts now, and it was fun to watch Jill's curiosity bubble over.

It was only a few minutes before the men returned. On the barrow, rolled round its posts, was the barbed wire.

'Gosh!' shouted Jill, her eyes shining. 'They've taken the fence down.' She looked at me in amazement. '*You* did that, didn't you? But... but *how?*'

'Simple,' I said. It's not often one gets a chance to swank a bit. I made the most of it. I struck a stern, grown-up attitude. 'Knowledge of the law, that's all.'

'What law?'

'English law. Just an old thing called Ancient Lights.'

'Ancient *what?*'

'Ancient Lights! If you've had sun, and light, and air reaching your house for more than twenty years, nobody has a right to block it off. If they build something that *does* block it off, you can get the court to make them pull it down again.'

'Well?' She still didn't understand.

'I went to see Mr Molyneux. I told him what the tower was going to do, and warned him what a court would say about it. That got him worried, because he's already spent hundreds of pounds on the tower. So then I said maybe you'd forgive him on one condition.'

Jill looked out of the window at the men with the barrow-load of barbed wire. 'And that was the condition? Crumbs, you're brilliant!'

They say pride comes before a fall, and so it was only justice that I fell down the stairs, as I stalked proudly out of the house.

But as soon as Patsy had recovered and the vet had passed

her as fit again, we were riding on Blandy Common once more.

And just to show that things sometimes *do* turn out all right in this crazy world, we met Mr Molyneux there, leading his daughter on a new pony. She became our best friend.

And even Mr Molyneux himself turned out to be not such a bad old stick, once we got to know him properly. From that tower of his you can see every star in the sky.

Leave It to Lady

by David Gammon

'*Help!*'

The cry drifted faintly to Sandra above the pounding of the pony's flying hoofs, and seemed to come from the dark wood ahead of her. She reined the pony to an easy stop, and, relaxed in the saddle, scanned the line of trees and the heather-covered slopes with curious eyes. Dartmoor lay still and sombre beneath the overcast sky.

A rabbit hopped from the cover of a bramble patch, saw her, and bolted back inside. Stonechats twittered softly in the gorse, while high above her a buzzard circled on wide, tireless wings. Nowhere was there any sign of another human being. From within the gloom of the oak wood came a harsh croak. Sandra smiled faintly. 'A raven! Was that what I heard, Lady?'

The way the mare set her ears back showed she knew she was being spoken to. A Dartmoor pony of fourteen hands, she was a graceful, sturdy bay, rich brown with black points, and blessed with an effortless action that made her a delight to ride. Although the pony actually belonged to her Aunt Kay, Sandra loved every proud inch of her, and the mare knew it. She responded to the question with a snort that seemed to say, 'Never mind – let's get on!'

'All right!' Sandra laughed. 'I was only asking.' A gentle squeeze with her legs set the eager animal into motion. Sandra often came to stay with her aunt and knew this part of the moor quite well. They followed the edge of the wood, and as they swung round the end of the copse she was confronted by the very last thing she had expected to see. A maroon and grey saloon car was sitting at an awkward angle on an overgrown cart track that ran across the bottom of a hollow. A tiny stream wandered nearby between clumps of blazing yellow gorse.

The car was empty, and the door on the far side hung open. There was nobody in sight anywhere. Her curiosity aroused, Sandra rode the pony down the slope and round the car to the other side. And then she saw the man.

He lay on his back on the grass alongside the open door, his eyes closed and blood spreading across his face from a gash high on his temple. Dead? It was impossible to tell, but Sandra knew it was her duty to find out. She swung down out of the saddle, stepped close and bent to touch the man's shoulder with a cautious hand. 'Hello,' she said.

The man groaned. She went quickly to the stream to wet her handkerchief. As she came back she noticed that the left front wheel of the car was deep in a mud-filled pothole. She supposed it had brought the car to a stop with a jerk that had thrown the man against the windscreen. As she reached the man's side she glanced into the car. She saw nothing unusual – except that there was no key in the ignition switch.

She bathed the man's wound carefully and wiped the blood off his temple and cheek. He groaned again. 'No – not the – formula,' he muttered. 'I won't – won't!' He was silent a moment, then spoke again. 'Roy! Oh, Roy, if he dares...' His eyelids fluttered, then slowly opened to reveal eyes as blue as her own. 'Oh! Who – are – you?'

'Sandra Barlow,' she told him with a reassuring smile. 'You've had an accident.'

His eyes glazed over. 'Yes – had accident,' he mumbled.

'Was anybody with you?' she asked.

His reply was barely audible. 'Yes – I mean no – nobody. On my own.'

He looked for a moment as if he might cry. Then his eyes closed, and his face emptied of all expression. Scared he was going to slip back into unconsciousness, Sandra said, 'My aunt's home isn't far, if you can sit on my pony.'

'Can't – must stay here.'

'No, you need attention,' Sandra insisted. 'Come on.'

She helped him to his feet. He was quite bemused and only just managed to stand. Without the patient co-operation of the pony she would never have got him into the saddle. He sagged there, and, unwilling to ask Lady to carry a double load, she walked at the pony's side, with one hand grasping the man's arm. It was a slow and tiring journey.

He rallied once and said thickly, 'Haven't been on a pony for years. Where're we going?'

'To my aunt's home,' Sandra told him. 'She'll know what to do.'

And Aunt Kay certainly did. She was a strong, capable woman, whose passion for photographing wild life had taken her all over the world, and looking after a man silly enough to knock himself out seemed to her a minor problem. She thought all men rather silly, and had never married. Having finally had her fill of globe-trotting, she had bought a house on Dartmoor and settled down to write a book. When she wasn't enjoying the company of her few relatives – Sandra in particular – she was off exploring one or other of Dartmoor's many bogs, happily wading around in the cushion of springy peat and sphagnum to photograph the delicately brilliant flowering plants that grow there. Sandra thought her the most wonderful woman in the world – next to her mother, of course.

A man was lying on the grass by the open door of the car.

'There – that's that!' Aunt Kay said, coming downstairs after dressing the stranger's wound and settling him in one of her spare beds. 'He's sleeping like a babe. You know, without women to look after them, men would have become extinct long ago! We'll see how he is when he wakes up, and then decide whether to call the doctor.'

Sandra smiled. 'He's not seriously hurt, then?'

'Oh, he took quite a clout,' Aunt Kay admitted. 'What was he doing, driving along that bumpy old track?'

Sandra had wondered about that, too. 'Didn't you ask him?'

Aunt Kay shook her head. 'Never had a chance! I patched him up, then brought him round with tot of brandy. He gaped at me as though I was a Bantu witch-doctor, mumbled something that sounded like "My boy, my poor boy!" and went off into a deep sleep.'

'It's a real puzzle,' Sandra said with some relish, perching herself on a corner of the big refectory table.

'I heard him mention a formula, and somebody named Roy... I suppose Roy could be somebody who went for help after the accident,' she mused. 'That would explain why the car keys were missing.'

'Why would he take the keys? And would he go without any attempt to help his companion?' Aunt Kay countered bluntly. 'Take my word for it, there's more to this than meets the eye!'

Sandra offered no argument; she was quite intrigued by the prospect of a mystery to solve.

'If you like, I can sit in his room and read – then we'll know the minute he wakes,' Sandra suggested.

Aunt Kay chuckled. 'Don't want to miss anything, eh? At fourteen I was just like you. If you want something to do, go back to his car and collect any bits that could be stolen.'

Sandra hopped off the table; she needed no urging to do

anything that involved riding Lady, she loved it so much.

A quarter of a mile from Aunt Kay's house the lane forked, the right branch leading to the village of Widcombe, and the other going out on to the open moor. At the junction was the cottage where the Cleves lived. When Sandra reached it, Granfer Cleve was tying up some sweet peas in the front garden, while young Billy, a red-headed ten-year-old, was sitting on a big stone outside the front gate extracting some teeth-jarring sounds from a mouth organ. He stopped and rose to his feet, grinning a welcome, as Sandra rode up.

'Hello, Sandra. Like my playing? That was The Sailor's Hornpipe.'

His grandfather, a white-bearded spry old man who made Sandra think of Santa Claus, looked at the boy in blank astonishment. But Sandra just smiled and said, 'I thought I recognised it.'

The boy nodded appreciatively, and to her relief put the instrument in his pocket. 'Going far?' he asked.

'Out on the moor to a car stuck in the mud.'

'Can I come?'

She saw no reason why not, and modded, knowing Billy had a shaggy little skewbald he had modestly named Conqueror. 'If you hurry up,' she told him.

Billy let out a whoop that would have turned any Red Indian green with envy and dashed off to the back of the cottage. Granfer Cleve scowled at the bloom he had been startled into breaking off, shook his head in resignation, and came to lean on the wall.

'Motor-car bogged down, eh?'

His accent was as broad as the moor itself.

'On an old cart track,' Sandra told him. 'I don't know where the man thought he was going, but he ended up with a nasty crack on the head.'

The old man nodded knowingly. 'Led off by they dratted

pixies, like as not. Proper terrors, they be. Though 'tain't as bad as the old days, mind ee. Time was when a man daren't be out nights...'

He was interrupted by another whoop from Billy, who arrived on Conqueror with a brisk clatter of hoofs. 'I'm ready!' he shouted.

Checked on the very threshold of one of his spine-chilling stories, the old man glowered at his grandson. 'Well, watch what you'm about, now,' he growled, realising he might as well go back to his sweet peas. 'There's a mist coming up.'

'We won't be long,' Sandra assured him. 'And Aunt Kay told me that if ever I get lost all I've got to do is give Lady her head and she'll bring me home.'

'Aye, her's a smart little mare, right enough,' Granfer Cleve conceded. 'Knows the moor nigh as well as me, I don't doubt.'

Sandra and Billy rode off along the lane and out on to the open moor. A flat and fairly open stretch tempted them into a race which she allowed Billy to win. When they were back to a walk, he asked her about the car. She told him as much as she knew, and explained that she was going to collect any personal belongings left lying around.

Chatting away about the odd affair, they reached the copse of oaks in no time at all. The sky was still overcast, but while the motionless air seemed a little cooler, there was no sign of the mist Granfer Cleve had warned them about. Sandra led the way down the flank of the wood, and Billy, jogging along behind, decided it was a good moment to try something new on his mouth organ. At the first discordant blast Lady put her ears back and let out a ringing neigh of protest. Sandra urged the mare into a trot, and as she rounded the corner of the wood and looked down into the hollow she caught a fleeting glimpse of a dark figure slipping away into the gloom of the trees. She reined to a halt in surprise.

Billy drew level, and stopped torturing the instrument to say 'What's up? Oh, there's the car.'

'I saw a man run into the wood,' Sandra said. 'I'm sure he came from the car. I expect he heard you playing.'

'And it scared him?'

'No doubt about it!' Sandra said, and was quite sure Billy wouldn't take it the way she meant it.

They waited by the corner of the trees for some minutes without seeing any further sign of the man. From out across the still slopes of heather came the golden bubbling cry of a curlew. To wait any longer seemed pointless, and when Billy said, 'He's hopped it,' she nodded and led the way down the slope. As far as she could see, the car was just as she had left it. But when she dismounted and walked close she saw how mistaken she was. The interior of the car had been pulled to pieces.

'Jumping jackdaws!' Billy exclaimed, peering in through a window. 'What a mess!'

The loose covers had been ripped off the seats, and the back seat had been dragged out of position. There was a jack and a pump in the space below. The floor was strewn with papers – a magazine, a motoring handbook, a couple of leaflets advertising car radios, and an opened packet of cigarettes. She also saw amongst the litter a pair of driving gloves, expensive sunglasses and a small folding camera. The shelf under the instrument panel had been swept clear, and the glove locker was open and empty.

'Mess is right!' she muttered, picking up the camera.

'That man you saw was a thief, then!' Billy said excitedly.

'I'm not so sure,' she answered thoughtfully. 'If that's it, why didn't he take the sunglasses and the camera? He must have been searching for one particular thing.'

'What, then?'

'I don't know. I'm only guessing. But I remember the injured man did say something about a formula.'

'A *formula!*' Billy echoed, suddenly excited again. 'Perhaps he's one of these nuclear scientists and the man you saw is an enemy agent – someone from the mysterious East.'

Sandra smiled, but said nothing. She put the camera on the seat, and wandered uncertainly round the car. While she didn't have a thing to go on, she had a feeling that Billy's wild theory might not be as far from the truth as one might suppose. It was becoming plain that there were aspects of this affair that were anything but ordinary.

Lying in the grass at the rear of the car was one of those iron braces used to remove wheel nuts. She didn't have to wonder what it was doing there when she saw the bent edges of the boot lid and the scratches on the paint. The man must have found the brace with the jack under the back seat, and used the screwdriver to try and force the boot open. Then, hearing them coming, he had dropped it and bolted for cover.

Billy's pony had strayed past a gorse bush to drink at the stream, and Billy, going after him, stopped abruptly to stare into the bush. He eased one hand in past the bristling green spikes and grasped something that had caught his eye. He withdrew his hand with the same care. 'Hey, look at this, Sandra!' he called.

Sandra walked over to inspect what he had found and saw with astonishment it was two car keys on a ring with a square leather tag. The tag held a small white card behind a plastic window, and she took the keys and read aloud what was printed on the card. 'Dr Chas. Lee, Bristol. The missing car keys!' she cried. 'Good work, Billy! Let's try them.'

She went quickly to the back of the car, the boy trotting eagerly beside her. The first key she tried in the boot lock didn't fit. But the other one did.

'What would they be doing in a bush?' Billy asked, puzzled.

She turned the key and said, 'Your guess is as good as mine.'

She swung up the lid. In the boot were two suitcases of different sizes. The larger one was locked, but the smaller one had a faulty catch and was held shut by a leather strap. Spurred on by increasing curiosity, she undid the strap and opened the case. To her great surprise it was packed with a complete selection of boy's clothing.

They were the sort of clothes a boy would wear on holiday, and were of good quality. By their size, she guessed the boy might be six or seven. In the bottom of the case she found an assortment of table games and a few story books. Written in a childish hand on the fly leaf of one of the books was the name *Roy Lee.*

Sandra let out a little 'Ah-ha!' of satisfaction. Things were beginning to fit together. The man she had found was evidently Dr Lee, and Roy was his young son. Yet if that was so, why had the man prevaricated, and where was the boy now? She thought about that, and the possible answers filled her with sudden doubts and fears.

'Who's Roy Lee?' Billy demanded. 'You never said there was a boy with the man.'

'No – because there wasn't,' Sandra replied.

'Well, where is he?'

'That's what I'd like to know!' she said grimly. 'I only hope Dr Lee has the answer. Come on – let's take the cases back.'

She rebuckled the strap and pulled the two cases out on to the grass, closed and locked the boot, and then the two doors of the car. She placed both cases on the roof of the car. Stopping to give Lady a caress and a few words of affection, she had an odd feeling of being watched. She swung up into the saddle and stared searchingly about her, especially along the edge of the wood. If the man was there, watching, he was well concealed. She moved Lady alongside the car, passed the smaller case to Billy and took the other herself. Billy said, 'We might have to start a search for the boy.'

She gave him a long look and said, 'I hope not.'

They rode up the slope and along the edge of the wood in silence, Sandra being quite preoccupied with the confusing aspects of this strange business. They were going up over a rise with the wood well behind them when Billy spoke again. 'Hey, Sandra – do you know something?'

'What's that?' Sandra asked, still lost in her own thoughts.

'There's a man following us!'

She was so startled she nearly dropped the suitcase. 'Are you sure?'

'Of course I'm sure,' Billy retorted. 'I looked back and saw him dodge behind a tree.'

She checked the pony and turned quickly for a look along the route they had followed. Nothing stirred. The wood was too far away for her to make out any detail. She eyed Billy dubiously – and he knew what she was thinking. 'All right,' he said, scowling in a way that reminded her of his grandfather. 'Don't, believe, then! But I *did* see him!'

She smiled and nodded, realising she had been unfair. 'It's all right, Billy,' she assured him. 'I do believe you. I was just so surprised, that's all.'

But though she looked quickly over her shoulder a number of times after that she saw nothing to confirm the boy's story.

Billy rode with her to her gate, where she took the case from him and thanked him for his help. Pausing only to loosen Lady's girth and turn her into the yard, Sandra took a case in each hand and walked into the house.

To her surprise she found Aunt Kay and Dr Lee having lunch together. Except for the neat dressing over his wound and a pallid and somewhat haunted look on his face, the man appeared to have completely recovered. Sandra put the two cases down just inside the door.

'Hello, Dr Lee,' she said. 'Glad to see you're better. I've brought your suitcase back from the car – Roy's, too.'

They turned to stare at her. For a brief moment the man looked quite relieved as his gaze rested on the two suitcases. Then the tense, harassed look came back.

'Roy's case,' he muttered. 'You didn't see...' He broke off abruptly, looking confused.

'You mean he should have been there?' Sandra demanded, and walked forward to the table. Aunt Kay looked sharply from one to the other and was wise enough not to interrupt.

'Er – no, of course not,' Dr Lee replied, making a poor attempt to appear relaxed. 'I couldn't think how you'd – got the cases. They were locked in the boot, and the keys... How did you...?

He was having great difficulty putting his thoughts into words. It came to Sandra in a flash of intuition that he was puzzled because he *knew* the keys had not been in the car. 'A friend who was with me found the keys – hanging in a gorse bush!' she explained. 'Did you put them there?'

'Hanging... No, certainly not.'

'Well Roy, then?' she persisted. 'Somebody must have put them there.'

All this was too much for Aunt Kay. 'You two might know what you're talking about, but I don't – and I'd like to! Who's Roy?'

'Dr Lee's six- or seven-year-old son,' Sandra said promptly. 'Dr Lee's name was on the key tag, and in a story book in the smaller case I saw the name Roy Lee. The clothes in the case gave me his age.'

'Yes, well that's all very clever, I'm sure,' Aunt Kay said with a trace of impatience. 'But if you're right, where's the boy now? A child can't just disappear like that, you know.'

They both looked pointedly at Dr Lee. He shrugged and said, 'I'm a research chemist, and I'm on my way to the Arco Laboratories, near Tavistock. I expect to be there about two weeks on important business, so I brought my son along and dropped him off at my sister's home in Exeter for a holiday. My wife will be joining him there in a couple of days.'

'Then why have you still got his case?' Aunt Kay wanted to know.

The man smiled faintly. 'That's the stupid part. In all the excitement of seeing my sister, I left without putting out Roy's case.'

'Just like a man!' Aunt Kay said, shaking her head. The grandfather clock in the corner gave its preliminary clunk, wheezed asthmatically, and then bonged twice. 'Goodness – two o'clock,' she went on. 'Sit down, Sandra and I'll bring you your lunch, dear.'

She rose to her feet and went out into the kitchen. Dr Lee looked at Sandra and managed another half-hearted smile. 'I'm very grateful to you for bringing the cases home – and for that matter, for bringing me home in the first place.'

'I'm glad I could help,' Sandra assured him. Then, far from convinced that the whole story had been told, she could not resist saying, 'I still don't understand how your car keys ended up in a gorse bush.'

Aunt Kay bustled back with a plate of cold ham and salad and a tall glass of milk. Sandra sat down at the table, suddenly discovering how hungry she was.

'I can't tell you how the keys got in the bush,' said Dr Lee, 'unless in my daze I threw them there.'

Sandra looked at him.'It couldn't have been the man who searched your car, because if he'd had them he wouldn't have been trying to force the boot open with your wheel brace.' She said it with a quiet directness that carried its own emphasis, and Dr Lee reacted as if he had been struck. He stared at her with his mouth hanging open. Gulping, he said, 'A man! You didn't say anything about a man searching my car!'

'Yes, don't *you* start holding things back!' Aunt Kay said significantly.

'Billy Cleve went along with me for the ride,' Sandra explained, 'and as we came in sight of the car I saw a man sneak off into the wood. The car was in a mess, and had plainly been searched. And when we finally left with the suitcases, Billy thought he saw the man following us.'

'And was he?' Dr Lee demanded tensely.

'All I can say is I didn't see him. It might have been Billy's imagination.'

'Can you describe the man you saw earlier?'

Sandra shook her head, and waited until she had swallowed. 'Not really. I got an impression he was tall, thin and dark. That's about all I can say.'

'Tall and thin. Yes...' Dr Lee muttered to himself, his gaze downcast. For long seconds he was silent; then, with a heavy sigh, he looked up. 'If you'll excuse me, I'd like to go to my room. I want to – rest.'

.You haven't finished your lunch,' Aunt Kay protested.

'I can't eat any more.' He got up, stood for a moment uncertainly, and finally crossed to the doorway and picked up the two cases. Aunt Kay told him to leave them, and said she would carry them up. He thanked her, assured her he could manage all right, and went slowly up the stairs.

Aunt Kay shook her head and sighed. 'He asked me not to call a doctor, but he doesn't seem well to me.'

Sandra went on with her lunch, her mind busily trying to make sense of this jumble of odd facts. But which ever way she put the bits together, it never came to anything that made sense. Aunt Kay sat down on her own chair, and they looked at each other.

'A real Dartmoor mystery, if you like,' Sandra said with a smile.

'He's a sorely troubled man,' Aunt Kay replied on a note of sympathy.

Sandra nodded. 'Yes, and it's quite obvious he's keeping something from us.'

'Perhaps,' Aunt Kay acknowledged. 'And if he wants us to know, he'll tell us. I don't believe in minding other people's business.'

Sandra didn't doubt that was a good policy, although, like most rules, she felt this was one of those times when it might make sense to break it. But what *didn't* make sense, she told herself crossly, was leaving Lady out in the yard still saddled. She hastily drank the last of her milk and rose, and when her aunt asked her where she was going, she said she thought she would give the pony a good grooming and clean out her stall.

As far as she was concerned, nothing that had to be done for Lady was work, and she tackled the various tasks with real pleasure. After unsaddling and rubbing down the mare, she arranged the tack along the rail for cleaning and got busy on the stall. She was in no hurry, and the time passed pleasantly enough. Once, she heard a sharp double-whistle and stopped to listen, certain it was no bird. The whistle wasn't repeated, so she decided it must have been a farmer calling his dog, and went on with her work. Some minutes later, when she started for the yard to get the wheelbarrow, the heard the drone of men's voices. She came to a standstill in the doorway as she heard a hard, threatening voice say, 'You're in no position to barter. If you want the kid back, you be at the top of the Tor two hours from now with the papers. And Lee, for the kid's sake – no tricks!'

Dr Lee was standing in the gateway into the orchard talking to another man. Even as Sandra spotted them, the man, his ultimatum delivered, turned away and was almost instantly lost amongst the trees. A tall, thin man! She realised with a thrill of excitement that it was the same man she had seen scurry into the wood. Dr Lee turned and started slowly back across the yard, his head bowed, his shoulders sagging dejectedly. Sandra could see, now, the terrible situation that confronted him, and her heart went out in sympathy. The thin man was holding Roy to ransom for the formula – whatever it was. No wonder Dr Lee had made up that feeble story about leaving his son at Exeter and forgetting about the case. He didn't dare tell the truth.

'Don't you think you ought to go to the police, Dr Lee?' she asked as he walked past the stable doorway. 'I couldn't help hearing what that man said to you.'

Her question startled him, and he stopped to stare at her with wide. fearful eyet. 'Oh, no – no! That's out of the question!' he gasped. 'There's no knowing what he'd do to Roy. I must submit – give him the formula.'

'It is yours to give?'

He looked astonished. 'It's my discovery – a cheap process for converting sawdust into a highly-combustible fuel. If the tests at Arco had proved successful, a big syndicate planned to buy world manufacturing rights.'

'Who is this man who's kidnapped your son?'

'An assistant at the lab named Falk. He wants the formula, and will sell it to some foreign group. He knew when I was coming and waited for me on the moor road; he was able to identify my car from my previous visits. He waved, and called to me to stop; I recognised him, so of course I did stop.'

'And he made you drive off along that old track?'

'He had a gun. When the car bogged down he got out,

and threatened to shoot me if I didn't give him the papers. The sound of your pony startled him. I threw away the car keys, shouted for help, and tried to grab him. He knocked me out with the gun.'

Sandra nodded. 'So he did the only thing left – took your boy and ran for cover. He must know this part of the moor well enough to have found a good hiding place.'

'Because he came back to search the car without Roy, you mean?' Dr Lee said.

'Yes; and he followed me here when I brought back the cases and found you again,' Sandra summed up. 'He's a determined beast, isn't he?'

'He's an unscrupulous criminal,' Dr Lee answered grimly. 'That's why I can't risk trying to trick him. He can have the formula if he'll release Roy.' He paused. Then, giving her a stern and direct stare, he said, 'You must give me your solemn word not to tell anybody about this – not even your aunt.'

Sandra returned the look. 'I give you my word, Dr Lee,' she said simply.

'Thank you,' he acknowledged, then abruptly turned and stalked off towards the house.

Sandra stood and watched him go, and thought about what he had told her. What a dreadful thing! She noticed that the distances had faded into a haze that could only be the forerunner of the mist which knowing old Granfer Cleve had warned her was coming. And she realised that if the mist came down while Dr Lee was out on the moor he would lose his way. Whether he knew it or not, she decided, he needed help – and the way things were, who but she could help him?

The Tor where Dr Lee had to meet the thin man was nearly a mile to the north-east of the spot where the car had bogged down, and somewhere near there, she guessed, the man had his hide-out. Now if only she could find that hiding place...!

She saddled up the pony again with an affectionate apology. 'You mustn't mind. Lady,' she said quietly. 'I've got to help a little boy in terrible trouble, and I can't do it without you.' Lady, of course, didn't mind at all, and was delighted to go off again with her young mistress – and said so. At least, Sandra felt sure that was what the pony's quiet whinny meant.

Sandra slipped across to the house to put on a warm hacking jacket and pocketed a couple of apples. Aunt Kay was busy baking, and when Sandra mentioned she had decided to go riding again, she got a warning not to dare to be late back for tea as something special was on the menu.

She rode down the lane, and as she had hoped, found Granfer still pottering about in the garden. She reined the pony to a halt as he eyed her. 'You know the moor well, Granfer, don't you?' she asked.

'There's nobody knows it better, I reckon,' he allowed.

'Where could a person hide or take shelter anywhere near Little Tor?'

The old man thought about it, scratching in his beard with the point of the pruning knife he was holding. Sandra watched in wide-eyed fascination, expecting to see the blood spurt at any moment.

'Only place I knows be the old grave,' he said at last.

'Grave?' she echoed blankly.

'Aye, one o' they community graves the ancient people used to build. Some explorer chaps opened her up 'bout ten year ago, and took away all the bones and things.'

Sandra realised he was talking about a cromlech, and asked him how she could find it. He told her, adding, 'But don't go there now, Sandra, 'cos mist be coming down, and the pixies favours them old places. Don't want to get pixy-led, do ee?' The old man was very serious and looked worried.

She knew the old stories about pixies leading moorland travellers away into the bogs. While she didn't believe a word of it, of course, she was too polite to say so to Billy's Granfer. She thanked him and rode on, with the exciting feeling that she now knew where the thin man was holding Roy Lee!

By the time she reached the wood the mist had become quite thick, limiting visibility to about fifty yards. Buttoning up her jacket, she told herself that as long as it didn't get any worse, it would at least help to conceal her approach. She skirted the wood and struck off along a fairly well defined footpath that led to the Tor. The mist drifted slowly about her, touching her with chill fingers that made her glad she had worn her jacket. The pony plodded on indifferently, and the only sound was the quiet clip-clop of her hoofs. Occasionally, Sandra spoke softly to the mare, leaning forward to pat the proud arch of her neck. And Lady, ears back to catch her mistress's voice, would set the bit rings jingling with an approving toss of her head.

When the ground began to rise towards the Tor, Sandra kept careful watch for the descending trail Granfer Cleve had described to her. It angled off to the right into an area of thick gorse, large rocks, and the occasional stunted tree. Somewhere off in the greyness a dog fox barked sharply, a wild, cruel sound that made her shudder. She tensed as a great dark shape loomed out of the mist, only to relax with a sigh of relief as she recognised it as the big rock the old man had told her to watch for.

She halted the pony, and swung down out of the saddle. 'There, this is far enough for you, Lady,' she said in a guarded undertone. 'You wait here till I get back.' She hitched the end of the reins to a gnarled elder stump and continued her way on foot. The track was almost lost in the confusion of gorse, heather, rocks, and long grass, and she had to grope her way as the mist pressed in close about her. Something moved near her feet, and she halted with a gasp as a large adder slithered across the path and vanished into the grass. She braced her shoulders and moved on, knowing the cromlech wasn't far ahead. She wasn't superstitious and certainly didn't believe in pixies, but... well, the old moor did nurse some dark and ancient secrets.

Somewhere just in front of her, stones clattered sharply, and she ducked behind a bush. A man spoke, his voice hard and low. 'All right, boy. Half-an-hour and you'll be with your father again – if he hasn't got lost in this infernal mist!' Straining her eyes, Sandra saw a shadowy figure move from right to left and go up the slope out of sight. The faint scuff of his feet slowly died away.

A thrill of elation went through her as she realised success was almost within her grasp. She went forward slowly. A long, low mound of grass came into view on her right, a big hole gaping in its side like a black wound. The cromlech! With her heart thumping like a bongo drum, she approached the ragged opening and peered inside. She couldn't see a thing in that lightless cavity. 'Roy!' she called softly. Muffled, inarticulate sounds came out of the darkness. Of course, she told herself; the boy was gagged.

Wishing she had brought a torch she crouched down and felt for the floor of the ancient grave with one extended leg. It was about two feet below the level of the opening. Tense but determined, she climbed down inside and shuffled her way to where the sound had come from. Her foot touched something soft, and she stopped, reached down with her hands – and found the trembling boy.

He was, as she had guessed, bound and gagged. She patted his head comfortingly, and felt for the knot in his gag. 'Don't cry out,' she warned. 'I've come to take you back to your

Lady turned her nose towards home and started walking.

father, Hold still and I'll have you loose in no time!'

She fought the knot with straining fingers, knew she now had to hurry if her plan was to be a complete success. The boy began to whimper, but rallied as she reassured him. He was stiff and cold from his ordeal, and she had to lift him out through the opening. He clung to her, tottering awkwardly along at her side. The pain of returning circulation started him whimpering again, and he cried out as he stumbled. Sensing what he was going through, she hoisted him on to her back, and, teeth clenched, struggled doggedly on.

The pony greeted her with a low whinny of recognition. Sandra spoke reassuringly to the mare, and explained to Roy how much the loyal animal had helped. She swung the boy into the saddle and gave him one of the apples. Still panting from her exertions, she bit into the other apple Being very partial to apples, Lady gave her a reminding nudge. 'Oh, all right,' Sandra said with a laugh; she took another bite, and gave the apple to the pony. Lady chomped with noisy appreciation.

'That bad man hit my daddy!' said Roy tearfully.

'Yes, but your daddy's all right,' Sandra told him. 'And the man will be punished.'

She was in the act of unhitching the pony when she heard the dull sound of stumbling feet. The mist was now so thick she could barely see a yard. 'Sit still,' she told Roy. 'I won't be a minute.' She scrambled hastily up the slope to reach the track to the Tor. A dark, panting figure appeared out of the mist. As she had hoped, it was Dr Lee. He looked wet and miserable and just about exhausted. Mud on his clothes showed he had fallen more than once.

'Dr Lee!' she exclaimed cheerily. 'It's me – Sandra!'

He stopped, and stared in astonishment. 'What are you doing here?'

'I decided you could do with some help,' she told him, feeling pardonably pleased with herself.

'You shouldn't have come!' he snapped angrily. 'Your meddling could endanger the life of my son! Go back at once!'

She bit back a sharp retort, knowing she must make allowances for the terrible strain he was under. 'You haven't handed over the formula yet, have you?' she asked instead, anxiously.

He frowned. 'I haven't reached the Tor, have I? The mist slowed me down. I must hurry on.'

'There's no need,' she assured him. 'It's all over, now.'

'But that devil has my son!'

'Not any more!' she assured him cheerfully. 'I rescued Roy! Come – I'll take you to him!'

He couldn't quite believe her, and followed her almost reluctantly. But when he saw his son sitting on the patient pony, apparently none the worse for his experience, his emotions overflowed. It was a wonderful and exciting reunion. Sandra unhitched Lady's reins and stroked the velvety nose. Not to be outdone, the pony affectionately nuzzled her chin.

'Sandra,' Dr Lee said, coming to her. 'I can't thank you enough... I don't know what to say...' He was so carried away he took her face in his two hands and kissed her forehead.

'Then don't say anything,' Sandra said lightly. 'Let's head for home without wasting any more time. That man Falk's got a gun, don't forget!'

'Yes,' Dr Lee nodded. 'The sooner we set the police on his trail, the better.'

'Besides,' said Sandra, 'Aunt Kay is baking one of her specials, and she'll skin us both if we keep tea waiting!'

They laughed together at that, and even young Roy joined in, though he wasn't at all sure what they were laughing about. Dr Lee, his face suddenly sober, looked about him and shook his head. 'We're fooling ourselves. Even you can't find your way through this blanket!'

'No – but my pony can!' she told him proudly. 'All we've got to do is leave it to Lady! She'll help us, we can be sure.'

And with a little neigh of understanding, Lady turned her nose in the direction of home and started walking.

They stumbled through the mist for about half an hour as Lady picked her way through the marshes.

'Are you sure that horse knows the way?' Dr Lee began to look worried when –

'Look!' Triumphantly Sandra pointed ahead to where the lights of Aunt Kay's kitchen window shone out through the mist.

Racing Rivals

by Marjorie Stace

As Christine Grayson came up to the top of the hill, the farm-house lights went on below.

She pulled her horse, Jet, to a standstill and sat there for a moment, high and proud on the hill-top, silhouetted against the darkening sky.

Christine sighed contentedly, for this was always one of the happiest moments of her life, looking down upon the neat, small farm-house where she lived with her mother, while Jet, her very own horse, blew deeply through his velvet nostrils after the climb up the hill.

After a short while, Christine pressed her heels gently against Jet's gleaming black sides.

'Come on now, Jet! I'm feeling hungry and I expect you are, too, after that gallop.'

With eager response, Jet moved forward, down through the clover-scented fields to the lane that led to the farm. Christine, still wearing her farm dungarees and open-necked shirt, smiled contentedly, delighting in Jet's long smooth stride and proud head carriage.

Black as a raven, Jet was; but sometimes in the summer, when he was sleek and satiny, there was a kind of blue sheen on him.

To Christine, who had hacked and schooled him as a four-year-old, he was more than a horse; he was a real companion.

They had wonderful fun together when they were out, Christine pretending they were all sorts of different people. Sometimes, Jet would be a ranch horse and Christine a cowpuncher riding slack and long-legged in the saddle. And once she'd been a highwayman and Jet a mettlesome, high-spirited creature flying at full gallop across the broad heath, under the light of the moon.

The lovely thing about Jet was the way he always seemed to enter into the spirit of these games.

It was nearly dusk as they turned off the grassy slope out into the lane. Jet stood motionless while Christine looped the reins over her arm and bent low in the saddle to secure the five-barred gate, so that the cattle couldn't get out. Then, just as they moved off along the narrow highway, a great rumbling came from behind. Jet's head flew up, his ears flickered back to catch the sound, and he edged nervously into the side of the lane.

Christine looked over her shoulder at the massive car with a horse-box behind bearing down upon them. The Carleys! She might have known it! Really, it was too bad of them to bring it down the narrow lane when the wide main road ran right to their gates!

She held the reins lightly, keeping her hands quiet and low as Jet fidgeted against the hedge until Christine's legs felt the prick of bramble and thorn. Jet was wonderful in traffic, but this great car and huge horse-box, filling the whole lane, were enough to frighten anything, and Christine didn't blame Jet for being apprehensive.

There was a grinding of gears as the driver changed into bottom, and crawled level. Christine could see Jim Hennegan, the Carleys' trainer groom, sitting in front, next to the driver. Then, as the box drew slowly away, Laura Carley's head appeared out of the rear window of the car.

'Got two firsts!' she shouted gloatingly, in a voice which

'Got two firsts!' Laura shouted gloatingly.

made Jet throw up his head, just as Christine had got it down nicely to the bit again. 'Juvenile Jumping and Hunter Class!'

Christine could see the saddles on the rack inside the box, and the bridles hanging by the window, their red rosettes still tied to them. Also, just visible, were the summer-sheeted quarters of Red Mask, Laura's prize-winning chestnut hunter.

Christine smiled at Laura, hating her for her cool detached glance at Jet, a glance which took in all Jet's bad points and made no allowances for the good ones. She knew just what was in Laura's mind, could almost hear her words, which were a faithful imitation of Jim Hennegan's: '*A blood weed that 'un; too light of 'is bone, got nothing in front, both 'is front legs at one corner...*'

Jim was right, of course. Christine, who knew more about horses than Laura ever would, admitted it. But there were so many other things about Jet: his turn of speed, his courage, his love of hunting; the way he drowsed on a summer afternoon and dipped his head and blew against your hair. To Christine he was a picture-book horse, and often, in her mind's eye, she clothed him in crimson and gold trappings and rode him out across the open heath, pretending he was a charger and she a Knight in search of the Holy Grail.

Laura Carley, whose father was so rich that he didn't even mind losing money on his farm, didn't have fun like that. She was too busy winning silver cups and rosettes at shows. She didn't even school her own two horses, as Christine had schooled Jet. Jim, the expert horseman whom Mr Carley employed, did it all for Laura. Christine had often seen him, before a jumping event, 'waking up' Red Mask. Then he'd hand over to Laura who simply had to go into the ring and sit there, as she'd been taught to do, while Red Mask cleared the jumps.

'Don't move yer 'ands now, Miss,' Jim always warned her.

'You just sit there quiet-like and keep yer 'ands low. Don't you interfere with 'im, and 'e'll go a clear round.'

Once, the actual jumps at a local show had been lent by Mr Carley. For the Carleys had a complete schooling ground at White Gates Farm. 'Nothing but the best for my girl, no matter what it costs,' Mr Carley always said.

Christine remembered these words as the big car and shiny horse-box disappeared, leaving her and Jet in a cloud of dust.

'Coming to Exney on Saturday?' shrieked Laura, just before it turned the bend.

Christine shook her head. There was no class for Jet; at fifteen hands, he was too big for the pony classes, too small for the hacks, and couldn't compete against professionals in the jumping. For although Jet was as clever as a cat out hunting and jumped well, he was no good in the show ring. He just hadn't the temperament. He hotted up.

'I'd soon put him right for you!' Jim had said sneeringly one day, after Christine had brought Jet out of the ring lathered with sweat and treading hot bricks.

But Christine didn't want Jet 'put right'. She liked him as he was – a perfect ride, a good-natured companion and a brilliant hunter.

Then Laura, impeccable in her expensive jodhpurs and velvet cap, had looked at Jet and said, 'But my dear! Why do you keep him? I mean, what use is he to you? Wouldn't it be better to sell him and buy something you could show?'

But even if Jet had been a show horse, Christine wouldn't have had the time for it. Many mornings when Laura had been setting out in the great car and horse-box for some show, Christine had been setting out on the tractor to plough or harrow Top Field or The Leys.

At first, she had envied Laura. But later she hadn't at all, for somehow her mother had managed to save up enough money to buy the beloved Jet for Christine's fourteenth birthday. And now, when Christine's long day on the farm was done, she would saddle and bridle him and off they would go, out of the valley, up over the hills, where the breeze was cool, to the broad open stretch of heath, the pine-scented woods and the quiet coverts; across sparkling streams, and through tiny, quaint villages.

At these times Christine tried to forget her resentment against Laura Carley and the challenge she presented. Jet was a better horse than Red Mask, Christine said to herself, even if he was a little on the small side. And one day she would prove it. How, she didn't yet know, but do it she would! Not for her own sake, but for Jet's. Oh, it was easy for Laura, who had everything, and whose father said, 'It doesn't matter what it costs as long as my girl wins.'

How could one compete against that?

When Christine thought of her own father, her face set sternly. Perhaps, if he hadn't gone off to ride in Australia all those years ago, when she'd been only five years old...

Firmly, she put him out of her mind. She would never forgive him for leaving her mother to manage the farm on her own, *never*.

Most of the struggle was over now and things were going fairly well, but they had been anxious years for Mrs Grayson; and even now it meant hard work for her and Christine to keep the place going. But it was work they both loved, it was their own place, and on top of everything else, Christine had her beloved Jet. Only the constant irritation of Laura Carley dimmed Christine's contentment.

She led Jet into the stable, took off his saddle and bridle, slipped a halter on to his small, thoroughbred head, brushed the saddle-marks off him, then turned him out into the nearby paddock.

She watched him for a moment, delighting in the way

he went away to the far side of the enclosure and stood under the tree, head held high, blowing into the soft, scented air. Then his head went down and he began to crop the short, sweet grass.

Christine turned away and went towards the house. One day she'd prove Jet's real worth. One day... somehow...

Not a Ghost

'Your father was a brilliant horseman, you know,' said Mrs Grayson, as Christine and she sat over supper in a kitchen bright with blue and white checked curtains and gay with coloured pottery.

Nan Grayson looked young for her age. She was slight and neat, and very capable. Her eyes were as blue as corn flowers, her hair was short and golden and curly, and her laugh was gay. Mostly, she wore comfortable old slacks and a sweater, or open-necked shirt. But on summer Sundays and special occasions, she wore a printed cotton dress and white sandals. Many times she had been taken for Christine's elder sister, and indeed, the two often behaved more like sisters than mother and daughter. Christine, in fact, often felt quite protective towards her mother. One of her day-dreams, when she'd been younger, had been rescuing her mother from some awful fate and being able to give her all the luxuries she'd had to give up when she married Victor Grayson. Things like a fur coat instead of her old tweed, and a shining car like Mrs Carley's instead of the old rattle-trap, which often had a bull calf or sacks of potatoes in the back. In some way, Christine wanted to make up for what she took to be her father's heartless neglect.

Now, at sixteen, Christine's day-dreams had taken the more practical form of working on the farm. She helped her mother with many of the outdoor jobs so that she could spend a little more time doing things in the house, like making new chintz curtains for the sitting-room and mending the towels and sheets, which she'd been meaning to do for ages.

Once, Nan Grayson had said, 'What I'd do without you, Christine, I don't know.'

'You'll never have to,' Christine had answered.

But Mrs Grayson had smiled knowingly and said, 'Ah, but one day you'll fall in love and get married...'

'I *won't!*' scowled Christine, going very pink, 'ever!'

'I'd be sorry if you didn't, darling,' her mother had replied.

'Well, not for ages and ages, anyway!'

Now, at the mention of her father, Christine's face set sternly. All she remembered was his smile and his hands as they swung her up into the saddle of Buttons, her first pony. But in many ways he was still there, at Shallows Farm.

Up in the attic there were albums full of his pictures, press photographs showing him riding the winner of the Foxhunters' Chase at Cheltenham, falling at the last-but-one at Sandown, taking Beecher's Brook at Aintree in grand style, unsaddling in the winning-pen at some point-to-point. And there were some of his colours, the quartered purple satin cap, the salmon jersey with cross-belts, the fine silk scarf and the thin, feather-light racing boots.

Resolutely, Christine put him from her mind. He'd gone away and left Shallows, left her mother and herself. He had no place in their lives now.

'Have a nice ride?' Mrs Grayson got up to clear the supper things.

'Heavenly! Jet was Rolande taking the good news from Ghent to Aix.'

'Well, I hope you didn't gallop him as hard as poor Rolande was galloped!' smiled Nan Grayson.

'No, of course I didn't. Only on the turf. The ground's too hard, really!' She paused then added casually, 'Laura

Carley overtook us in the lane. She'd been to a show. Bridles simply covered with rosettes, of course.'

Mrs Grayson ran hot water into the sink. She knew exactly how Christine felt about Laura Carley. For wasn't Christine Victor's daughter?

It was only a matter of time now before Christine's courageous spirit, her desire to compete, to prove her own horse the better one, came uppermost. It had to be. She was Victor's daughter, however hard she tried to forget it. Her father was there in her, in the way she sat a horse, casually, naturally, not stiffly correct, but one *with* the horse, relaxed yet firm. It was there in her handling of Jet, in her love for him which was combined with an honest assessment of his good points, and a pride which didn't blind her to his faults.

In these moments, Nan Grayson was a little afraid. She wished she knew more about horses so that she could help and advise Christine. For she wouldn't be satisfied for ever with the childish games she made up for Jet and herself; that much was clear. She would no more be able to knuckle down under Laura Carley's pinpricking, gloating triumph than... Well, than Victor would have been able to. Resentment would flare up into action one day. Yet Christine didn't stand a chance against the Carley fortune. 'If only Victor were here,' thought Mrs Grayson. 'He'd know what to do all right!'

But Victor Grayson was thousands of miles away, riding for a wealthy Australian owner.

Mrs Grayson put away the stack of plates, then took the heavy torch off the dresser.

'I'm just going out to the battery,' she said.

'Want any help?'

'No. You go up to bed. You look tired after that ride, and tomorrow's going to be a heavy day with the potatoes to get up.'

Outside, the sky was dark purple and the scent of clover and dog-rose was heavy.

Nan Grayson went past the small paddock where Jet was busily cropping the dewy grass. It was very quiet out there, very peaceful. A dog barked distantly, and somewhere a bucket clanked on stone.

Beyond the paddock trees lay the Carleys' land, and beyond that their house, big and over-stuffed with fat satin cushions and unsuitable pale-coloured carpets that showed every scrap of mud.

By now, Red Mask and the grey would be in their modern stables, rugged-up against the cooler night air, tucking into a good feed of oats. The comparison between their lot and Jet's was painful, although Christine always stoutly maintained that Jet was the happier, living as nature intended him to.

The chicken battery was built alongside the paddock. Later on, when Mrs Grayson could afford it, she meant to move it nearer the house, pull down that useless old sty and...

Suddenly, she caught her breath, and stood stock still, staring.

He was standing on the other side of the paddock fence, leaning on the top rail, looking towards the farmhouse. There was no mistaking that tall familiar figure, the long legs which Christine had inherited, the straight back, the jut of the chin, the gay curl to the brim of his hat...

Aghast, she moved towards him. A ghost! He must be a ghost!

But no. He turned, saw her and lifted a hand in greeting.

'Hullo, Nan,' he said huskily. Then he added with a smile, 'Like the proverbial bad penny – I've come back.'

He moved towards her, and it was then that Nan Grayson noticed the stick he carried and the way he limped.

It was some time before Nan Grayson could bring herself to break the news to Christine. Meantime, Victor Grayson was staying at the village inn.

'I'm afraid she resents you,' Nan Grayson had said, one evening at the inn.

'I can't blame her for that,' her husband had replied, as he limped to the mantelpiece for matches.

Watching him, Nan Grayson had been struck once more by the likeness between Victor and Christine.

'Why didn't you let us... let *me* know you were back?' she said.

'I meant to, eventually. I was trying to think of a way of doing it without it being a shock either to you or to Christine.'

'Yes, I see.'

'You haven't told her yet?'

'No; I'm being cowardly I suppose...'

'Nan...' He had looked at her steadily. 'Would you rather I went away again?'

'No, of course not, Victor.'

'Would it make things easier... because of Christine? We have to consider her first of all, you know.'

'She'll get used to the idea of having a father again. I'm sure of it... She needs you, Victor. I'll tell her tonight.'

'Tonight or tomorrow or the next day, my dear...' Victor Grayson had shrugged. 'It's up to you. But when you *do* tell her, please say that I want to come home, that I want to make amends, will you? And tell her that all these years I've been thinking about you both, and longing to come back. I would have done, too, if I hadn't had that fall which crocked me up for good. I meant to make a fortune, Nan, and come back here and give it all to you – and Christine. You do believe me? I didn't want to come back a failure,' he finished simply.

Nan remembered his words on her drive back in the noisy little rattle-trap. She remembered, too, his limp – all the more tragic in one so essentially strong and vigorous. Victor couldn't ride professionally again – ever. That was the simple truth of it. 'And...' he had added sadly. 'I haven't even made the fortune I wanted to. I'm a failure after all, my dear.'

Nan Grayson remembered her own words, too, as she drove back to the farm, where Christine would be waiting. 'To-night... I'll tell her tonight...'

She found Christine cleaning tack in the dilapidated old cart-horse stable, which one day Mrs Grayson planned to make into fine, new stables with proper ventilation and electric light.

'Hello; where've you been?' called out Christine.

'Into the village.'

This brief explanation satisfied Christine. All her attention was directed towards soaping the reins of a snaffle bridle that hung from a nail in the beam. 'One day,' thought Nan Grayson, 'we'll have one of those proper iron hook things that you can hang lots of bridles on at once.'

Christine finished the reins and turned to a bucket of water in which two snaffle bits, a bridoon, a curb chain and a pair of much too small irons were soaking. All the stuff was old fashioned; all of it, except the curb chain, dull steel instead of nickel plating – which the Carleys had and which shone and glittered in the sunlight, and only needed a quick rub-over instead of all this hard and unrewarding polishing. And it wasn't as if, at the end of it all, Christine's tack really looked clean. The old, forward-cut saddle had been bought second-hand from a farmer and the girth and leathers were black with age instead of being a lovely glowing walnut colour. It was a shame that such a beautiful little horse as Jet had to be cluttered up with all that second-hand ill-fitting tack. Everything was too big. The saddle flaps gave him a poorer shoulder than he really had; the reins, cracked and split despite Christine's persistent efforts with neat's-foot oil, were thick and heavy. The leathers were too broad, and both single and double bridles had needed extra holes punching in them before they fitted Jet's small head. The total result was clumsy, instead of neat and workmanlike.

Mrs Grayson knew that the right sort of tack can make a lot of difference to the appearance of a horse, just as the right sort of dress or hat can make a lot of difference to a woman.

'If I sell those pigs well, she shall have some new tack; a set of leathers and irons, perhaps,' thought Nan Grayson. Certainly, Christine needed another pair of stirrups, for it was actually dangerous to have them too small, in case the horse came down and her feet didn't slip free.

But there was still the blacksmith to be paid for the last set of shoes, and a small account to settle with the vet. Those things had to be seen to before new leathers and irons could be bought.

Engrossed in these thoughts, it was several minutes before Mrs Grayson realised that Christine was quiet and preoccupied. Usually she chattered away while she cleaned tack, whistling and singing in a cheerful off-key voice.

Mrs Grayson was alarmed. Had she heard that her father was back in England, and was living only a few miles away? Had somebody seen him, and made some remark to Christine, not dreaming that she didn't know?

She was just about to tell her the truth when Christine said, 'Laura Carley's going to ride in point-to-points next spring.'

So that was it!

Mrs Grayson breathed a silent sigh of relief. 'Oh?'

'Jim Hennegan says Red Mask is good enough.'

'Darling...' began Mrs Grayson, awkwardly, then stopped.

But Christine, lost in her own thoughts, went on.

'Laura's thrilled to bits, of course. As soon as showing is finished they're going to turn Red Mask out for a month, then get him in and put him into training.'

Mrs Grayson caught the stifled note of envy in Christine's voice and decided this wasn't the moment to break the news to her that her father was back. There was no knowing how Christine would take it, but either way it would mean terrific readjustment; and knowing how she resented all mention of her father, it was fairly safe to assume it would take her some time to get accustomed to the idea. Wisely, she decided to make no mention of Victor for the moment.

'That means Laura will be out hunting this season, then?' she said instead.

'No. She's going abroad with her mother for a holiday.'

Nan Grayson frowned. For if Red Mask were to run in point-to-points he'd have to be ridden out hunting before he could qualify for the Master's certificate, passing him as a bona fide hunter.

'Then how...?' she began.

'Jim Hennegan will bring him out while Laura is away.' Christine rubbed furiously at an obstinately dull buckle for a moment. Then she said suddenly, all in a rush, 'Mother, I'm absolutely certain Jet could win a point-to-point! I know he's a bit on the small side, but he jumps well and he's got the speed. And he ought to have stying power!'

Nan Grayson looked away. It hurt her to see the eager light in Christine's eyes. For, of course, it was hopeless.

'Darling, I'm afraid it's no good,' she said gently.

'But *why*, Mother?'

'It would mean Jet would have to go into training and neither you nor I know enough about it, and we certainly can't afford to send him to an establishment. You know that.'

Christine sighed and turned back to her cleaning. Her mother was right, of course. It had been a lovely but impossible dream, to think of racing Jet. She had been absurd even to think about it. Racing was so different from everything else. It required different technique, different schooling. The horse had to learn to spread himself, to jump out well, not stand back and jump off his hocks as in show jumping.

Besides, Jet would have to be got fit. At the moment, he was soft. He needed regular work to harden his muscles, not just the odd rides Christine took him on when she'd finished work on the farm. He'd need proper schooling over made fences, and proper feeding. He'd have to be got in, too; and that would mean his box would have to be mucked out twice a day on top of all the work there was to do on the farm... Christine could see that the obstacles were absolutely insurmountable.

Yet somehow, however hard she tried to put it out of her mind, the dream persisted. But it was only a dream, one that could never become a reality. For, as her mother had so wisely said, it would be too much of an undertaking.

It was all very well for Laura, who had Jim Hennegan to do the work for her. Jim had trained horses to run under National Hunt rules.

All the same, Christine couldn't help dreaming. Every night, after she'd put out the light, she lay there imagining Jet racing against the other horses, saw him flying over the emerald grass, his small ears pricked forward, his intelligent eyes fixed on the jump ahead.

Sometimes, in her dreams, Christine made a mistake at the stiffest jump, but Jet saved them both by cleverly putting in a 'short one' just in time.

And then she saw Jet draw away from the rest of the field, heard the wild, excited cheering as the crowds of spectators swept down from the packed hill-top to see the finish. She heard the frenzied clapping, as Jet flashed past the post to win by several lengths.

Sobbing quietly, Christine buried her head in the pillow. She knew Jet could do it; she just *knew*.

But what was the good of just knowing without being able to prove it?

Fears for Jet

'Ah, I mind the time when your father rode in 'orse shows,' said old Amos Partridge reflectively. 'Every day 'e was off somewhere, ridin' for this owner or that. Never 'is own animals, o' course. Always belonged to someone else like, someone 'as couldn't ride like your dad could. Why,' he paused to straighten his back and rest the muscles a moment, 'I seen 'im win first prize in the Open Jumping on one 'orse, and second prize on another 'orse belongin' to someone else.'

Old Amos had always worked at Shallows, ever since he could remember. There wasn't a thing he didn't know about the place. He was a splendid worker, too, and although many farmers round about had said to him, 'Any time you want to change your job, Amos, you know where to come. And I'll raise your wages on top of it,' – he'd stayed at Shallows.

Shallows Farm was home to him; he couldn't imagine working anywhere else. Often on a summer evening he'd wander back after he'd had his tea at six o'clock, and walk over the fields he'd spent all day in; or he'd run his eye over the pigs, 'Just to see if they's all right,' as though some dreadful disease might have got at them since he last saw them at five o'clock.

He and Christine did all the ploughing and planning between them, leaving Mrs Grayson to operate the milking machine.

Amos often talked about Master Victor, remembering his past glory, his local fame and each of his sensational triumphs.

But Christine, who couldn't share his indulgence, had no wish to listen.

'He went away and left us,' she always reminded him.

Amos, who'd known Mr Grayson from a baby up, would shift his ancient beaver hat to the back of his head, scratch at the scant grey hair, and say, 'Ar... 'e were restless and ambitious, Miss Christine. Farmin' were too slow for 'im.'

All her life Christine could never remember Amos saying a word against her father. Neither could she ever remember his wearing anything other than the ancient brown beaver hat and the heavy leather belt with its brass buckle. In winter he merely added a cast off jacket of Victor Grayson's, with a long flared horseman's skirt, sloping pockets and double vents that flapped in the wind.

On Sundays and fête-days, Amos wore a bright blue suit that was too small for him, a flannel collar, a knitted silk tie and a stiff grey trilby.

He was enormously strong, despite his fifty-five years, and very loyal. Nan Grayson thought the world of him; and to Christine, Shallows Farm just couldn't be Shallows Farm without him.

The most surprising thing about Amos was his daughters. He had three and they all looked like film stars. One of them worked in the local store, one was an usherette in the cinema eight miles away, while the youngest had gone to London to try and become an actress.

Amos ignored them all. The light of his life was Shallows, and after that the marrows and peas he grew in the front garden of his cottage for competition in the annual Flower Show.

For year after year he'd won these events – till the Carleys came to White Gates and brought Frank Gosford with them as head gardener. Frank Gosford – a 'foreigner' from the next county! Thereafter the battle had raged furiously. But the bitter rivalry went beyond marrows and peas to passionate championship of their respective employers. In this respect, Amos was unfortunately rather handicapped, since Frank was apt to boast at the local inn about Miss Laura's triumphs.

'Well,' he'd say, smugly. 'we won the Lightweight 'unters today!' as though it had been all his doing. Then he'd glance at Amos as if to say, '*Beat that if you can!*'

Amos couldn't, of course. But when 'Master Victor' returned it would be a different story.

Meanwhile, Amos was forced to dig into the past in order to compete with Frank's stories and take him down a peg.

'Ah' he'd say, 'I mind the time Master Victor won the Championship at that very same show...'

Impressive at first, but it soon lost its power. The long-past wasn't as good as the present, and once or twice of late, Frank and the others had openly yawned and begun to talk of other things.

But when 'Master Victor' came back to Shallows – then Amos would have his say!

For Amos never doubted he would return. Shallows was his home, just as it had been his father's before him, and a man could only stay away from his home so long. He had to come back sooner or later; the ties were too strong.

But Christine made a face and started up the tractor in order to cut off his words; for it annoyed her to hear him praising the father whom she could hardly remember, and whom she had vowed never to forgive.

It was well into August now, and often Christine was too tired even to take Jet for their evening ride. Instead, she would go out to him after supper, and just lean over the paddock rail, watching him. She could spend many minutes like this, looking at him, while the evening breeze rippled through his thick black mane, as he tugged contentedly at the grass. Sometimes, he threw up his head to listen to some sound beyond Christine's hearing. Then he would stand motionless, even his jaws still, with perhaps a blade or two of grass sticking absurdly out of his mouth.

It was on just such an evening that the bombshell fell for Christine.

Her mother had walked out of the house to join her at the paddock rail, and together they stood there, silently watching the black, gleaming horse. Then Mrs Grayson said, 'Christine... I've got something to tell you.'

Christine's heart leapt. It was about the point-to-points!

'About...' she began breathlessly.

'About your father.'

Christine's spirits sank. 'Oh!'

'He's back in England,' her mother said.

Christine turned, amazed. 'In... *England?*'

'Yes. In fact, darling, he's in the village, staying at the Crown.'

Christine stared at her mother incredulously, her thoughts in wild tumult. Then one fear emerged from the confusion.

'He isn't... coming *here?*' she asked.

Nan Grayson looked away from the worried grey eyes, that were such an astonishing replica of Victor's.

'Not if you don't want him to,' she said.

'I *don't!*' burst out Christine.

'Darling... he wants to come home. He misses us both and he's lonely. He asked me to tell you that he thought about us all the time out there, and he would have come back sooner, but he wanted to make his fortune first and then come home and surprise us. But things didn't work out like that. He had this terrible accident and had to give up riding, the sort of riding he's used to. At the moment, he's just amusing himself schooling a young horse or two for Mr Fawcett, the dealer.' She turned to Christine eagerly. 'He's got such wonderful plans for this place, darling. Wait till you hear...'

'I don't want to hear,' murmured Christine.

'But Christine...'

'I don't want him to come, Mother! He'll spoil everything. It'll all be different. And we're getting on all right, aren't we?'

'Of course we are, darling. It's just...'

'No! Please, Mother, *please* don't let him come! Don't let him spoil everything!'

Nan Grayson saw, then, how the prospect of Victor's return really upset Christine and wisely dropped the matter.

'Very well, Christine. If that's how you feel that's all there is to it. It is his wish that your feelings should come first,' she said gravely. Then she walked away.

When she'd gone, Christine climbed over the rail and went across the paddock. Jet threw up his head at her approach, and whinnied.

Christine laid her head against his warm arched neck. Her thoughts raced confusedly. At all costs her father must not come back to Shallows. For, in some way, she felt that his return would separate her from Jet. Her own happiness and Jet's safety were threatened. For fathers had a terrible, supreme power. What if he disapproved of Jet? What if he ordered him to be sold?

The mere thought was so awful that Christine put her arms round Jet's neck and hugged him to her.

'I'll never part with you!' she vowed passionately. '*Never!*'

That was how Amos found them when he came running up the lane to the farm.

'Miss Christine! Miss Christine!' he shouted from some distance away. 'I've seen 'im with me own eyes! Master

Victor, 'e's back, Miss Christine! Back in the flesh! Spoke to me, 'e did! "Well Amos," 'e ses, "'ow's things at Shallows?" Just as if 'e'd never gone away!'

Panting, he stopped by the paddock gate, looking at Christine with his small, blue, lively eyes and smiling in a way that took many years off his age.

Christine took one look at him, then pressed close against Jet.

'Don't!' she sobbed. 'Go away! Go *away!*'

'Why, whatever's the matter?'

'Go away!' implored Christine.

Puzzled, Amos went on into the farmhouse to tell Mrs Grayson.

Fifteen minutes later, when Christine could at last bring herself to leave Jet and go into the house, Amos had gone. Her mother sat sewing in the window.

Christine sank wearily into a chair. The clock ticked loudly on the wall, and one of the dogs got up and crossed the kitchen to resettle at Christine's feet. Otherwise there was silence. For the first time in her life, Christine had nothing to say to her mother. For the first time in her life, a shadow lay between them – Victor Grayson!

Trouble for Christine

A week later, Christine came down from the fields into the farmyard to find Laura Carley waiting for her. Laura looked cool and serene compared with Christine, who was tired, and covered with dust from Top Field.

'Hello!' Laura called out piercingly, in a voice that made even the tractor engine seem like a soft purr.

Christine switched off the engine and there was a lovely new silence in the yard. She swung down to the ground as Laura said, 'Just thought I'd pop over and say good-bye.'

'Good-bye?' Puzzled, Christine turned to face Laura.

'Yes. Don't say you've forgotten!' Laura added, as though Christine had nothing to think about other than the activities of Laura Carley. 'Mother and I are off to Italy on Monday.'

Christine swallowed against the dust parching her throat.

'How lovely; I do hope you have a marvellous time,' she said, trying to sound enthusiastic, trying not to envy Laura but not succeeding very well.

'Oh, it's Mother's idea, really. She feels she wants a holiday, you know...'

'What from?' wondered Christine, thinking of Mrs Carley's leisured existence.

'Left to myself, I don't think I'd bother,' Laura continued. 'Still, I may as well go as there's nothing happening here till the point-to-point season starts.'

Automatically, both girls wandered towards the paddock where Jet stood beneath a tree, swishing his tail languidly and resting a leg. 'He would!' thought Christine, wishing that at that particular moment he could have been standing on all four legs, his ears pricked forward and his head held high. Then she despised herself for these unworthy thoughts, but somehow Laura always made her feel like this.

Laura nodded towards Jet.

'He looks a bit poor for this time of the year,' she said seriously. 'Perhaps there isn't enough grass in this paddock?'

Christine gritted her teeth, but managed to say, 'He's all right. How's Red Mask?'

Laura brightened visibly.

'Terribly well. What a horse and a half he is! But then he *ought* to be. Father gave five hundred guineas for him.'

Her gaze went coldly back to Jet.

'Beats me why you don't sell that thing, Chris, and get yourself a proper horse. Jim was only saying the other day...'

That thing!

For two pins Christine would have hit Laura Carley. She clenched her fists tightly, her jaw set rigidly.

'Jet is a wonderful horse,' she said stoutly, 'even if he didn't cost five hundred guineas. It doesn't matter to me, anyway!'

'All right, all right,' smiled Laura amusedly. 'Don't fly off the handle. I only meant you could have more fun with something else, something up to a bit more weight perhaps...'

'Jet is up to my weight and that's all that matters to me.'

It was difficult keeping her voice casual, difficult to answer Laura as though she didn't attach much importance to her words when every one of them was a hammer-blow to her heart. 'If only you knew Jet as I know him,' she thought. 'He didn't cost five hundred guineas – he cost fifty, because he was small and they didn't think he'd live. That's why we got him cheap, considering his breeding. But mother had to go without things and save and save for ages so that she could afford to buy him for me...'

'Oh yes, of course, I suppose that's what really matters to you,' agreed Laura quickly, as though suddenly bored with the subject. Clearly, she thought it a waste of time to argue with someone so obviously blind to the animal's faults. She turned her elegant back on Jet and hooked her arms back over the rail.

'Well... point-to-points next,' she said almost wearily, as though racing was just another field waiting for her to come along and conquer. 'Which,' thought Christine, 'is probably true, although she needn't sound so beastly conceited about it.'

'We've got Red Mask's shoes off,' went on Laura. 'Then I shall have him in when mother and I get back from Italy, and put him into training.'

Listening to her, no one would ever dream that Jim Hennegan had anything to do with it at all.

'Oh...and that reminds me,' added Laura as though

she'd just remembered. 'We shall need something to pace him by to get him used to galloping against another horse. It doesn't have to be as fast as Red Mask or anything like that; I mean, it's not a real race, but just to give him the idea. So I wondered if you'd care to bring Jet up some time? Red Mask will leave him standing, of course, but that won't matter, will it? As I said before, it's only schooling...and it might be fun for you.'

Somehow, Christine found words, somehow they came out more or less politely, even though inside she was seething at the insult to Jet.

'If I'm not too busy here...' she managed.

'Good,' Laura lounged away from the rail. 'Well, I'll pop over again and see how you feel about it nearer the time. 'Bye.'

Without another glance at Jet she sauntered to the five-barred gate dividing the yard from the farmhouse garden. With her hand on the latch she turned and called back, 'I'll send you a postcard from Italy.'

'Thanks,' said Christine, hating her not so much for her conceit, as for her scornful disregard of Jet.

The moment Laura was out of sight, Christine could bear it no longer. Hurt and resentment were packed tight inside her. Somehow they held while she ran the tractor into the shed, called out 'goodnight' to Amos and shouted through the kitchen window to her mother that she didn't want any tea. Somehow, she managed to hold back the tears while she gulped at water from her cupped hand held beneath the tap in the yard. Then she dashed into the stable, picked up Jet's saddle and bridle and went into the paddock.

Jet moved nervously as she slipped the reins over his head. He sensed her distress and indignation.

'You're not a *thing!*' panted Christine as she tightened the cumbersome leather girth. 'And Red Mask would *not* leave you standing! How dare she? How *dare* she?'

Furiously, she wrenched the irons down the length of the leathers, then swung lightly up into the saddle.

'Christine?' Mrs Grayson came to the kitchen door, her face anxious, and alarm in her voice.

But Christine didn't stop.

'Back soon!' she called over her shoulder as Jet moved out of the paddock.

Out in the lane, Christine pressed him up on to the bit, urged him to walk out, made him carry his head. Jet responded willingly, as though he understood her desire for him to appear suddenly at his very best.

Through the gate they went, up the hill, and on to the wide expanse of open heath.

Before them stretched the broad dusty track that led right across the heath to the village. Jet gave a gentle little buck as if to say, 'Come on, what are we waiting for? I'm feeling rather full of myself!' He tossed his head playfully.

Christine heard Laura's supercilious words again: *Red Mask will leave him standing, of course.*

Swiftly Christine shortened her leathers till her knees were high on the saddle, jockey-fashion. She looked about her, but there wasn't a soul anywhere to be seen on the heath, while before them lay the deserted track...

Jet only needed a light pressure on his sides and he was off. As the pace increased, a sense of exhilaration seemed to possess both horse and rider. Christine crouched low in the saddle as Jet thundered over the hard ground, his small feet flying out beneath her, his mane flowing free.

Faster...faster...faster they went, Jet's pounding hooves sending up small clouds of dust.

'Faster! Faster!' sobbed Christine, as though to drive Laura's slighting words right out of her head.

But Christine was not alone on the heath, as she had thought. A solitary, unseen rider coming towards her had pulled in to

A man watched, unseen, while Christine flashed by on Jet.

the side of the track. Now he sat his horse quietly, screened by the trees of a copse. Impassively, he watched through narrowed critical eyes as Christine and the little black horse flashed past.

A second later he tensed in the saddle and sat motionless, listening. But the hoofbeats had stopped altogether, so that there was only an unnatural silence instead of that rhythmic pounding...

Quickly, the man urged his horse out into the open. Then he saw them; the little black horse was struggling up from the ground in a great cloud of dust, and a few feet away lay Christine, dead-still in the long grass by the side of the track.

Strange Meeting

The world was a huge, spinning catherine wheel to Christine when she at last opened her eyes. Out of the blur came a voice which she did not recognise, but which sounded somehow reassuring.

'You're all right. Don't try to get up for a minute. Stay where you are.'

'Jet...' murmured Christine, closing her eyes again.

'Don't worry about the little horse, he's all right. I caught him for you, and he's tied up to a tree. Not a mark on him, either. Bit winded, that's all.'

Thankfully, Christine sank down into the swirling vapours. When she re-emerged it was to find the catherine wheel fading and a face bending over her; the eyes were grey like her own, but narrow and shrewd with age and experience.

'Are you feeling a bit better now?'

'Yes... thanks...' She struggled to sit up. Miraculously the world righted itself. Trees and bushes became normal and there was the broad track down which she'd galloped. But the man was talking to her again.

'...caught his foot in one of those old roots,' he said.

Christine turned and looked up at him.

He unbent and stood upright, tall and slim in his flared riding coat, his lean face deeply tanned by sun and wind. Then, as he moved towards his horse, she saw the limp.

Swiftly the realisation came to her. This man was... *her father!* He couldn't be anyone else. She knew almost everyone who rode in that part of the country, and this man was a stranger. Besides, there were his eyes – so like her own that she might have been looking into a mirror!

Immediately, she was on her guard. He needn't think that just because he'd caught her horse she was going to throw her arms round him. She was grateful to him for catching Jet and tying him up, but she would have been grateful even if the man had been anyone else, any other complete stranger.

A little unsteadily, Christine got to her feet.

'Thank you for...catching my horse,' she said stiffly. 'Just let him try and reason and plead with me!' she thought.

'That's your horse?'

'Yes... my own,' she said, proudly defiant. 'Let him dare say a word against Jet,' she thought.

But Victor took her completely by surprise. Instead of reasoning with her, pleading with her, or saying a word against Jet, he said furiously, 'Then what the devil do you mean by galloping him over ground like this?'

'You don't know who I am, do you?' Christine replied.

'Of course I do!' stormed Victor angrily, 'and I must say I thought a daughter of mine would have more sense than to gallop a horse like that over this kind of ground.'

He unhooked his horse's reins from a low-hanging branch and swung up into the saddle, with an ease and grace which Christine couldn't help noticing and admiring. But all she could think of were Victor Grayson's words; words that might mean nothing...or so much. '...a horse like *that*...' he'd said. Then suddenly she realised that he'd also said, '...a daughter of mine...'

Furiously, Christine took hold of Jet's reins, and turned round.

'Fortunately, it's no concern of yours what I do!'

For answer, Victor Grayson simply dismounted, limped over to where Christine stood with Jet, and ran his hand expertly down the horse's legs.

'How old?' he said briefly.

'Six, rising seven,' Christine replied, as she watched him curiously.

'Ridden him in a point-to-point-yet?'

'Wh – what?'

'Had him in a Ladies' Race yet?'

'No – no.'

'Why not?'

'Because...' Christine's lip trembled. Covertly, her hand stole out to Jet, as though asking his forgiveness for what she was about to say.

Somehow this was no time for false pride; this was the moment for unsentimental truth. 'Because he's not good enough,' she said.

'Nonsense!' The word was like a whip-crack. 'Hunt him at all?'

'Twice a week last season.'

'Does he carry you well?'

Christine smiled. 'He keeps up with the best,' she said softly. 'And there isn't a jump he turns from.'

'Hm.' Swiftly, smoothly, Victor Grayson remounted the young horse he was schooling for Mr Fawcett, the dealer. Then he pulled the brim of his hat lower over his eyes.

'In that case,' he said quietly, 'all you want is a good trainer!'

With a brief unsmiling nod he moved off down the track towards the village, leaving Christine to watch him in amazement.

Then slowly she remounted Jet and walked home in the opposite direction. Once, she turned in the saddle and saw the straight, supple back before it disappeared in a dip of the heath. No amount of personal antagonism could mar her admiration of the supreme ease and style with which her father sat a horse.

That night, she was quieter than ever at supper, sitting there staring into space, her thoughts miles away. Suddenly, she said, 'Mother, I...I...met *him* up on the heath this evening.'

'Him?' Startled, Nan Grayson looked across the table. 'You mean...your father?'

Christine nodded.

'Jet caught his foot in an old tree root and came down...'

'Darling, you're not hurt?'

'No, I was only stunned for a bit. Served me right, actually, for galloping Jet like that. Anyway, I landed in the thick grass so it was all right. When I came round, he was there. He had caught Jet for me.'

There was a long silence; then Nan Grayson said softly, 'Well?'

'It...doesn't make any difference to the way I feel, though. I sort of thought I ought to tell you, that's all.' Christine rose from the table, then added haltingly, thoughtfully, 'He wanted to know if I'd ridden Jet in a point-to-point. When I said no, he said why not? He doesn't seem to think it's a silly idea, like Laura Carley and Jim Hennegan do.'

'Well, he ought to know,' said Mrs Grayson. 'He's been riding race horses for a good many years.' She looked at her daughter hopefully, wondering if this turn of events this, unexpected meeting of father and daughter might, after all,

Christine put on some of her father's old racing things.

alter things. But Christine was clearly too confused and too prejudiced to see the matter in its right perspective.

That night, instead of going straight to bed, Christine went up to the attic.

The single unshaded light bulb lit up the profusion of broken chairs, ancient, dusty books, a rusty hip-bath, several deed boxes, a doll's pram and a pile of empty dress boxes.

Christine made straight for the old leather trunk in the furthest corner, lifted the lid and drew out some of her father's racing things.

Wonderingly, she pulled on the jersey with the cross-belts, and placed the hard helmet with its brilliant satin cover on her head. Then she went to the mottled mirror that stood against the wall and looked curiously at herself.

Miraculously, the attic walls melted away and she was out there on the course, flying over the turf hearing the roar of the crowd... *Jet wins! The little 'un wins!*

Then Laura Carley's words came back to spoil it all: 'Beats me why you don't sell that thing and get yourself a proper horse...' And suddenly, Christine saw Red Mask, the powerful chestnut hunter, a horse that even the most unemotional dealer would call a nice-ish animal. Red Mask had quality, all right; he also had Jim Hennegan to train him. It was a hopeless combination to try and beat single-handed.

Christine sighed and took off Victor Grayson's old colours.

Yet her father had called Jet 'that horse', almost as if Jet was...well, valuable; and he hadn't seemed to think the idea of running him in a point-to-point at all absurd.

But it was absurd, Christine told herself firmly, and the sooner she forgot about it the better.

She put away the colours, switched off the light, and went down to her room on the next floor.

Tonight, she'd be sensible and not think of Jet winning races. For the whole thing was quite out of the question.

She got into bed and fell asleep instantly...only to dream of Jet coming to the winning-post. But this time he was chestnut-coloured instead of black, and Christine was wearing her old dungarees and wellingtons. And Laura Carley was laughing at her, and exchanging winks with Jim Hennegan.

At the Market

There was an excitement about market days which never failed to thrill Christine.

The shouting of the drovers, the bleating of sheep, the hoarse bellowing of the cattle; the chaffing among the farmers as they leaned over the various pens talking; the auctioneer's rapid fire of sales-talk and the clanging of his bell as he moved from one section of the market to another.

But it wasn't all noise and bustle; there were the quiet corners where the grading went on, the small, circular arenas where the prize beef of the country stood before experts in white coats. Here, there was no shouting and exhorting, but only a joke or two between the white-coated men, or a whispered exchange with a farmer whose cattle were due to step over the scales.

At certain times of the year there was a sale of horses in the market, some of them wild ponies brought down from the hills and moors, some thickset working horses and a few hunters from Ireland.

Today, early in September, was one of these occasions. Christine, waiting till the Shallows Farm pigs had been sold (at a price that would make her mother frown despairingly), was glad when Amos said, 'Well, I'll go and 'ave me pint now, Miss Christine.'

'All right, see you at the car at one-fifteen then.'

Neither Amos nor Christine drove the rattle-trap. Amos because he'd never learned, and Christine because she wasn't yet old enough to hold a licence. But Mr Osborne obligingly drove it for them, which saved him a journey by bus to market and back. Mr Osborne had no real business in the market, but he liked to go because it interested him and made what he called, 'A nice little trip out.' It was an arrangement that suited Nan Grayson, as it left her free to get on with things at Shallows while Christine and Amos were away.

Now Christine, with half-an-hour to spare, went through the crowded market to the long lane where the horses were being sold. As usual there was a double row of people, two and three deep, on each side of the lane, watching intently as each horse was trotted out in hand.

Christine recognised many faces, including that of Mr Fawcett, the sour-faced local dealer who had only the highest class hunters in his yard, and Micky Shaw, the cheerful little dealer who bought all the 'dodges' or 'wrong 'uns' cheaply and sold them to unsuspecting mugs.

There were gypsies, too, with fever-pink cotton neckerchiefs, brightly coloured waistcoats left unbuttoned and beaver hats.

Christine, hemmed in by backs, wriggled her way through to the high rails of an empty cattle pen and clambered up to the top rail.

A skewbald pony in a rope halter was being run out in hand by a gypsy. When it reached the top of the yard, where the trucks and horse-boxes were parked, a whole horde of gypsies surged forward, shouting and waving sticks and fiercely exhorting the skewbald to '*Garn! Garn!*' as it turned to trot back up the lane to the auctioneer's dais.

Christine saw its frantic bewildered eyes – and shuddered. Never, never would she risk exposing Jet to a similar fate, for once he ever passed out of her keeping this might easily happen to him.

The skewbald was sold at 'twenty pund' and a big dappled grey with milky mane and tail was led into the lane.

'...magnificent Irish mare, likely to win a point-to-point!' shouted the florid-faced auctioneer, rattling off particulars of the breeding and ending up with, 'What'll you bid me? What'll you start me off at? Come along, my friends – two hundred guineas? What about one-and-a-half, then?'

Horse after horse came into the lane. Then, suddenly, Christine realised with a start that she ought to be going. But at that moment the crowd surged back against the cattle-pen to make way for a lively young horse that looked ready to use his heels.

Christine clung to her perch, unable to get down till the people moved forward again.

It was then that she heard the two men talking. The words 'Miss Carley...' caught her ears and she realised that one of them had said, 'I hear that Miss Carley, up at White Gates, is running her horse in the point-to-points this year.'

'So I've heard. Might win, too, the way it's bred.'

'Riding it herself, is she?'

'So Jim Hennegan says.'

'Ah.' The man chuckled softly. 'I'd like to see Vic Grayson's girl riding against her. That'd be the day. Often see her out hunting, y'know. Got her father's style all right, she has.'

The other nodded. 'You'd have thought she'd have entered that little black horse of hers, wouldn't you?'

'You would. Don't know how any daughter of Vic Grayson's can hold back. When you think of the old days...'

The men moved away.

'...at ninety-five guineas,' shouted the auctioneer. 'A hundred, gentlemen? At ninety-five, then...'

Free now, Christine was able to slither down off her perch. When she reached the rattle-trap Amos and Mr Osborne were already there.

'Ah! Here she is!' exclaimed Mr Osborne jovially. 'We

were just wondering if you'd bought one of those wild Irish hunters to ride in the point-to-point, weren't we, Amos?'

Christine knew Amos wouldn't have been wondering any such thing. She got in the back of the car, leaving Amos the seat beside Mr Osborne, for she had no wish to be teased about when she was going to be a jockey like her father. She'd had enough of that sort of thing for one day. Her feelings were already too confused by the words she'd just heard.

As the car turned out of the market she slid down against the worn leather and allowed herself to feel justly indignant. What idiots those two men were! Didn't they realise the wanted, above all things, to ride Jet in the Ladies' Race? To prove he had the speed, ability and courage to win a point-to-point.

But people never looked at the other side of things. They thought that all you had to do was say. 'I think I'll put my horse into training,' and that's all there was to it.

Well, isn't it...? flashed back a voice in Christine's head so suddenly that she sat up with a jerk. *What's so difficult about getting a horse in, feeding him oats, schooling him over a few fences, giving him a gallop every day? All this fuss!*

Christine gazed incredulously at the back of Amos's hat. Suddenly all kinds of impossible plans had started to form in her head: plans for stuffing up the holes in the old stable with wodges of sacking so that Jet wouldn't feel the draughts; plans for buying a load of straw with her savings in the Post Office; plans for taking Jet down to Mickey Shaw's place to be clipped out... plans... plans... plans...

She was shining-eyed with excitement when the car at last turned in to the Shallows farmyard. A determined, self-confident smile was on her lips. She'd do it! And somehow her mother must be convinced that they had a chance...

Mrs Grayson came out of the milking shed as the car stopped. In the late September sunshine she looked tired and worried. Her hands steamed from the hot water she was using to scrub out the big churns.

'Well?' she asked Amos anxiously.

Amos shook his head sorrowfully. ''Tweren't a good day for pigs, missus,' he said sadly. 'Couldn't get more'n twenty pound a piece for 'em.'

'But Amos – that hardly shows us a profit!' said Nan Grayson despairingly. Then she smiled, for of course it wasn't Amos's fault. 'Never mind, perhaps we'll do better with the next lot.' She sighed and went back into the milking shed.

Christine wandered across to the ramshackle old stable, her spirits deflated. She couldn't mention Jet's training now, it the face of her mother's anxiety and disappointment over the pigs. She'd have to wait for a while, till things looked better. Meanwhile, she could still go on planning...

'Oh, Christine!' called Mrs Grayson through the milking shed window. 'There's a postcard for you from Laura, dear. On the dresser. She's coming back next week.'

Thoughtfully, Christine went into the farmhouse kitchen. If Laura were returning next week that meant Red Mask would be got up from grass.

Christine smiled to herself. All the needed to do was to keep an eye on the chestnut, find out what was going on up at White Gates stable, then try to do the same with Jet. Naturally, no two horses were alike and what suited one might not suit another; but if the based her training routine on Jim Hennegan's and added her own common sense it ought to work out all right.

It would mean seeing more of Laura, and getting her to talk about Red Mask and what they were doing with him, how much work they were giving him and how they were feeding him... But Laura was always willing to speak about the five-hundred-guinea wonder animal, so that wouldn't be difficult.

With her plans made sketchily but determinedly, Christine went out to help her mother with the milk churns.

The Dismal Failure

It was easy to tell when Laura and her mother returned from Italy. There was a brisk excitement about White Gates Farm. Things began to happen.

Red Mask had gone from his field, and both Jim Hennegan and Frank Gosford had been seen up on the gallops building a row of rough schooling fences a nice distance apart, and with some good going in between.

But so far there was no sign of Laura.

'Brought a cousin back wi' them,' old Amos reported to Christine one morning, at they went about their work in the farmyard. 'Spending a few months at White Gates, so I 'ear from Frank Gosford. A foreign branch of the family, so 'e ses...' He mumbled and rambled on, but Christine had long ago lost the thread of this piece of gossip. She was concentrating on the possibility of probing Laura for information about Red Mask's training routine.

But the first the saw of Laura was two weeks after her return. Hounds were meeting a mere ten minutes' hack from Shallows.

Christine decided to get Jet up and see as much of a hunt as she could in between her duties on the farm. She wouldn't be able to spare the whole day, but at least she might manage a morning and hope that hounds would find in the first covert.

Laura was already there when Christine arrived at the meet, but she wasn't in riding clothes.

'Too much beastly standing about,' she said in a bored voice. 'I really couldn't be bothered. You know what it's like once they get into Witham Wood. Such a waste of time.

Jim's bringing Red Mask out for a bit, just to qualify, so Paul and I thought we'd wander down and see them off.'

Christine was suddenly very glad she never felt like that about hunting, as if every bit of the pleasure had gone from it.

'I see you've still got your pony turned out.' It was Laura's voice again, scathing and critical.

Pony!

The old anger and irritation, which nobody else but Laura seemed able to arouse in Christine, rose hotly now. How dare Laura call Jet a pony! But before she could say anything, Laura had turned to the dark, good-looking boy of seventeen who stood beside her.

'By the way,' she added, 'this is my cousin, Paul. He's from South America, actually, but we met him in Italy and brought him back with us. He's going to spend a few months at White Gates before going up to Oxford.'

Christine managed a brief, cold smile. Any cousin of Laura's would be sure to be unbearable!

'Hello,' said Paul eagerly, in a perfectly English voice. 'I've been admiring your horse.' He put his hand gently on Jet's velvety neck. 'In our part of the world we are more accustomed to this light, thoroughbred type of animal. We have no use for the big, heavy hunter type.'

A thrill of gratitude swept through Christine. That was indeed a nasty one for Miss Laura Carley! Apparently, she thought so, too. 'If you're referring to Red Mask,' she snapped furiously, 'you just wait until he wins the Ladies' Race!'

Paul smiled and winked up at Christine. He was about to retort when two things happened. Red Mask, newly clipped out and shod, came trotting down on to the green, and the Master gave two short notes on the horn to indicate that he was moving off to draw the first covert.

Christine joined the cavalcade of horsemen and women making for Witham Wood. Jim Hennegan was a long way in front, talking to Fred Polson, the second Whip; but soon, when he was free, Christine intended to draw alongside and question him about Red Mask's training.

But it was a forlorn hope. For no sooner had the hounds been put into covert than the chestnut turned back, threaded its way through the waiting field, and went trotting up the lane leading to White Gates.

After that day, with the memory of Laura's coldly critical gaze wandering over Jet's rough winter coat, and the memory of her voice calling him a pony, Christine felt even more determined to enter Jet for the Ladies' Race. But now it was a desperate kind of determination. The gallops up on the heath drew her like a magnet. She could think of nothing else. Suppose she rode Jet up there one morning when no one was about, and tried him over Hennegan's fences, just to see how he went?

Three mornings later, she slipped away, caught Jet, and rode him, rough-coated and in his oldest bridle, up towards the heath. Climbing the narrow track, she began to feel excited. Soon she would be in sight of the schooling ground.

At the top of the track, where it suddenly opened out on to the heath, she drew Jet to a standstill. For there, to her horror, was the Carleys' enormous limousine with Mr Carley standing beside it. Laura and Paul were with him, and Jim Hennegan was up on Red Mask.

Christine tried to draw back, but Jet chose that moment to lift his head and announce their presence with a great piercing whinney that shook his whole body.

The Carleys turned swiftly and saw her, making Christine acutely conscious of the fact that she was wearing her oldest farm clothes and riding a horse which she had not even had time to brush!

'Come to watch the fun, lass?' called out Mr Carley. 'You're a bit late; we've just finished.'

Christine felt the old stab of irritation. Why should Mr Carley think it was any fun for her to watch Red Mask? However, now that she had been discovered, there was nothing for it but to go over to them, or be unforgivably rude.

'How...how did the chestnut go?' she stammered, wishing she'd never come.

'Oh,' laughed Mr Carley, rubbing his hands together smugly, 'I don't think we'll have much competition to fear, eh, Laura?' Then he looked at his watch. 'Well, I must get down to the office.' He looked up at Jim Hannegan. 'Have you got everything you want?'

'I think so, sir.'

'Got enough corn? Don't run short now. Order what you like. Feed, anything. Don't worry about the money. As long as Red Mask wins that race...'

A few minutes later, the great gleaming car had moved off down the heath road, and Laura and Paul were walking back to White Gates behind the rugged-up quarters of the chestnut.

Left alone on the gallops, alone on that flat, limitless stretch of heath beneath a lowering, grey sky, Christine walked Jet up to the first gorse-fence. Should she try him over it? Why not? It wasn't so very different from hunting, was it?

Suddenly, her mind was made up. She trotted back to an imaginary starting-post, then, shortening her reins, she turned and drove her heels into Jet's sides with a desperate purposefulness.

Down the length of good, grassy going Jet galloped. Coming into the first fence, Christine steadied him for the take-off, felt him balance himself and then leap high over the fence, with a foot or so to spare. On the other side he pecked a bit, then recovered and went on to the next fence.

But before he could jump it, Christine pulled him up.

It was no good. She knew it. All Jet's speed had gone. They had no more than 'muddled' along the grassy ribbon of gallops. It was a poor attempt and she was heartily thankful that no one had been there to see the awful exhibition both she and Jet had made of it. Bitterly, despairingly, she apologised to the little black horse. For he was only too willing to do all she asked of him, but the trouble was, she didn't know enough herself! With a sob of hopelessness, she admitted it. The game of make-believe was over. The dream had ended. It was no use breaking her own heart, and Jet's, in trying to accomplish the impossible. She could never compete with Laura in the Ladies' Race – and that was final.

'You'll never win a race that way.'

'Wh – what?' Startled, Christine spun round in the saddle to find her father riding alongside.

'You're 'show-jumping' him over the fences,' went on Victor Grayson quietly, seriously. 'That's no good at all. You've got to make him spread himself, take the jumps in his stride, not stand back at them. Forget about clearing them. Forget about height. It won't matter if he brushes the tops. You want him to jump out, not up. You lose too much ground, too much forward travel by clearing fences with a foot to spare. See what I mean?'

With a shock of excitement, Christine realised that his voice was briskly assured, serious, as if the whole thing was a problem worthy of proper consideration. She saw perfectly well what he meant, she knew what was wrong, but knowing what was wrong wasn't at all the same thing as knowing what to do about it, how to cure it.

'Yes, but...' she began eagerly. She stopped when she remembered who he was.

But now her resentment confused her, because she was finding it more and more difficult to dislike him. In one way, she could even understand his going off to Australia to ride.

For his whole life had been bound up with horses and somehow the chances had not been as good for him in England, and the Australian offer had seemed like a golden opportunity not to be missed. She could understand the lure and the pull of it, but there was her mother to think of now. There must be no risk of *her* being hurt again. Now she set her face into a cold, proud aloofness.

'I'm...I'm not trying to win a race,' she said stiffly.

'Aren't you?' smiled Victor Grayson. 'In that case I'm wasting my time.'

He turned his horse's head and went off down a bridle path to the left.

Immediately, Christine felt a deep sense of loss. She wanted desperately to turn to him, to beg him to help her. For never had she felt such confidence in anyone before. Somehow, she felt he knew more about horses than Mickey Shaw, Jim Hennegan and the vet all put together. But there was the past between them. For her mother's sake she mustn't risk it.

Bewildered and unhappy, she rode on to Shallows Farm alone. She knew now that by herself she could achieve nothing.

But with her father's help...

A Quarrel

That evening, immediately after supper, Christine got her old bicycle out of the stable and cycled into town. When she arrived at the inn, her father was having supper alone, in his own room. Nervous and hostile though she felt, Christine couldn't help feeling sorry for him as he sat alone at the round table. There was something so awfully bleak about his room; nothing homely and warm and cheerful, like the kitchen at the farm.

'Why...Christine...' He half rose, surprised at first, then clearly alarmed. 'Is anything wrong? Your mother...?'

'No. It's nothing personal.'

Relief relaxed the sudden tension of Victor Grayson's face. 'Sit down, then,' he said gruffly.

'No, thank you,' said Christine proudly. 'I...I won't sit down.' Defiant and desperate, her heart thudding, she stood by the door, her mind groping for the right words.

'Please yourself,' shrugged Victor Grayson. 'Mind if I get on with my supper?'

'No...of course not. It's...about Jet.'

Victor Grayson looked up quickly, his eyes narrowing shrewdly. 'The little black horse?'

'Yes.'

'Well? Go on, girl.' he prompted impatiently. 'What's the matter with him?'

'Nothing...' She paused. aware suddenly of the terrific thing she had come to ask, but remembering also Laura's biting scorn and her scathing remarks about Jet. A pony, she had called him: but her father called him the little black horse. In a breathless rush, Christine went on. 'I want to race him! I...I...want to ride him in the Ladies' Race in our local point-to-point!'

'I see,' he said calmly. 'Well?'

Christine swallowed and plunged on.

'I don't know how to train him, I just *know* he stands a good chance, but I...' She shook her head as the tears threatened to blind her. 'I wondered if...if...you...' She faltered to a stop.

'You wondered if I'd train for you. Is that it?'

'Yes,' whispered Christine.

'I see.' Victor Grayson rose from the table and limped to the mantelpiece for cigarettes and matches. .'You know what that would mean?' he demanded quietly. 'You realise I'd have to come to Shallows?'

'Yes. I do realise that,' she admitted. Suddenly her father turned.

'All right. Christine,' he said quickly. 'Don't worry. If I undertake to train your horse for you I won't regard it as a lowering of the flag. It would be on a strictly professional basis. But I warn you – it will mean hard work for you, and for the little horse.'

'Then...you'll do it?'

'I don't know yet... It all depends. I'll have to have another look at the horse before I make up my mind.'

'There's one other thing,' said Christine unhappily. 'The Carleys' horse, Red Mask...'

'The chestnut?' Victor Grayson smiled reflectively. 'Yes. Nice pattern. What I'd call a Leicesterhire horse.'

'That will be favourite.'

Victor Grayson nodded slowly. 'So that's the competition, is it?' he said softly. Then he chuckled. 'Well, we'd have to see what could be done about that, wouldn't we, Chris?'

Christine's eyes were brilliant with excitement and a hope she dared not yet even acknowledge. 'Then you really think we stand a chance?' she breathed.

'Don't you?' said her father.

'Oh yes. Oh, *yes!* But I...I thought I was the only one who believed it.'

'Perhaps you are. I don't know yet. I'll come up tomorrow, afternoon and have a look at your little black horse. Then I'll tell you what I really believe.'

He turned away, as though there was nothing more to be said.

Awkwardly. Christine hesitated in the doorway.

'Thank you...for not saying no right away,' she said, dignified, but embarrassed. It was then that her eye caught sight of the open suitcase on the bed, a suitcase already packed. Questioningly, she looked at her father.

'Good night, Christine,' he said sharply.

Slowly, Christine closed the door behind her. So it was

true! Only yesterday her mother had said something about her father leaving the district for good, going north to a big training establishment. Now he was staying. For her sake? Would it depend on Jet?

Thoughtfully, she went down the winding old oak staircase and out into the cobbled yard where her bike was propped against the wall.

The next afternoon, Victor Grayson stood in the middle of the paddock while Christine turned Jet loose. He had already looked him over in the old, ramshackle stable, his shrewd, professional eye ready to notice any bad points. After his long examination and several sharp questions to Christine, he'd said, 'Well, you can turn him out again. I've seen all I want to.'

There was nothing to tell from the tone of his voice what his decision would be. Now, as Christine came back to him, carrying Jet's old snaffle bridle, he said quietly, 'All right, Chris. You've got yourself a trainer.'

Christine was so happy she could think of nothing to say to express her feelings.

'The first thing we've got to do is get the little horse fit,' her father went on. 'We'll get all the flesh on to him that he can carry, then we'll set about hardening him up with plenty of work.'

Together, in close consultation, they paced the farmyard. Now a new note crept into the atmosphere between Christine and her father; suddenly everything was brisk and business-like and purposeful.

'It means giving him as much corn every day as he'll eat,' explained Victor Grayson, 'and, of course, he'll have to come in right away.'

Christine listened to him with growing dismay as he went on about corn, loads of straw for bedding, chaff...

'We... I... couldn't afford...' she began awkwardly,

realising for the first time how much Jet's training was likely to cost, and that this was likely to mean the end of everything as far as racing him in the point-to-point was concerned.

'Don't worry about the cost for the moment.' Wisely, Victor Grayson knew better than to offer to pay for Jet's training expenses as a gift. Christine would never accept that from him. Not for the moment, anyway. She had the same streak of integrity, of independence, that he had; the same determination that had prevented him from returning until he'd made a success of his efforts in Australia. His failure was probably his just reward, but at least he was honest enough to admit his mistake and his defeat.

Now he went on in his quiet, grave voice. 'I'll see to all that for you, and you can settle up in easy instalments later,' he smiled, 'when you've won the race. All right?'

'Well, if you're sure...' Christine said gratefully.

'I'm sure.' He tugged at the curled brim of his green felt hat and turned suddenly away. 'Bring the little horse down to the yard tomorrow afternoon and we'll clip him out. Amos will patch up the old stable tomorrow morning, and it'll do for a bit till the really cold weather sets in. Got any rugs?'

'N-no...'

'All right. I'll get hold of one for you.'

'Thank you,' said Christine breathlessly. 'And thanks for...'

But he was already limping away, down the farmyard that had once belonged to him, and to his father before him.

The next afternoon, Christine was getting Jet up from the paddock when Laura Carley rode into the yard.

'Oh! Are you off for a ride?' she called out, trim and rather too formally dressed for an hour's exercise round the lanes. Casually, she flicked the grey's beautifully brushed mane. 'Good. I'll come with you. Jim's so busy with. Red Mask that I thought I'd give this one an hour or so.' She gazed critically at Jet's plushy, mud-spattered sides. 'I say, that pony looks as though it's come straight off the moors, doesn't it? Look at all that mud on him!'

But for once, her words failed to sting Christine.

'Yes, doesn't he?' she agreed. 'That's why I'm just taking him down to be clipped out.'

Laura's mouth fell open with amazement. 'Clipped *out?*' she repeated incredulously. 'Wh-what for?'

Christine swung lightly up into the slumsy old saddle. 'Well, I can't very well put him into training with his winter coat still on him, can I?' she asked reasonably.

'Into... *training?*' queried Laura, looking incredulous. 'Training for *what*, may I ask?'

'Point-to-points, of course,' said Christine calmly. 'Look I've got to fly. Sorry!'

A burst of laughter broke from Laura. 'So you actually think you can get round a point-to-point course on that thing!'

That thing!

Christine's hands trembled on the reins. She had just about stood enough from Laura Carley. But worse was to come. Now she said quietly, 'My trainer seems to think so.'

'Your trainer? And may one ask the name of "your trainer",' sneered Laura, 'or is it to be kept secret till the great day?'

Christine's heart pounded uncomfortably, but her head was high as she answered steadily, 'No, it's not a secret. It's my father, Victor Grayson.'

'Victor Grayson!' said Laura in a scornful voice. 'Well, he may be your father, but everyone knows he's finished now as a horseman; he's just a broken-down ex-jockey...' She broke off in alarm as Christine rode straight at her. The grey scuttered back a few paces, then went trotting madly out of the yard. Laura made a grab for the reins and got the horse back under control before the bend in the lane. When she turned, her face was red with indignation. She had lost her smart hat, her whip and her dignity. Christine, who'd had no intention of touching either her or the grey, could not help feeling somewhat amused and pleased to see her so put out, for once.

'How dare you ride at me!' shouted Laura threateningly. 'I'll make you pay for that, Christine Grayson! I'll show you who's the power round here!' She glared at Christine. 'You and your precious father and your tuppenny ha'penny pony!'

Then, with a furious kick at the grey's sides, she trotted off down the lane.

'What's the matter? What's going on?' cried Nan Grayson, coming out into the yard. 'I thought I heard Laura Carley.'

'You did,' said Christine.

The next second she had flung herself off Jet's back, thrown the reins over the gate post, and run sobbing into the farmhouse.

'Darling...whatever...?' Anxiously, Nan Grayson followed her daughter into the kitchen.

'I hate her! I *hate* her!' sobbed Christine incoherently. 'She...she...called him a... a...broken-down ex-jockey...'

'Who dear? *Who?*' Nan's arms went around the heaving shoulders.

'But he's *not* and I hate her...and Jet's not a tuppenny ha'penny pony...'

'Of course he's not, darling.' Slowly, Nan rocked Christine to and fro till the sobbing became a snuffle and finally ended up in a watery kind of smile.

'Oh, dear,' sighed Christine worriedly at last. 'I dare say I've done something awful now and Laura won't rest till she gets her revenge. I didn't mean to touch her, or her horse, but I just couldn't stick the awful things she said any longer. All I was going to do was tell her to get off the farm, but the grey took fright...' She smiled wanly. 'Laura's voice was enough to scare the wits out of any horse. Did you hear her?'

'Don't worry,' said Nan Grayson cheerfully. 'There's nothing she can do, however vindictive she feels.'

The Gypsy's Warning

During the next few weeks many changes took place at Shallows Farm. Jet no longer roamed the small paddock, but was now installed in the old stable. Amos, under Vic Grayson's directions, had boarded up the holes, but it still looked ramshackle, dark and dirty. Then one day in mid-October, Christine came in from the fields to find a miraculous change. For during her absence her father had been busy with the distemper brush. Now the stable walls were a fresh, clean white, the window above the hay-rack was polished clean, the floor was ankle-deep in new straw, and an electric light had been run across from the milking shed.

In all this new splendour stood Jet, lively-eyed, his legs sleek and satiny beneath the moth-eaten old rug borrowed from Mr Fawcett.

In this new and worthier setting, the little black horse looked more than ever like one of those old-fashioned coloured prints of a thoroughbred in a stable. But, despite the extra vitality resulting from the improvement in his condition, he was just the same good-natured Jet. And still, in the evenings, when the last oat was eaten and Christine moved quietly and efficiently about the stable, bedding him down for the night, he dipped his dozing head and blew softly into her hair, as she bent down to refill his water bucket or toss over the straw he had trodden flat.

These were some of Christine's happiest moments with her horse, and Jet seemed to enjoy them too. For the day's work was done, and in the peace of the evening there seemed to be a quiet understanding between the girl and her horse, who watched her with a dreamy and trustful gaze.

Sometimes, tired though she was, Christine could hardly bear to leave Jet. She would stand gazing at him with pride and love, delighting in the slope of his shoulder beneath the tattered old rug, the Arab quality of his small head, the carriage of his fine silken tail, and the perfect conformation of quarters and hocks and 'tea-cup' feet.

Every day Victor Grayson limped up to the farm. By now, a regular daily routine was in force for Jet. Feeding, mucking-out, grooming and exercise were matters of clockwork precision. There were no more casual rides lasting anything from half-an-hour to three hours, taken whenever Christine could get away from the farm. At eight o'clock, rain, gale or sun, Jet was out at exercise. One hour to begin with, increasing as his condition improved and his muscles hardened. Hunting was only allowed as and when Victor ordered.

By the time Christine got back with him her father would have arrived, ready to groom and muck-out while Christine got back to her work on the farm. But first she had to give him a detailed account of how her horse had gone. Even the smallest thing had to be mentioned.

Like a hawk, Victor Grayson watched Jet's progress, noting every change in temperament and condition.

By now there was a comfortably impersonal relationship between father and daughter. They were trainer and owner. Nothing personal was ever discussed; but Jet, the little black horse that Nan Grayson has scrimped and saved to buy, formed a link between them, and through him both father and daughter began warily to discover each other.

Once, when Christine greeted her father, panic-stricken because Jet had left half his early-morning feed, Victor Grayson had simply smiled where another trainer might have shared Christine's anxiety.

'But I read in a book that if they're off their feed it's a bad sign!' cried Christine. 'It means they're either ill or fretting!'

'You read that in a book, eh?' teased Victor Grayson mildly. 'Well, we're not training from a book! Now don't worry. Your horse is doing well. He's fine, believe me.'

'But he left half his feed!' wailed Christine, doubting her father's knowledge.

'If you have a favourite bar of chocolate,' said Mr Grayson, 'don't you often tuck into most of it right away and then put a little bit on one side to eat later?'

'Y...ye-s...'

'Well, Jet is no different. Look...' He led the way into the stable where Jet, rugged-up after his exercise was now happily finishing the remains of his breakfast.

Every morning it was the same story.

'I still don't see...' worried Christine. 'Do I give him too much or too little?'

'Neither. Whatever you gave him he'd leave half of it till later,' smiled Mr Grayson. 'You see, Christine, horses, particularly clean-bred ones, have their little fads and fancies, just like ordinary people. Your horse knows what he likes. It's a case of personality. I dare say he loves coming back to that bit of feed he's left in the manger. Look how he's tucking into it with relish, really enjoying it!'

'But surely if he finished up the first lot before we went out I could give him some more when we came in?'

'No, no! That wouldn't be at all the same thing,' explained Victor Grayson patiently. 'It would spoil it for him. Don't you see? There's something *special* about that bit he's left. He knows he's left it. He knows it's there. He's probably even thinking about it while he's up there on the heath!'

'I see...'

'The great thing is not to fuss him over it. Let him have his way. Don't worry him by trying to change such a harmless little fad. The main thing is to have him happy, Chris; to appreciate that he's got his own special character. The big mistake a lot of people make,' added Victor Grayson gravely, 'is in thinking that a horse can be trained absolutely on automatic lines. Basically, of course, there's got to be a rigid routine. But there's also got to be a margin allowed for an animal's personality.'

Suddenly, Christine saw what he meant. And she saw, for the first time, the truly professional attitude to horses; the attitude which was half skilful knowledge and half real love and understanding.

She saw nothing of Laura, or her cousin Paul, during those busy, exciting weeks.

Once, coming home on Jet, she passed Jim Hennegan in the narrow lane. The encounter left her shaken. For to her polite 'Good morning', Hennegan had shouted out sneeringly, 'Is it the Grand National you're after winning on the pony, then?'

The words hadn't upset Christine so much as the sheer venom and malice on Hennegan's face.

Later, when she told her father, he simply said, 'That's a good sign, Chris. Perhaps he's getting afraid of the competition, eh? Hennegan's got a cushy job there, but Carley won't be any too pleased if his horse loses the local race. Those people who think money can buy everything don't like to be beaten.'

A week later Christine was to remember those words. She was coming out of the saddler's when she met Paul.

'Hello!' he cried with real pleasure, his grin more friendly than Laura's had ever been. 'I've been hearing lots about you!'

Christine's eyes widened. 'About *me?*'

'Yes.' Then suddenly his grin faded, and he looked quickly about, as if someone might overhear his next words. 'Laura's really worried about your riding against her in the Ladies' Race.'

'But – why? I mean, Red Mask is a very good horse...'

'Yes,' put in Paul quickly, 'but Laura is not a very good horsewoman – and Jim Hennegan knows it! Don't think I'm being disloyal to my own cousin, but...' he paused, then added earnestly in a swift rush of words, '...but unless you're really keen I'd give up, if I were you!'

'Give up?' gasped Christine incredulously. 'I wouldn't dream of it!'

'Then take my advice and watch out. The Carleys hate to be beaten. I can't say any more.' He jingled the leathers and irons he was carrying. 'Laura wants these quickly so I'd better get on, I suppose.'

'Well, goodbye and thank you.'

'Good luck,' he said seriously. 'And don't forget the gypsy's warning, will you? I...' he broke off awkwardly. 'I'd hate anything to happen to your horse.'

The next second he'd gone, and Christine was left to wander slowly back to where her mother waited in the rattletrap.

'Who was that good-looking boy you were talking to?' asked Nan Grayson.

'Laura's cousin, Paul.'

'Oh! One of the enemy camp!' smiled Nan, as she put the rattle-trap into gear.

'No,' said Christine thoughtfully. 'Paul's not an enemy. He's a friend.'

Then suddenly, she began to wonder. *Was* he? Or had he been told to try and persuade Christine to abandon the race?

Once again, Christine celarly heard Mr Carley's voice: '...don't worry about the money...as long as Red Mask wins!'

Now she remembered all kinds of odd things; Laura's angry threat, Jim Hennegan's spiteful words, her father's comment about the Carleys not liking to be beaten...and now Paul's warning.

Now, for the first time since she had seriously considered racing Jet and begun training, Christine felt really afraid.

A Plot

With the date of the point-to-points approaching, the general excitement increased. Posters advertising the races were hung in shop windows; people stuck printed slips across the back windows of their cars; and in the market, speculations as to the chances of the various horses were rife.

'Reckon we'll see a proper battle between Vic Grayson's girl and that Miss Carley!' Christine heard one farmer chuckle.

On all sides, people wished her luck; some because she was 'Vic Grayson's girl' and it would be good to see a Grayson in the saddle again; some because they'd known her from a baby up. She was 'their Christine'.

'Oi'll be 'avin' my shillin' on you, Miss,' grinned an old shepherd. 'So you mind and win, now!'

'I'll do my best,' promised Christine.

That's how it was, wherever she went. Now it was more than just her race and Jet's; so much seemeed to depend on it. It was as if somehow she would be letting them all down if she lost.

To Amos it was like a dream come true. For now, to every boast of Frank Gosford's about Red Mask, Amos could go one better about Jet. Once, it almost came to blows between the two men, and the landlord of the inn had to ask them to be a bit quieter about it.

Never for one moment did Amos consider the possibility of Christine losing the race. To him, it was as good as won!

By now Jet was in top condition, and he could do a good gallop without fear of blowing up. Under Victor Grayson's training he was taking his fences better too; putting in a short one when necessary, without losing too much speed. And all the time, the confidence of both the horse and the rider was increasing, until they felt sure they could win.

Then came the morning when Victor Grayson met Christine on the gallops with one of Mr Fawcett's new horses. 'Let's see how Jet goes in company, shall we?' he said casually.

Christine's heart leapt. For in a way it would be like a race. like the real thing.

And so they rode their fences side by side, father and daughter, the little black horse and the big Irish bay. The sound of the thudding hooves gave Christine a tremendous feeling of exhilaration, as she tried to take the jumps really well. Only vaguely, out of the corner of her eye, did she see her father, his old hat crammed down hard upon his head, as his horse rose hugely beside her over the fences.

'You'll do, you'll do!' Victor Grayson laughed teasingly, when they pulled up at last, breathless and red in the face. 'Where d'you think you are – Aintree? If you make the running like that on the day, my girl, you'll have Jet blowing up before you reach the second fence!' Then his eyes narrowed as he looked past Christine to the belt of trees fringing the gallops. 'Hullo...' he murmured. 'Who was that, I wonder? I could have sworn I saw someone on a grey horse.'

'A grey horse? Oh, that was probably Laura, or Jim Hennegan,' said Christine casually.

'Hmm,' murmured Victor Grayson thoughtfully.

'Why?' asked Christine, as Jet trod hot bricks after the exciting gallop. 'What's the matter?'

'Nothing,' replied her father swiftly. 'Come on, we'd better get those rugs on...'

But Christine wasn't deceived. As they turned for home she knew that something was worrying him, something to do with whoever had been watching their trial gallop from the trees. Was it something to do with Laura?

Up at White Gates Farm, Laura lounged in a corner of the stable, watching Jim Hennegan 'do over' the grey horse.

'But are you sure?' she insisted anxiously.

'As sure as there's shamrock in Ireland, Miss,' replied Hennegan, ceasing the breathy whistling which always accompanied his grooming efforts. 'The little black is going a gallop as 'ud put him in the picture at Cheltenham.'

'But you don't really think they've got a chance, do you, Jim?'

'*Chance?*' snorted Hennegan. 'It's no chance – it's a cert! The little back horse'll do us out of the cup yet, Miss, unless...' He broke off and applied the body-brush with even faster and firmer movements.

Laura stood watching him, appalled. Never had she considered Christine and Jet as serious competition. Why, the whole thing was beyond belief, outrageous...

Yet, was it?

You only had to remember the stories they still told of Victor Grayson's brilliance as a jockey, and after all, Christine was his daughter. She was a Grayson, too; like father, like daughter, so they said.

But surely Jet hadn't the stamina, even if Christine were a fine horsewoman? A blood weed, that's what Hennegan had always called him. Yet if Jim said they had a chance, then they had. He would know. He wasn't one to make a mistake.

Anger rose up chokingly in Laura. To be beaten by a top-class horse from an adjacent hunt would be bad enough, but to be beaten by what her father called, 'an impoverished farmer's daughter on a tuppenny ha'penny pony' – that would be terrible indeed.

She'd never be able to live it down. She would be a laughing-stock. Her father would be furious. 'After all the money I've spent,' she could imagine him saying, 'you let yourself be beaten by that circus turn-out!'

For that was what Christine and Jet would look like. A circus turn-out, with Christine wearing patched-up, second-hand old boots and the cap she'd worn ever since those earliest Pony Club days, and Jet in a comical saddle far too big for him...

Oh, no! The whole thing was unthinkable! Besides, she had to show Paul that she could leave Christine and Jet standing, for his remarks about 'these big, heavy hunter types' still rankled.

Up till now, she'd had no doubts about her own success.

Oh, she'd known that Christine was playing about with Jet, trying to train him, pretending she could win a race with him. But Laura had never taken it seriously. At the back of her mind she had nursed a vague plan for making Christine look silly if she so much as got as far as the point-to-point course; show her up in some way, teach her a lesson for that scene at Shallows Farm, taunt her in public about the 'pony', about the blood weed, about her ancient and ridiculous tack, shatter her self-confidence till she retired from the race, humiliated and miserable.

But that was all. It would be revenge enough, anyway, when Laura herself appeared in the paddock, resplendent in her new racing colours, the gleaming lemon satin cap and purple hooped jersey, with Red Mask being walked round the paddock in his new monogrammed rug. And it would be triumph indeed when she came up after the race to be led into the winning pen, while Christine – if she did take part in the race – came trailing in last, tired and defeated.

She had never really regarded Christine as competition until now. Why should she? She had everything on her side. The best horse that money could buy, an experienced trainer, and everything done to smooth her path. Besides, she was so used to winning every time that to lose now would be unthinkable. Why, only the other day her mother had said jokingly to the other ladies at her bridge party, 'I don't know what I'll do when Laura starts winning point-to-point cups as well! We'll have to have another room built to hold them!' And the other ladies had smiled and said, 'Laura is certainly a brilliant rider, my dear.'

The memory of those words came to Laura now, causing her to clench her fists till the knuckles whitened. She *had* to win that cup! Even if she lost every other one afterwards, she must win this one, the Lord Herleigh Cup.

Then Jim Hennegan's words came back to her: 'They'll do us out of the cup yet, Miss, unless...'

Unless?

Unless what?

Laura turned to him quickly and found him watching her shrewdly.

'Unless what?' she whispered hoarsely.

Hennegan shrugged. A crafty little smile twisted his lips, as he slowly collected the body brush, curry comb and rubber. 'Unless we do something about it,' he said softly, thoughtfully.

'What *can* we do?' demanded Laura bitterly. 'How can we do anything?'

'Sure, there's ways...'

'*Ways?* But the race is only the day after tomorrow!'

'That still gives us time.'

'Time?' gasped Laura. 'Time for what?'

Jim Hennegan fixed her with a strange, steady look. 'Time to make sure the *right* horse wins,' he said quietly.

The Eleventh Hour

'Nervous?' asked Victor Grayson, turning up the collar of his coat against the pelting rain.

Christine slipped the bolt of Jet's box and nodded. 'Yes, I am a bit,' she confessed.

'Good!' said her father surprisingly. 'That's how you ought to be on the night before a race. I always was.' He caught Christine's anxious glance up at the low dark clouds. 'Don't worry about this weather. Your little horse likes a bit of heavy going.' He smiled at her; one of his rare, warm smiles. 'Try and get a good night's sleep, Chris,' he advised quietly. Then, abruptly, he tugged at the brim of his old felt hat and added huskily, 'Good night, my dear... and good luck for tomorrow.'

'You'll be there, won't you?' asked Christine hastily, suddenly aware of how awful it would be if he were to desert her now, at the eleventh hour.

'Yes. I'll be there,' he promised slowly. And afterwards? Afterwards when the race was over, he'd be gone, never to return. It was no good, he could see that now. There was no place for him here. Nan wanted him back, but Christine didn't. And it was Christine who counted now. He'd see her through tomorrow's race, and after that he'd go north. And this time it would be goodbye for ever.

For one moment he allowed his gaze to linger on the shadowy hulk of the farmhouse, the house where he'd been born. His home. Never had it meant so much to him as it did now when he had to leave it for good.

'I'll see you there,' he said harshly, to hide the emotions he didn't want Christine to see. 'We'll walk round the course first. Amos can bring the horse down.' He turned away, and stumbled against the stable door.

'What is it? What's the matter?' cried Christine in alarm, as her father gripped the edge of Jet's box, his face twisted with pain.

'Nothing!' he panted. 'It's all right! It goes... like this... sometimes! I'll be...all right!'

Slowly, the red-hot pain eased and he cautiously relaxed.

'It's that old leg, Chris. It got smashed against the rails. There's nothing more they can do about it,' he explained simply. He stood upright now, angry with himself, because he had that queer sort of pride which hated anyone to see his pain, to pity him. Least of all Christine.

Ruefully, he remembered the incident of that race, the one that was to be his last, when he'd ridden on to the rails in order to save young Tim Tilney from the fate that an older jockey had planned for him. They'd been coming down to the last fence but one and his horse had been going a double handful. Just in the nick of time, he'd seen what old 'Foxy' had been up to and had forced himself up alongside young Tilney, between Tilney and the rails. There had been yells and shouts and the terrible sickening crunch of his bones against the rails. Then he'd fainted, and the next he knew he was lying on the warm grass with a doctor fussing over him.

Well...it had been worth it. Young Tilney was doing well now, winning nearly every time out. But if he, Victor Grayson, the old hand, the experienced jockey, hadn't seen what was coming, Tilney would almost certainly have been finished with racing for ever, his spirit broken, and the most promising young jockey of the day lost to racing for ever.

With a sigh, Victor Grayson turned away. One last glance at the place which had always, even when he was all those miles away in Australia, been really home to him, and he limped off, his tall, spare figure proud and upright as it disappeared into the mist of rain and falling darkness.

'Bed!' announced Nan Grayson firmly.

Christine looked up from her place on the hearth rug, where she was giving a final polish to her black garter straps.

'But I'll never sleep! I know it!' she cried in protest.

'Oh, yes, you will. You'll be surprised. There's nothing like excitement for making one tired.' Nan Grayson yawned and smiled. 'Besides,' she added, 'if you give that leather another rub you'll wear it away!'

Christine looked about her at all her possessions, and her gaze lingered critically on the saddle resting along the back of a kitchen chair. It was a beauty. Not new, of course, but just right, small and light and beautifully cut. The sort of saddle you could 'sit into' straight away. It belonged to her father, and he had brought it up yesterday. 'Let's see how this one fits,' he had suggested in his own casual way, as if he'd produced nothing more exciting than a new brow-band. Then he'd put it on Jet's back and stood away to see the result. Christine had glowed at his pronouncement. 'With that horse,' he'd said admiringly, 'you'd have a job to put a saddle on wrong!'

'This place looks like a tack room,' said Nan Grayson suddenly. And indeed, it did. For apart from the saddle over the chair-back, its irons glinting in the firelight, there were boots, garter straps, breeches, an ancient velvet cap, bridle, whip and jersey draped over every available space.

At the sight of the jersey, Nan smiled musingly. She remembered the last time Victor had worn it. He'd won on Cinnamon, a great raking bay mare belonging to Colonel Fenright. No one else had been able to get her down to the start, even; but Victor had managed it, soothing the fretting, sweating creature, settling her, giving her some of his own confidence.

Perhaps it would bring Christine good luck to wear this same jersey with its salmon-coloured cross-belts?

Then she shook her head sadly. For although Christine had spent hours washing and darning it, it still looked absurdly large on her, engulfing her slender figure. Yet a new one would cost more than they could possibly afford.

Anxiously, Nan Grayson hoped that Laura Carley wouldn't notice the jersey and make some acid remark about it. Not that Christine would mind, because all her thoughts would be on Jet instead of herself. All the same, Nan wished she could do as much for Christine as the Carleys could do for Laura.

'There!' Christine stood up and stretched. 'That'll have to do!' Her mother was right; the kitchen did look like a tack room, a particularly cosy one. But there was one thing missing. If only he could be there, sitting in the old armchair by the fire, his bad leg resting on the fender, recalling old races of the past.

With a stab of pain, Christine remembered how terribly tired he'd looked as he'd limped off to his bleak room at the inn; how tired and how lonely...

'What's that?' cried Nan suddenly.

For a long moment they stood still, listening. But there was no sound.

'I thought I heard a door,' said Mrs Grayson.

'Probably the wind slamming the old barn door,' shrugged Christine. She looked at her watch. Ten o'clock! And her mother was right. She was tired after all.

With a long last look at her things for tomorrow, Christine kissed her mother goodnight and went upstairs. It still seemed amazing to think that by this time tomorrow the race would be over, and everyone would know who had won the cup.

Jet in Danger

Christine awoke to the sound of voices coming from somewhere below her window. It was still dark. Instinctively, she sensed that something was wrong. A glance at the luminous dial of her watch told her it was only five minutes past twelve. At that very moment a screaming whinny shuddered out into the silent night.

In a flash, Christine was out of bed, pulling on slippers

and dressing-gown as she flew down the stairs two at a time.

'Christine!' cried Nan, coming out on to the landing 'What's the matter?'

'I don't know, but I'm going to find out!'

'I heard something...'

'So did I!' Grabbing the torch that always stood on the draining-board by the back door, Christine rushed out into the yard. Her heart was thudding violently. If anything had happened to her darling Jet...

A thin ribbon of light showed under the stable door. Before Christine could reach it, a figure came stumbling out into the night. Breathing heavily, it tore off into the darkness.

Heedless of puddles, Christine flew across the yard in her thin slippers. On the threshold of Jet's box she stood still, transfixed with horror. For there, in the straw by Jet's restless heels, lay Victor Grayson, the blood coursing freely down the side of his face.

'Hullo...' he panted, blinking dazedly up at her and trying to struggle to his feet. '...nothing to worry about ...not as bad as it looks,' he said breathlessly.

'Victor!' Nan Grayson's shocked voice cut into the horrified silence. With an old tweed coat thrown over her pyjamas, she came running into the box. 'Whatever's happened? Your face...'

'Now don't fuss, old girl...' Nan Grayson helped her husband to his feet. 'Woa, lad,' he said soothingly to Jet, who seemed thoroughly frightened. 'Woa, lad; woa, horse; woa, then...'

'But,' began Nan in alarm, '...your face...'

'It's only a graze.' He looked very pale as he leaned against the side of the box. 'I'm a bit winded still, that's all!'

'But what *happened?*' implored Christine, as her mother ran back to the farmhouse for towels hot water, iodine, and the bottle of brandy she kept for emergencies.

'Nothing, fortunately,' panted Victor. 'But if I hadn't been here it would have been a very different story. Take a look at this!'

Christine gazed down, recoiling with horror from the hypodermic in his hand. Speechlessly, she looked at the long needle, glinting wickedly in the light.

'What...?' she began fearfully.

'Bromide,' went on Victor Grayson grimly. 'A couple of shots of this and your little black horse wouldn't have got over the first fence tomorrow!'

With a low sob, Christine went to Jet's head. Quieter now, he allowed her to press her face thankfully to his smooth neck and run her hand through his mane.

'But who was it? And... how did you know? And... why were you here?' breathed Christine, in a tumble of questions.

'That's the funny part of it,' frowned her father, mopping at the blood on his face with an already soaked handkerchief. 'Somebody tipped me off, or I wouldn't have known.'

'*Somebody?*' Christine gazed at him wonderingly. 'But... who?'

'That's what I don't know. When I got back to the inn they told me there was a 'phone call just come through for me. It was a man's voice... young fellow, by the sound of it. Wouldn't give his name. Just said it would be better not to leave the little black horse unguarded tonight. That's all.'

'Who could it have been?'

'I don't know. He rang off when I asked his name. Obviously doesn't want it known. Anyway, I had my supper, then got a couple of rugs from Fawcett's place and came back up here for the rest of the night.'

Suddenly, Christine remembered the noise her mother had heard just before she had gone up to bed. So it hadn't been the barn door slamming, after all! It had been her father, coming back to sleep in the stable and to keep guard over Jet.

'I didn't want to worry you,' Victor was saying, 'so I just made myself comfortable in here; I was sound asleep when suddenly I woke up, because Jet was a bit restless.' He patted the rugged-up quarters. 'He knew, all right! He gave the warning. The next thing I knew was a torch shining by the door.' He managed a rueful smile. 'I'm a bit out of condition, Chris, but surprise tactics helped, despite the old leg!'

'Who was it? Who could have been so utterly vile as to think of doing such a thing?' asked Christine, her face white.

'Can't you guess?'

'Not...*not Laura Carley?*'

'I don't know. But the man who broke in here tonight was Jim Hennegan!'

Nan Grayson, bustling back with a bowl of steaming water, made Victor sit down in the straw again while she washed the cut above his eye.

'Well?' she demanded practically. 'What do we do about it? Telephone the police?'

'No!' said Victor curtly. 'No harm has been done, thanks to whoever it was who rang me up.' He glanced shrewdly at Christine till she felt a blush creeping hotly over her face. 'You've got a good friend there, Chris.' He slowly winked his unbruised eye. 'I suspect it's an admirer. Anyway, if we go to the police it means he'll be involved, and that's a poor way of showing our gratitude to him after what he did. Mister Hennegan has had a bad fright, and Miss Carley won't be feeling any too happy, either.'

Nan looked up at Christine over Victor Grayson's bandaged head. 'You're not going back to that inn tonight!' she said firmly. 'Chris and I will make up the bed in the spare room...'

'You will not,' cut in Victor Grayson. 'I'm staying here for the rest of the night.'

'But that's absurd! It's utterly ridiculous to stay out here.'

'Oh, no it isn't! If that customer comes back I mean to be ready for him this time.'

'I never heard of such stupidity...' protested Nan.

'Look...' put in Victor patiently, 'it's not the first time I've slept in a stable, and until you've done it you don't know how comfortable it can be.' He smiled. 'Remember when I used to sleep in travelling horseboxes after race meetings? Well, then...' He winked at Christine again. 'I bet anything you like Chris envies me! I bet she'd swop places with me, eh, Chris?'

Christine gave a hesitant little smile, remembering all the times when she had, indeed, longed to curl up in the deep straw in Jet's clean, warm box!

'Now don't you worry,' went on her father, snuggling down under the two heavy blankets. 'I'll be perfectly all right here. And Chris,' he ordered sharply, 'you cut along to bed now, or you won't even be in the running tomorrow. Off you go!'

As Christine and Nan left the box he added softly, almost casually, 'By the way, for your information, Chris, the mysterious voice on the phone had a slight foreign accent. Good night.'

Two minutes later he was asleep.

In the paddock

By the time Christine and her mother arrived at the point-to-point in the ancient rattle-trap, the hill above the course was already densely populated. Crowds of people were hanging about by the bookmakers' stands, while others stood round the saddling enclosure.

The lines of cars and shooting brakes were parked so that their owners had a view down over the course that stretched across the top and sides of the hill then down into a dip.

As the rattle-trap bumped across the ground to the parking place, Victor Grayson came limping over to it.

'Come on, Chris! We've got time to walk the course before the first race.'

'I'll take your things to the changing tent,' offered Nan.

Beneath the hill, the course wound across country between fluttering red and white marker flags; across the emerald; grass of the good going, and the ploughed field of the bad across 'made' fences, open ditch and water.

On all sides, as Christine and her father hurried down to the course, people smiled at them and called out. Many of them wanted Victor to stop and talk, but he merely smiled and nodded and went on. For this was 'the job' to him and he had no time for chatter until after Christine's race.

From way out on the course the shouts of the bookmakers were only thin noises blown by the wind and growing fainter. Soon they were lost altogether as Christine listened to her father's words of advice.

Jump by jump, he took her over the twice-round course.

'Watch this one, Chris. You'll come into it at an angle. See?'

Every so often he made her look back over the way they had come, and she was amazed to find that they hadn't come in a straight line, as she had thought, but in a cunningly contrived bend.

'You want to look out for that, Chris. Try and lie up on the inside there.'

Gems of advice. Whatever would she have done without him!

Back on the hill, Nan came hurrying towards them.

'Amos has just arrived. He's taken Jet over to that quiet bit of covert on the far side of the hill.'

'Good,' nodded Victor Grayson. 'I'll go on over while

Chris changes. See you later Christine!' He waved.

In no time at all, or so it seemed to Christine, the first two races were over. As the runners for the Ladies' Race were being read out over the loudspeaker, the horses were being led round the saddling enclosure.

To Amos, leading Jet, this was the great day, and he wore his best clothes to do it justice.

But the rows of eagerly watching spectators had scant attention for the little black horse in the tattered moth-eaten old rug. Their admiring gaze was held by the Carleys' massive showy chestnut, in his brand new monogrammed rug.

Christine, standing in the middle of the enclosure, looked lovingly at Jet. How small he seemed, walking quietly between the great chestnut and a big bay mare from an adjacent hunt! Small, yes, but only she and her father knew that Jet had the breeding and the heart to win this race.

'Good luck,' said a voice coming up behind Christine.

'Paul!'

For a moment their eyes met in understanding. Then suddenly Paul smiled.

'I'm glad to see the little black horse looking so well!' he murmured.

'It's...it's thanks to you, isn't it?' said Christine softly.

'Or to your father!' said Paul quickly. Then, 'I must go. Laura's just come into the paddock. But I just had to come and wish you luck.'

'Thank you,' said Christine, from the very depth of her heart. For without his friendship Jet would probably not have been even a starter.

Suddenly, another voice cut into the gentle murmur of chatter in the enclosure.

'Good heavens! Someone's got a pony running!' it cried scornfully, loud enough for everyone to hear.

Laura!

Slim and elegant, everything about her shone expensively as she walked between her cigar-smoking father and Mrs Carley, whose mink coat somehow looked out of place among all the duffles and sheepsking.

But this time, her acid remarks only made Christine even more confident of success. Once she had longed hopelessly to show Laura and that sneering Hennegan just how good a horse Jet really was. Now it was no longer a hopeless dream. She was actually going to race against Laura Carley for the Lord Harleigh Cup; she was going to ride Jet against Red Mask.

A few seconds later the horses turned in, their rugs were drawn off and the girths were tightened.

Christine peeled off her coat and bent her knee for the leg-up, heedless of the amused smiles at her over-large jersey and the shabbiness of her tattered cap. 'Come straight off the tractor, I shouldn't wonder!' sniggered someone in the crowd.

Nan Grayson's cheeks blazed, but Christine seemed not to hear. Her hands were firm on the reins, her round young jaw set purposefully, her grey eyes steady as she listened to her father's final instructions.

'Now remember – hold the little horse up in the hard going. Save him as much as you can, but push him on in the good going.'

Christine nodded down to him while Jet lunged, fighting for his head, his small feet dancing impatiently, eager to be off down that strip of shining grass leading to the start.

For a moment longer, Victor Grayson looked up at the girlish figure silhouetted against the grey clouds. A lump came into his throat. How brave she looked, sitting confidently up there in her old cap and his own old colours; and how very determined!

'Good luck, my darling,' he whispered softly, almost to

himself. He looked up at her and winked encouragingly.

Christine gave him a brief, quivery little smile, then turned Jet's head to the break in the ropes.

'Oh, Victor,' breathed Nan tremulously, as they stood side by side watching Jet join the string of horses disappearing down the hill to where the official starter was waiting. 'I know she's going to win! I just *know* it!'

For a moment there was no answer; then Nan received a shattering blow. For Victor Grayson said quietly, 'No, Nan; I'm afraid the Carleys' chestnut will have the edge.'

'Wh-*what?*' Nan looked at him, aghast. 'But you said she was good enough to win!' she cried.

'She is,' said Victor, 'but the little black horse just won't be able to stay the pace. He's a game one; he'll try his hardest, but the going's a little too heavy down in the dip!'

The race

Down at the start the horses were already waiting. Christine recognised a big grey mare named The Pennant, a bay horse named Varsity, and another, whose name she didn't know, ridden by a tall dark girl with four seasons' experience behind her.

As Christine drew into line, Red Mask came charging alongside, causing Jet to throw up his head nervously.

Christine turned, and for a long moment the eyes of the two girls met in a steady, challenging glance. This was their first race, their first ride against each other. And for both, there was more than the Cup at stake.

'Good luck,' said Laura, as her glance swept scornfully over Jet's small, restless body. 'I think you're going to need it!'

Christine bit her lip and turned away. She just wouldn't answer, wouldn't rise to the bait. But her hand stole up along

Jet's black gleaming neck in a soothing caress unseen by Laura.

The last two horses came cantering down to the start, and Jet pranced and pivoted with excitement.

The official starter walked on to the course and as he glanced along the line of horses, Jet swerved nervously away, his quarters flashing restlessly this way and that. Quietly, Christine urged him back into the line, feeling in the little black horse's tense, quivering body all the power and highly-strung excitement of his breeding.

Time and again, as the others stood patiently waiting, Christine had to urge Jet forward into the line, only to have him shoot forward seconds before the flag dropped – as though his anxiety to be gone was just too much for him.

As he came up for the third time, a hushed tension locked the vast crowd in silence. Would it be all right this time?

Then, suddenly, the flag dropped at exactly the moment when Jet was level with the other horses, and a great roar of '*They're off!*' broke from the hill-top.

Jet plunged forward to lie fourth as they came to the first fence. He met it right, spread himself and landed well out on the other side. Now the course wound gently left-handed – the cunningly contrived bend! Christine was watching for it.

At the next fence the horse ahead refused and ran out. For a sickening moment it looked as if a collision was inevitable, and a shocked gasp went up from the spectators. But Jet balanced himself in time, swerved with cat-like agility, and jumped straight off his hocks. Before them now was half a mile of beautifully firm turf. With a smile of pure joy, Christine let Jet gallop on. Lightning fast now, they pulled away from the rest of the field. They were well in the lead when the fence ahead loomed nearer. Christine tightened her hold on the reins. As she cleared the top, another horse came up behind her, the big grey, full of going, jumping boldly and well. Christine took a deep breath and went on.

Now the course rose uphill to a fence with a very nasty take-off. Beyond it lay the dreaded ploughed land, the deep, heavy going that would impose a great strain on Jet's fine, slender legs. Christine's heart ached. Had she already taken too much out of Jet on the good going? Had she been too anxious to take the lead too soon? Landing in the deep, soft earth she felt the little black horse slow down as the wet soil imprisoned his legs, fettering them as if with heavy chains. But his spirit was still strong, and for a desperate moment, as the other horses came up behind, she wondered if she should disregard her father's words and urge him on.

The temptation to keep the lead tore at her.

...'*hold the little horse up in the heavy going, save him as much as you can...*'

But could he be wrong? It would be so easy to press on, for Jet's courage and spirit were such that Christine knew she had only to ask him to go on and he would. It was all there, in his small, compact, thoroughbred body. As first the grey, then Red Mask drew level and overtook them, Christine hesitated. The temptation to go against her father's instructions was almost too much for her when Laura looked back over her shoulder and gave a smug smile. Jet was willing; she had only to ask him...

Then her sense of discipline asserted itself. A good jockey rode as the trainer told him. Surely her father, with his years of experience, would know best? She must trust him now... she *must*.

Bitterly, she watched Red Mask take the lead from the grey mare. Saw him take the fence ahead, saw his head come up on the other side. But now another shocked gasp went up as the grey crashed sickeningly on landing...and Red Mask went on alone.

As Christine reached the fence, the other horses came up

to lie alongside. Now there was half a furlong of good going. Desperately, Christine crouched low in the saddle. Could she regain the lead?

A wave of excitement burst from the crowd as, several lengths in front, Red Mask took the open ditch. A murmur ran through the watching people: 'Come on, Red Mask! Come on the chestnut!'

Another sharp intake of breath signified that yet another horse was down, but Christine dared not look to see who it was. All her attention was fixed on Red Mask. Could Jet do it? Could he bridge the distance between them?

Quiet and still, Christine sat there as he cleared the open ditch. Then, miraculously, Jet began to gain on Red Mask.

At the last fence but one, Jet was lying six lengths behind his rival. And now the winning-post was in sight.

Feverishly, the crowds began to pour down on to the course to see the finish. Their wildly excited cries filled Christine's ears as she lay close to Jet's neck.

A low sob broke from Christine, but she gritted her teeth against it. She couldn't do it! She just couldn't! If *only* she hadn't lost the lead in the heavy going!

As she took the last fence a great tumult of hunting-cries broke from the hill-top, mingled with the cheering from the people clustered round the jump.

Fifty yards to go — and Red Mask between her and the winning post! Christine's hope and faith faltered.

Then, suddenly, there flashed into her mind the stories of her father's past glory, and of his fame as a jockey. The greatest steeplechase jockey of his day, some said. Would he have given up? He would never ride racing again — but his will to win, his driving power, his unbeatable courage must still live on — *in her*.

He had said she could win. He believed in the little black horse; he had told her so. Surely with all his experience, he knew better than she, who was only taking part in her first race? 'Let the others make the running,' was one of the things he'd told her. 'Ride a waiting race... let him out after the last fence...'

Suddenly, with renewed determination, Christine drove her heels into Jet's sweat streaked sides. 'Come on, Jet!' she sobbed imploringly. 'Come on...'

Jet's gallant spirit matched her own. With nostrils flared and small feet flying he made the supreme effort. Steadily, his head crept closer to the chestnut's quarters; drew level with Laura's leg...

Twenty-five yards to go...

Grimly, they fought the desperate battle as the crowds streamed down to the course.

'*The little black horse! Come on, the little black horse!*' they shrieked frantically. And, as Jet flashed past the post a wild tumult of cheering, hunting-cries and shouts broke from the crowd: 'Jet wins! The little black 'un wins!'

Several lengths past the post, Christine pulled up and turned back as the crowds came running over the grass to greet her, congratulate her and lead her triumphantly in. Smiling faces were upturned to her, hands stretched out to pat Jet's sweat-lathered neck and heaving sides.

'A great race! A wonderful finish!' cried someone. And, 'Well done, Chris! Your own father couldn't have done better, girl!'

Dazed, she looked down at the milling crowd. She could hardly realise yet that it was all over and she had won. For a few seconds, she wasn't sure where she was, although Jet seemed to know instinctively the right direction to take.

Then, suddenly, a firm hand reached up to the rein lying slack against Jet's neck, and Christine found herself looking down into her father's eyes, while the crowd cheered and clapped round them.

Jet flashed by the post in a wild tumult of cheering.

'A brilliant race, darling!' said Victor Grayson softly. 'You rode magnificently!'

'It was Jet,' said Christine breathlessly. Then with a burst of honesty, 'And you! It was you! I just did as you told me!'

Victor Grayson grinned and patted Jet.

'But *that* was the hardest part of all, wasn't it?' he observed.

Then, as Nan came flying towards them, her eyes filled with tears even though she was laughing, he turned and led Jet up to the winning-pen.

The aftermath

To old Amos, this was almost the greatest day in his life. Never again would that 'foreigner', Frank Gosford, dare to murmur one word about 'our' horses up at White Gates. But for Amos the best moment was still to come — the moment when, later on in the evening, he would walk into the inn to receive the congratulations of the landlord and customers. He could already imagine the outburst of admiring greetings. 'Well,' they'd say, 'that was as fine a finish as we'd ever expect to see!' And Amos Partridge would be as much the hero of the hour as if he'd won the race himself.

Now, at Jet came walking freely up the hill and into the winning-pen, Amos beamed with joy and pride.

Beneath the gaze of the crowd clustered round the winning-pen, Christine slipped lightly down out of the saddle and quickly undid the girths. Just for a moment, as she pressed her head against Jet's side, she closed her eyes and murmured softly, 'Thank you, Jet. My darling, gallant little black horse.' But no one saw her lips move, for the words came more from her heart than her lips.

With a final pat, she left him shaking himself and blowing hugely through his nostrils, and went to weigh in. A few seconds later, she emerged from the tent and stood there, her old coat thrown over her riding clothes, her eyes searching the throngs of people massed on the hill-top.

'Well done, my dear...'

Christine turned to face the Master of the Chedbury Hunt.

'Thank you,' she murmured shyly.

'That was a brilliant finish.'

When he moved away Christine's eyes went back to the crowd, resuming their search.

'There you are, darling!' cried Nan, coming up to her. 'Amos is looking after Jet. When he's cooled off he's going to walk him gently to the farm.

'Good,' said Christine quickly. But even as she spoke her eyes still anxiously raked the crowds of people for a familiar figure. Then, suddenly, she said urgently, 'Where's...?' She broke off.

'Your father?' finished her mother.

Christine nodded.

'He's gone,' Nan said in a low voice. 'He left a message for you. He said...'

But Christine was gone, hurrying through the crowds and running across the grass.

'Christine!' called out Nan.

But it was no use. As Christine hurried across the grass, the noise and excitement of the point-to-point grew fainter and fainter. On and on she ran: past the lines of cars, past the packed refreshment marquees and the fenced-off paddock...

He would be making for the inn to collect his suitcase, and then the station where he would catch the north-bound train. She must stop him before he got that far.

Then, suddenly, she saw him, and her heart bounded in a great lurch, and her throat ached. He was limping away, over the field to the lane which led to the main road; a lonely figure, stooping a little, his lame leg dragging tiredly.

'*Daddy! Daddy!*' yelled Christine.

The next second she had flung herself sobbing into his arms, hugging him fiercely, as though she never wanted to let him go again, burying her face into his coat.

'There, there...' he murmured softly, stroking her tousled fair hair.

'You mustn't go!' sobbed Christine. 'You mustn't leave us again, *ever!* Come back to Shallows... *please!* It's your home and we need you. Please!'

Gently, Victor Grayson pushed her away. He stood back.

'Now look, my dear,' he began gravely, 'I've done what I promised to do. I've trained your horse for you. Now the job's done and I'm leaving.'

'No!' protested Christine.

Victor Grayson sighed wearily.

'I know this feeling. It's a kind of nervous reaction after your first race. It often happens. When it wears off you'll regret this. Now be a good girl and let me go.'

'No! I'll still feel the same tomorrow,' insisted Christine, lifting her tear-streaked face to him earnestly. ' I *know* I will.'

For a moment Victor Grayson hesitated. Then, 'You really mean that, Chris?'

'Yes, I do. I *do!*'

The next moment he was hugging her rapturously and neither was able to speak because they seemed to be laughing and crying all at once. Then together, without another word, they turned and walked back to the course.

Nan came hurrying towards them, an expression of anxious concern on her face.

'Christine, what on earth...?' She broke off in amazement at the sight of Victor and their daughter arm-in-arm.

'He's coming back to Shallows,' cried Christine happily, 'for ever!'

But before Nan could express her joy at this announcement a burly figure had joined them.

'Mr Grayson? My name's Carley. I've got the big house near your farm – as your daughter here knows.'

The three Graysons stared at him silently.

'Well, now,' went on Mr Carley briskly. 'I'll come straight to the point because it saves time, and my time is money.' He paused and squared his shoulders in the expensive tweed suit he was wearing. 'The question is, what will you take for that little black horse?' Steadily, he met Victor's eyes. 'No fancy price now,' he added warningly, 'but I'm willing to buy because my girl Laura must have the best. So let's get down to business and I'll give you a cheque now.'

Christine watched him in fascinated horror, her face frozen, her heart at bursting point, her eyes enormous with fear. Swiftly, she looked at her father and saw to her terror that he was smiling! Actually smiling at Mr Carley, as though it was a perfectly reasonable idea and not enough to make the whole world explode with indignation.

Cold fingers stretched over her heart and squeezed it in an icy grip, while all kinds of nameless fears shook her. This was the moment she had always feared and dreaded. Her father, she knew, admired the little black horse, but he didn't *love* him as Christine did. He couldn't be expected to. He'd ridden so many horses; he couldn't love all of them. But with Christine it was different. Jet was more than just a horse; he was a companion, a friend...

Suddenly she felt her father's arm link through hers again, so that in some way it seemed as if they stood united against the power of people like Mr Carley.

'Well, that's very handsome of you, Mr...er, what was the name?' said Victor Grayson pleasantly.

'Carley,' snapped Laura's father, going pink in the face. He wasn't used to people not knowing his name.

'Oh, yes. Well, Mr Carley, you're really speaking to the wrong person. You see, Jet doesn't belong to me. He belongs to my daughter.'

'Don't quibble, man!' retorted Mr Carley furiously. Then, to Christine, 'However, if that's the case – what'll you take for him, my girl? Three hundred pounds? That's a fair enough offer, eh?'

Three hundred pounds!

To Christine, money had no meaning where Jet was concerned. Mr Carley might have said three thousand or even three million and it wouldn't have made any difference.

Then suddenly she realised what his offer really meant. It meant a great deal for her mother. It meant freedom from worry over bills. It meant a holiday and a car that went and didn't have to be pushed...

For a second longer, Christine hesitated. Then, with eyes blinded with tears, she turned bravely to Mr Carley.

'I...' she began chokingly.

'My daughter is a minor, Mr Carley,' said Nan Grayson swiftly, before Christine could get any further. 'She is not able to contract to sell the horse, and I forbid the sale. I'm sorry.'

'You mean...?' spluttered Mr Carley incredulously.

'I mean that Jet is not for sale – *ever*,' said Nan firmly.

To everybody's amazement, Mr Carley suddenly grinned.

'Well,' he grunted, taking a large cigar from its expensive case and nipping off the end. 'I don't know as I blame you.' He winked at Victor Grayson. 'You've got a fine little jockey there,' he added. 'My girl had better retire from point-to-points, eh?'

Victor Grayson smiled back at him.

'Perhaps she had,' he agreed, 'if she can't ever bear losing.'

The Trophy

The last race was over. Loaded horse-boxes trundled slowly and heavily across the uneven ground leading to the lane; the lines of cars had already begun to form, single-file, at the exits; on the now deserted hill-top the bookmakers were packing up their equipment.

But not everyone was leaving. In the paddock surrounding a large marquee, crowds of people were gathering, waiting for the presentation of the silver cups.

A long trestle table had been erected, and the cups arranged along it glittered in the evening sunshine.

As each person went up to collect his or her trophy from the Master's wife, a sudden outburst of cheering and clapping broke forth. But it was louder and longer than ever when Christine's name was called, and she went forward wishing that the ground would open up and swallow her. On all sides came cries of, 'Well done, Chris!' accompanied by a positive tumult of hunting cries. Blushing furiously, she went back to her parents.

'Congratulations,' said a familiar voice at her elbow.

Christine turned and looked into Laura's hard, bitter eyes.

'Thank you,' she said calmly. 'But it was all Jet's doing and my father's.'

'Wonders will never cease, will they?' went on Laura spitefully.

Christine was never one to gloat over other people's misfortunes and disappointments, but she found it hard to feel very much sympathy for Laura. Even now she was unsportsmanlike, and quite unrepentant. She was very annoyed that she had not won the race and, of course, that her father had not been able to buy Jet.

Chris's memory went back, with a deepening sense of gratitude, to her mother's loyal refusal to be tempted by

Mr Carley's offer – she realised now, more acutely than ever before, what it must have meant to her mother to turn that offer down...knowing very well, no doubt, that Carley would have paid almost any price to satisfy his daughter's whim.

Well, thought Christine as she stood there, uncertain of what to do next, but rather hoping Laura would have the good sense to go. Well, at least Mr Carley was something of a sport, and Laura's attitude might be quite a disappointment to him, too.

Laura suddenly turned to Paul, who stood just behind her. 'Come on, Paul. I'm starving and it's nearly dinner time.'

But Paul didn't follow her.

'You go on, Laura. I'll come up later.'

'But it's half-past six,' said Laura furiously, 'and you know how father hates it if we're late for dinner!'

Laura glared balefully at the little group, and seemed almost ready to explode. But there was obviously something in Paul's quiet determination that told her the situation was hopeless, as well as being thoroughly undignified. 'I see,' she said icily; and then, without so much as a nod, she turned and walked away.

For a moment, no one seemed to know what to say. Then Victor Grayson saved the day by saying, 'Perhaps Paul would like to come back to Shallows and have supper with us?' Then hastily, 'Er...if that's all right with Chris?'

Christine glanced up at him quickly. Was that a faint wink, or had she been mistaken? But at least his eyes, usually so grave and shrewd, were clearly twinkling.

'Oh, yes, I'd...I'd like that,' she said, realising what fun it would be to have someone of her own age to talk to about the race.

'Good,' said Victor, exchanging a quick smile with Nan. 'That's settled then, providing it's going to be all right with you, Paul? We'd like you to spend the evening with us.'

Paul's face was one huge grin.

'Oh, yes, sir!' he said enthusiastically. Then with embarrassment, 'I...I...mean thank you, I'd like to very much.'

It was dark when Christine went across the farmyard to say her last goodnight to Jet. He had finished up all his oats and now stood dozing contentedly on three legs. But his head went up as he heard Christine's quick, light footsteps, and he blew softly, a little gruntingly, through his nostrils when he knew who it was.

For a long moment Christine stood by his head till it sank down on to her shoulder, resting on it, so that she could feel the soft warm breath on her neck. Gently, she rubbed his small ears.

'My own lovely little black horse,' she murmured tenderly. 'The greatest, most gallant little horse in the world. Thank you for winning the race. I knew you could do it. I just *knew*.'

Quietly, Christine moved away, leaving him to his well-earned rest.

Out in the farmyard she bolted the stable door and then stood for a moment looking up at the star-brilliant sky. It was very quiet now. Every sound could be heard: Jet's feet shuffling in the straw as he shifted his weight on to another leg; a mysterious rustling in the hedge beyond the pig-sties; and from behind the drawn curtains of her home, the comfortable sound of voices talking and laughing.

Suddenly, Christine gave a deep happy sigh. Altogether, it had been the most wonderful day of her life. Then, as she heard her mother begin to sing softly by the open kitchen window, and heard her father call out to her from his chair by the fire, she felt sure it was only the first of many such days.

I Wanted a Pony

by Lilias Edwards

I'll never forget the morning the letter arrived from the Council. We were just about to start breakfast and Mum was at the cooker, preparing toast and scrambled eggs. She barely turned her head when Gran came in with a long envelope in her hand.

'Post for you, Margaret,' said Gran, waving the letter excitedly. 'It's from the Council.'

'From the Council?' Mum seized the letter, ripped it open, and gave a kind of gasp.

'This is it!' she exclaimed. 'At last! At last! Oh, I must 'phone Tom at once!'

She grabbed her purse from the shelf and ran off, leaving the rest of us staring after her as though she'd taken leave of her senses. Our mother, running into the street with two pink curlers still in her hair! It was unbelievable. And the eggs were scorching and the toast burning to a cinder!

I jumped up from the table and ran to save the eggs.

'What on earth is happening?' I asked, throwing the burnt bread into the pedal bin and putting two fresh pieces under the grill.

'It's a house!' said Gran. 'You've got a house at last. Oh my, I feel quite faint! I must have a cup of tea.'

I was all excitement myself then. We had been living with Mum's parents ever since Dad came back to Brantown to work, nearly five years before, and all that time we'd been on the waiting list for a council house.

Mum and Dad were always talking about 'when we have a place of our own', but, honestly, I had begun to think we never would. And here it was, at last!

'Oh, how marvellous!' I said, pouring out Gran's tea and spilling half into the saucer in my excitement. 'Where is it? How big? Shall I have a room to myself?'

'We'll have a puppy!' shouted John, jumping up and down.

'Poothy-cat!' said Billy, banging the table with his spoon. Billy was only four and couldn't quite manage the letter *s*. 'I want a poothy-cat!'

'No!' said John. He was seven and rather bossy. 'We'll have a *dog*.'

We had always wanted a pet but Dad had said, 'Wait till we're in a place of our own', and the only pets we had were two goldfish in a little square tank. They were quite pretty to watch but you can't really *play* with goldfish – not like you can with cats and dogs.

However, *I* didn't want a 'poothy' or a dog. I wanted a *pony*. I'll tell you more about that later. In the meantime Gran was sipping her tea and wiping her eyes.

'I shall miss you all very much,' she was saying; then she paused and sniffed. 'What's burning?'

It was the toast again!

* * *

We moved into our new house some weeks later. It was on a new estate called Green Hills and was right on the edge of the town, with fields and woods beyond. The house was lovely and it was really wonderful to have so much space all to ourselves.

The builders were still working on the estate, and although the back gardens were fenced off, the front gardens were *awful* – broken bricks and rubbish everywhere, no paths, no fences, no gates, and not even a pavement along the roadway. When it rained it was a sea of mud and when it was dry there was dust everywhere. But we knew it would all be lovely some day, with trees and gardens, and we were happy.

Our next-door neighbours moved in about a week after we did.

'Their name is Morris,' said Mum, who had been talking to them across the back fence. 'Two girls and a boy in the family, just like ourselves. The girl is about your age, Elizabeth. Her name is Ann. I hope she'll be a nice friend for you.'

Friend? Phooey! We quarrelled the very first time we met.

It happened like this: it was a Saturday morning and Dad had been digging in the back garden. It was hard work and after a while he stopped for a breather and came indoors for a cup of coffee. I was standing at the dining room window and I saw a small bird hopping over the newly dug ground, looking for worms.

'Oh look!' I said happily. 'We've got a robin in our garden.'

No sooner had I spoken than something struck the robin and he toppled over on his back, his little legs in the air. I rushed out and picked him up but he was quite dead. I turned round and saw a group watching me from the next-door garden – two small boys, one with a catapult in his hand, and a girl about my own age.

The boy with the catapult looked ready to burst into tears.

'I didn't mean it,' he said miserably. 'It was a mistake.'

'It was my fault,' said the other boy. 'I dared him to hit the bird but I never thought he would. Honest, he always misses, so I thought I was quite safe in daring him to do it!'

'You *horrible* boys!' I said furiously. 'Killing a robin!' I looked down at the pathetic little bundle of feathers in my hand. 'Oh, how could you!' I went up to the fence and held the bird towards them. 'Look what you've done!'

The boy with the catapult *did* burst into tears then.

'Don't be so cruel,' said the girl, beginning to get angry. 'You can *see* he didn't mean it.'

'He shouldn't be allowed to play with catapults,' I retorted, and with my free hand I snatched the horrible thing from him, threw it down and stamped on it.

I buried the robin at the foot of the garden, and then went indoors and upstairs to my room. I felt miserable about the bird and about having such horrible boys next door, so I sat down to console myself with my pony books. And now I'll tell you about wanting a pony.

I had wanted a pony for almost as long as I could remember, ever since I had first seen a dear little Shetland in a circus. Every summer, when we went to the seaside, I spent all my pocket money on pony rides. There was one man at Clovenbeach who got to know me so well that he let me help him and I had lots of rides for nothing there. I always had pony books from the library and I had pony pictures on my walls, and my most treasured possession was a beautiful china ornament that Aunt Betsy had given me – a lovely brown colt with a white star on his forehead.

All the family thought my pony craze was a huge joke and Mum said I'd grow out of it. But I was sure I never would, and now that I lived so near the open country I hoped I might find some place where I could work with ponies. In the books I read, girls could always get work to do in stables and riding schools and that's what *I* hoped to do now in the country.

It was that very night that I heard the sound of hooves. They woke me from sleep and at first I thought I must be dreaming, for the noise came from our *own back garden.* I lay and listened and sure enough, there it was again. Clop – clop! Clop – clop! An unmistakable sound.

I jumped up and went to the window and threw it open. Perhaps the sound startled the animal, for it trotted off along the side of the house and out to the front roadway. In the darkness I saw nothing.

I went back to bed and when I woke in the morning I was convinced I had dreamed it all.

But I hadn't! For when I looked out of the window there were hoof marks all over the piece of ground that Dad had dug the day before.

Dad was furious, but I was absolutely thrilled.

* * *

There had been more than one horse or pony roaming around in the night and everyone was up in arms about the havoc they had caused.

'I expect they came from that gypsy encampment in Scout Lane,' said Mr Morris, looking at the ruin of his carefully prepared lawn.

'Gypsies?' exclaimed John, his eyes growing round. 'Ooooh! Smashing!'

'Not real gypsies,' said Mr Morris. 'They're diddicoys. I saw them arriving yesterday. If they give us any more trouble I'll report them to the police.'

'What's a diddi – diddi...what you said?' John asked.

'They're wandering tinkers,' explained Dad. 'Scrap dealers. Rag and bone men. That sort of thing.'

I had been hovering about, listening to this conversation, and at the first opportunity I set off down Scout Lane to see for myself. Sure enough, in a field beside the road were several caravans, a battered old lorry, a small two-wheeled cart and a great deal of rubbish. Some grubby children, dressed in strange odds and ends of clothing, were playing with a mongrel dog, and close by were two large, heavily built horses and a small black and white pony. The pony was rough and unkempt and his white patches could have been whiter, but he was rather sweet. I left the road and stepped in to the field and at once the children stopped playing and stared at me in silence. The dog, on the other hand, began to bark furiously and a rough-looking man came to the door of one of the caravans and shouted at me.

'Clear off,' he roared, 'or I'll set the dog on you!'

I trailed home again, a bit crestfallen, but later that day some of the diddicoy children came up the lane with two big milk churns in an old pram. The first house they came to was the Morris's; but the family were out, so then they came to us.

'Water, please!' they said, and waited expectantly.

Mum gave me the job of filling the churns. It took absolutely *ages* because our biggest jug held only a quart, and by the time the job was finished I knew that the eldest child's name was Joey, that he had never been to school, didn't know how to read or write, and wanted to be a scrap metal man like his dad. I also learned that the pony's name was Bonzo.

'Bonzo?' I repeated. 'That's a funny name for a pony! Why Bonzo?'

'Why not?' asked Joey, looking surprised.

The children came every day for water, sometimes several times a day. It was a real nuisance but, as Mum said, 'You can't really refuse *water*, can you?' I can't imagine what they did with it all for they were never any cleaner than when I first saw them. However, I improved my acquaintance with Joey and eventually I ventured down the lane again. This time the children knew me and when I said I wanted to give the pony an apple there was no objection. Soon I was going down the lane at every opportunity, and before long I was allowed to trot round the field on the pony's back. There was no saddle so I had to go very slowly lest I should slip off; but it was enormous fun and I thoroughly enjoyed myself.

Then one morning, at breakfast time, Mum looked at me crossly.

'For goodness sake, Elizabeth, stop scratching!' she exclaimed.

'I can't help it,' I protested. 'I'm so itchy.'

'Let me see,' said Mum, and she pulled up my jersey and vest. And right across my front was a scattering of big red spots!

'Goodness!' said Mum. 'What's this?' She felt my forehead anxiously and looked at my tongue. 'Do you feel all right?'

'I feel fine,' I said.

'Well, you can't go out today,' said Mum positively. 'Perhaps it's only nettle rash, but one never knows!'

So I stayed indoors all day and tried not to scratch.

Next day I had spots all over my back as well and where I had scratched them they had risen into big angry blobs. What was worse, John had spots and he was scratching too! Mum was worried to death.

'I'll have to call the doctor,' she said. 'It must be something catching so I'd better not take you to the surgery.'

The doctor, of course, was new to us. He was a big man with bushy eyebrows and a bristly moustache and he looked searchingly at John and me.

'Well, you look healthy enough,' he said, taking my wrist and checking my pulse. 'Now, let's see those spots.'

When he looked at the spots his bushy eyebrows came down and I thought he was going to be angry. Then his eyes twinkled, his mouth twitched and he suddenly burst out laughing.

I trotted round the field on the pony's back.

I was most indignant. Here we were, afflicted by who-knows-what dreadful plague, and he was *laughing!*

'What is it?' asked Mum, looking puzzled.

'Fleas,' said the doctor.

Mum flared up instantly.

'That's impossible,' she said. 'We're a clean, respectable family...'

'Yes, I can see that,' said the doctor, still chuckling, 'but even a clean respectable person can pick up a flea. It all depends on where you've been.'

When he said this I felt my face redden guiltily. I looked away but not before Mum had noticed.

The doctor picked up his case and prepared to leave. 'I'm glad it was nothing worse,' he said kindly. At the doorway he paused and looked back, still laughing. 'Good hunting!'

Mum saw him off and then hurried back to us. 'I've never felt such a fool in all my life,' she exclaimed. She put her hands on her hips and looked at me sternly. 'Well?' she demanded. 'What have you been up to?'

'I haven't been doing anything wrong.' I mumbled.

'Out with it!' demanded Mum. 'Where have you been?'

'Down Scout Lane,' I muttered reluctantly.

'You don't mean...? Not to that dreadful diddicoy camp? Oh, Elizabeth!'

'I went to see the pony,' I wailed, scratching madly. 'It's ever such a nice pony, Mum.'

'You won't go there again,' said my mother firmly. 'Promise!'

Sadly, I promised.

Not that it mattered anyhow. A day or two later the police came and moved the whole camp. A big 'Trespassers Will Be Prosecuted' notice was set up and a wire fence was strung along the edge of the field.

And I never saw the diddicoys, Joey or the pony again.

* * *

All this had happened during the summer holidays, but presently it was time for school again. A new school was planned for the estate, but it was still nothing more than a sketch on someone's drawing board, and for the time being we had to go to the nearest local school and were squashed into classes already overcrowded.

I found myself in the same class as Ann Morris. We were still rather cool towards each other (though the boys played together happily enough) so I avoided sitting beside her and chose a seat next to a small dark girl with glasses. Her name was Mary Winfold and she was rather quiet – not a chatter-box like me – and we shared a desk for a whole week before I discovered she lived on a farm.

A farm! Visions of horses and ponies flitted through my mind. I asked Mum if I might invite Mary to tea.

When I look back on it now, I think I was a horrid sort of person at that time. I didn't ask Mary for her own sake, but only in the hope of a return invitation. All I wanted, really, was to get to that farm.

Mary came to tea on a Saturday afternoon. It poured with rain and we couldn't go out but Mary knew some marvellous paper-and-pencil games that kept us engrossed all afternoon. She didn't mind playing with the boys either and she made comical 'glove puppets' for them with brown paper bags. They thought she was wonderful and young Billy showed her his pride and joy – two woolly caterpillars in a jar filled with leaves.

'We're going to have a real pet soon,' said John importantly. 'A puppy, or a kitten, or maybe a white rabbit.'

Mary's face lit up. 'We've got kittens at the farm,' she said eagerly. 'My mother is ever so anxious to find good homes for them. If you would like one...' Her voice tailed away and she looked at us hopefully.

Until that moment I hadn't cared if the family pet were a budgie or a tortoise but now I was all in favour of a kitten.

'Oh yes!' I said enthusiastically. 'We'd *love* a kitten. Wouldn't we, Mum?'

'I like cats,' said my mother agreeably.

'The kittens are sweet,' said Mary. 'They're a kind of marmalade colour, with white fronts and paws.'

'They sound gorgeous!' I exclaimed. 'May I come and choose one?'

It was settled that I would, and on the following Saturday I went to tea at Mary's home. It was a lovely afternoon and I almost danced up the road to the farm. I was looking forward to Mary's company this time, and to choosing a kitten and to meeting all the farm animals – especially the horses and ponies!

The kittens were adorable and Mary's mother helped me to choose a sturdy little male. Then I asked if I might see round the farm.

'Of course!' said Mary, and off we went.

We saw some poultry, a rather smelly pig family, an amiable old collie dozing in the yard, a meadow full of cows, several fields of growing crops – but never a horse or pony!

'Horses?' exclaimed Mary, when at length I ventured a question. 'Oh no, we're fully mechanised, and none of us rides.' She looked at me curiously. 'You look quite disappointed. Are you awfully keen on horses?'

'I'm pony mad,' I confessed. 'Do you know of any pony places around here?'

'I've heard of a riding school at Westburn,' taid Mary. 'I don't know the address but you'd find it in the 'phone book.'

I had a lovely time at the farm in spite of my disappointment and in the evening Mary's father drove me home with the kitten buttoned inside my jacket, purring happily.

Mother intended to call the kitten Marmaduke. but Billy fell upon him with delighted shrieks of 'Poothy!' – and 'Poothy' he remained.

The boys and I were playing with him in the back garden a few days later, when Ann Morris saw us. She was in ecstasies over the kitten.

'Isn't he *sweet!*' she enthused. 'What's his name?'

'Poothy', I said, giggling at the kitten's antics.

'Poothy?' Ann looked surprised, then began to laugh. 'You're joking, of course.'

Really, she was a most irritating girl!

'No. I'm *not* joking,' I said coldly. and I swept up the kitten and marched indoors.

* * *

I found the Westburn Riding Stables in the 'phone book, as Mary had suggested, and I wrote to them, asking if I might work there on Saturdays. I enclosed a stamped addressed envelope and received a very scrawly note in return.

> *You may help at the stables if you are willing to work hard. In return, you will receive some training in pony management but no money payment. Meals are not provided so please bring your own lunch. You may start on Sat. any time from 8 a.m. onward.*

This was followed by an absolutely unreadable signature and then a P. S. *Advisable to wear old clothes.*

I was wild with excitement. At last I was going to be a 'pony girl'!

My parents thought I was crazy.

'You'll have to go to Westburn by train,' my mother pointed out. 'It will cost you quite a bit. You won't be able to go *every* Saturday, you know. It will be hard work.'

'Never mind, I'll go as often as I can,' I said blissfully. 'I can start this weekend if I empty my piggy bank.'

'But we arranged a picnic to Beech Common,' Mum reminded me. 'You're not coming?'

'I'd rather go to the Riding Stables,' I said happily.

And so, on Saturday morning, there I was in the train to Westburn, bursting with joyful anticipation.

And on Saturday evening I travelled home again, tired, dirty, smelly and in the depths of misery.

I'd had an *awful* day. I'd spent most of it cleaning out filthy stables that seemed to have been neglected for weeks. Nobody bothered about me except to say 'Do this' or 'Fetch that'. About one o'clock I had sneaked into a corner and gobbled my packed lunch. The only time I had tried to approach a strings of ponies I was roughly told, 'Out of the way, you!' During the afternoon, plagued with thirst, I sought out the kitchen and asked for a glass of water. The woman who gave it to me said, 'Give it up, ducks. You'll never get nowhere in this dump. The boss thinks kids like you are a huge joke; he'll let you work yourself to death but you'll never get any training. I know; I've seen it happen dozens o' times. You're just a bit o' free labour for 'im.'

I knew she was telling me the truth and soon after that I downed tools and departed. Nobody bothered to say goodbye.

I had a carriage to myself in the homeward train and I stood before the mirror trying to rub the dirt from my face and to straighten my dishevelled hair.

'You've been done!' I told my scruffy reflection. 'Well and truly done! I wish I'd kept my money in my piggy bank. I wish I'd gone to Beech Common with Mum and Dad and the boys. I bet they had a lovely time!'

A great wave of self-pity washed over me and tears began to trickle down my cheeks. I scrubbed them away with my handkerchief, leaving clean places in the grime, and just then the train slowed down at a wayside station. I sat down hurriedly in a corner and hoped no one would decide to share my carriage.

The train stopped, the door opened and in came the last person in the world that I wanted to see at that moment... Ann Morris!

'Oh, hello!' said Ann brightly.

'Hello!' I mumbled, putting my head down and hoping she wouldn't notice my reddened eyes.

There was a long silence, and then...

'Anything wrong?' asked Ann.

She spoke very softly and kindly and to my horror I could feel the tears threatening to come again.

'No, nothing,' I said. I fished out my grey handkerchief (once white!) and blew my nose vigorously.

'You've had a fall?' Ann queried. 'You've got a dreadful bruise under your chin.'

'It isn't a bruise,' I said. 'It's dirt.'

'Oh!' Ann fell silent then.

'I've been working at a riding school today,' I explained, trying to assume a jaunty air. 'A place at Westburn.'

'Westburn Riding Stables?' Ann exclaimed. 'Surely not! That's a dreadful place!'

'You know it?' I asked in astonishment.

'I've heard about it from my Aunt Wyn. She says they overwork their horses...'

'I bet they do!' I said grimly.

'...and the proprietor is a horrid little man with a face like a bulldog...'

'...and he snaps and snarls at everyone except the customers.'

'You shouldn't have gone there,' declared Ann.

'I know,' I agreed fervently. 'I was "had".'

'Poor you!' Ann sympathised. 'How awful for you!'

I was feeling heaps better now. It made a world of difierence to be able to pour out my troubles and Ann was so understanding. Bit by bit I gave her a full account of the day's misadventures.

'How awful!' she said at the finish. 'They ought to be prosecuted or something. Why did you go there, anyhow?'

'Ponies,' I said simply. 'I'm pony mad. I'd do anything...' I remembered the Westburn Stables and altered that hastily '...*almost* anything to be with ponies.'

'Perhaps my Aunt Wyn could help you,' said Ann.

'She keeps ponies?' I asked eagerly.

'Oh no, but... Oh, we're stopping again.'

'Goodness, I hope no one else comes in,' I said fearfully. 'I'm so dirty and I smell a lot.'

'Yes, you do pong,' said Ann honestly. 'Never mind, a hot bath and lashings of bath salts will put you right.'

'My mother will have a fit when she sees me,' I mourned.

No one else came into the carriage and the train chugged on again.

'About your Aunt Wyn...' I said hopefully.

'I've been seeing her today,' said Ann, 'and that's why I'm here now. If anyone can help you, *she* can. She's very knowledgeable about ponies and all the pony places round about. Next time I visit her you can join me if you like.'

'Oh, I *do* like!' I said warmly.

We sat smiling at each other, all our old enmity forgotten.

'I'm sorry I laughed about Poothy,' said Ann suddenly. 'I did honestly think you were joking.'

'No wonder!' I said. 'It *is* an idiotic name. Mind you, Mum wanted to call him Marmaduke and that was even worse.'

'Marmaduke!' cried Ann, and we both went into gales of laughter.

* * *

Mary was quite upset when I told her the story of my day at Westburn Stables.

'It was all my fault,' she lamented, 'but honestly, I didn't know...'

'Of course it wasn't your fault,' I said warmly. 'Anyhow, it all turned out for the best. If I hadn't gone to Westburn I wouldn't have met Ann in the train, and if I hadn't met Ann I wouldn't have heard about her Aunt Wyn...'

'And what's this Aunt Wyn going to do for you?' Mary enquired.

'Oh – ah – I'm not sure, but I think Ann has something special up her sleeve.'

'A pony, perhaps?' suggested Mary, and giggled at the thought.

A week or two went by before Ann suggested a visit to her aunt. This was just as well as it gave me time to save the necessary train fare and to talk my mother into letting me venture forth on another pony quest.

'I don't want you coming home again in such a disreputable state,' Mum complained. 'Your jeans will never be the same again.'

'It will be all right this time, Mum,' I coaxed. 'We're going to visit Ann's aunt and I'm sure she won't let us get involved in any trouble.'

'I certainly hope not!' said Mum grimly.

We set off, Ann and I, on a Saturday afternoon, taking the Westburn train but getting off one station earlier than on my previous expedition. Ann had been rather secretive about her Aunt Wyn and what she could do for me, so I really didn't know what to expect as I followed my friend out of the station and into a maze of suburban streets.

Aunt Wyn lived at No. 6 Cherry Tree Road (small brick terraces without a cherry tree in sight!) and was a small energetic woman with bright sharp eyes and a quick way of talking.

'So this is Elizabeth,' she said at once, taking my hand and shaking it briskly. 'How d'you do! So you had a bad time at Westburn? I'm not a bit surprised. Did you have a good journey? Tea's ready. I hope you're hungry. This way! Mind the step.'

She gave us the most sumptuous tea, talking all the time about everything under the sun – everything, that is, except ponies – and I somehow had the feeling that she was weighing me up.

'I don't understand,' I whispered to Ann, when her aunt had gone off to refill the teapot. 'I thought she was going to advise me about ponies.'

'All in good time,' said Ann, and her eyes danced with mischief. She held out a plate. 'Try one of these biscuits. They're delicious.'

After tea we washed up together, and then Aunt Wyn put on her jacket.

'I'm taking you for a walk,' she announced.

'To The Lodge?' asked Ann eagerly.

'To The Lodge,' agreed her aunt.

Ann looked at me and her look said – as plain as plain could be – 'This is it!'

We walked briskly down Cherry Tree Road (everything with Aunt Wyn was done at top speed), then along Laburnum Drive and Walnut Avenue and down Oak Tree Lane. The little brick terraces were left behind and the houses grew older and bigger as we went along and the open country seemed close at hand. At last we came to a high wall and then an old-fashioned gateway with a nameplate saying HAYWOOD LODGE. On the wall beside the gate was a framed notice and under it a collecting box set into the stonework. I wanted to stop and read the notice but Aunt Wyn hurried us through the entrance, up the drive and round the house to the grounds at the rear.

And the first thing I saw was a paddock and ponies!

'Oooh!' I said, thrilled to the marrow.

But still Aunt Wyn didn't stop. She led us into a big shed where an elderly man was busy with a small greyish-brown animal. It took me a moment or two to realise that the creature was a donkey – but what a donkey! He was so thin that his ribs stuck out like the bars of a cage, and his back was covered with sores. I drew back from him in horror.

'What – what kind of place is this?' I asked fearfully.

'This is Haywood Lodge Pony Refuge,' said Aunt Wyn. 'A place for poor neglected ill-treated creatures like this one.' She touched the wretched animal gently, then turned to the man in charge. 'I think he looks a bit better today.'

'Yes, he is,' said the man. 'I think he'll pull through, but it was a near thing.'

Aunt Wyn led us all through the out-buildings and we saw more animals in various stages of convalescence.

'Where do these animals come from?' I asked, almost in tears over an emaciated old horse.

'We try to rescue any horse or pony in distress,' said Aunt Wyn. 'Donkeys too, as you have seen. They come to us in many ways. This poor old fellow was a coalman's horse; when his master bought a lorry, he was left shut up in a small yard without exercise or proper care until someone reported it.'

'And who pays for all the animals to be kept here?' I asked.

'It's a labour of love,' said Aunt Wyn. 'Unpaid helpers and voluntary giving.'

She led us out to the paddocks then and several sleek plump animals trotted over to meet us.

The first thing I saw was a paddock full of ponies.

'Some of these were in dreadful shape when the Refuge took them in,' said Aunt Wyn. 'That little chestnut pony there – isn't he a darling? – he was bought for a girl who wanted a pony, but she soon tired of him. He was sold first to one person and then to another and finished up with a tradesman who overworked him shamefully. He's in excellent fettle now and we will try to find a new home for him – a *good* home with someone who will really care for him.' She looked at me earnestly. 'You know, Elizabeth, a pony is not merely a plaything to fill an idle hour; it's a living, breathing creature and to own one is a great responsibility.'

'Yes,' I agreed humbly.

'Not all our stories are sad ones,' Aunt Wyn went on. She went over to a big placid horse and patted him fondly. 'This is Dobbin. He's a grand old fellow. He used to be on a milk round and when the dairy company changed over to electric floats he was "made redundant", as they say nowadays. He was growing old and no one else wanted him, so his future was pretty bleak; but the milkman and his customers combined to buy him from the firm and send him here.'

'Tell me more about this place,' I begged as we continued round the paddocks. 'How did it begin?'

'Well, the house belongs to Mr and Mrs Hooper, a retired couple. Mr Hooper – he was the man you saw with the donkey – was always fond of horses. Some years ago he rescued one unfortunate pony and the whole thing snowballed from that. Eventually he had to buy this extra ground for the animals and now you have the Haywood Lodge Pony Refuge.'

'And all run on a voluntary basis!' I exclaimed, marvelling.

'We're nearly always in the red,' confessed Aunt Wyn, 'but we manage somehow. We have many good friends and they run bazaars, jumble sales, coffee mornings...' We had come back to the house now and she paused before a shabby sun-blistered door marked OFFICE. 'We have an association called "Friends of Haywood Lodge". Members pay a small yearly subscription and help us in whatever way they can.'

'I'll join!' I said eagerly. 'May I?'

'This way,' said Aunt Wyn, and opened the office door.

* * *

All that happened quite a long time ago. You wouldn't recognise our housing estate if you saw it now. We have pavements, fences and gardens, and the fruit trees we planted in our first year have grown quite big. Billy is at the newly built Primary School and I'm swotting for my O-level exams. If I do well, Mum says I can stay on and try for A-levels as well. No, I haven't got a pony yet, and perhaps I never will, but I don't fret about it as I used to do.

Anyway, we haven't got enough room to keep one. I think some of my enthusiasm must have passed on to Mary, who now has a sweet Welsh pony which I sometimes ride in the evenings after school.

On my window ledge, beside my treasured china pony, is a collecting box marked 'Haywood Lodge Pony Refuge' and I put something in every week. All my friends have boxes too (I reckon I'd make a good saleswoman!) and between us we make quite a useful contribution.

I go to Haywood Lodge with Ann and Mary as often as possible and we do all we can to help there. They sometimes receive animals that seem more dead than alive, and it nearly breaks my heart to see them; but it's so rewarding when they respond to treatment and begin to fatten out and perk up. I love every minute that I spend there. Just at the moment we have the cutest little Sheltie called Mandy... But no, that's another story!

The Ghost Horse of Hidden Valley

by Sheila Austin

'Nearly there now. Gosh, I'm so excited, I must get another look at the photo of the ranch before the train gets in!'

The sun caught Judy Rainford's copper curls as she rummaged in her handbag, hunting for the photo. The train roared on through the Arizona Plains and England seemed very far away. The desolation she had felt during those terrible months that had followed her parents' tragic death in a motor accident was beginning to fade into the past, and Judy was eager to start her life in this new, exciting country.

At last, she found what she was looking for – an old, yellowed photograph, crinkled and torn at the edges. It showed a ranch-house, massively built, with creeper-clad walls and courtyards; a beautiful hacienda, set in a grove of tall trees, and surrounded by ranch buildings – stables, paddocks, barns and bunkhouses – and beyond, stretching to the foothills of the distant mountains, were corrals and pastures where huge herds of cattle grazed.

'It's grand!' breathed Judy, her eyes sparkling. 'And to think that this, the Lone Pine Ranch, is to be my home! I'm longing to see it and longing still more to meet Aunt May and my cousin Bob. I – I wonder why she didn't mention Bob in her letters? Well, I'll soon...'

She broke off sharply. The train was slowing down – and the porter had told her that the next stop was Yaqui Crossing, her destination.

'Oh, help – I must hurry!' gasped Judy, as the train slowed down and came to a grinding halt.

Frantically she closed her handbag and reached for her heavy leather suitcase. She hurried to the door of the carriage, jumped down from the step to the ground, and dragged her luggage out.

She dropped it on the ground and looked about her. Then her heart sank – there was no sign of a vehicle or of anyone to meet her. She had hoped her aunt might be waiting or, at least, one of her cowboys, and she felt disappointed and alone.

Further up the train some cowboys had been driving a few cattle into the wagons. Now they had finished and, mounting their horses, they went galloping across the prairie into the distance, like a scene from a Hollywood Western!

Judy couldn't help smiling, though she felt nervous and rather helpless. There was not even a platform here – just a tiny office-like shed with a lean-to stable at the back.

From the carriage windows people were staring at her, some in admiration, others in surprise. Judy thought it was because she looked so English, standing there, on a deserted station in the middle of nowhere. It did not occur to her that she made a delightful picture in whipcord riding breeches, a cream blouse and khaki jacket, with her gleaming hair just showing from under the wide-brimmed hat she wore.

Then the train moved away, gained speed, and vanished. She was alone.

It was only at that moment that she caught sight of a man – obviously the railroad official who had been helping load the cattle – coming towards her, a sheaf of papers in his hand.

'Well, my goodness!' he exclaimed, as if sighting Judy for the first time. 'Where have you sprung from, missie?'

A sudden alarming doubt came to Judy.

'From the train, of course,' she said, smiling uncertainly. 'But – but this is Yaqui Crossing, isn't it?'

'Well, it is, and it ain't,' said the railman slowly. 'This is Yaqui Crossing district right enough, but it ain't the station, miss; that's about two mile further along the line. You shouldn't have got off here at all.'

'Oh that's torn it!' she exclaimed, her heart sinking. 'No wonder there's nobody here to meet me!'

'Where are you bound for?' asked the railman. 'Which ranch?'

'The Lone Pine. Mrs Carson is my aunt, and...'

'I know her well, and a mighty fine lady she is,' said the man, rubbing his chin reflectively. 'Well, you are in a nice fix, miss; it's better'n five mile to the Lone Pine, and rough going at that. And it looks mightily like a storm coming.'

He pointed to the distant mountains, now almost hidden beneath dark, ominous clouds. Even as he did so, they heard the low growl of distant thunder.

'Only thing for it,' the man added, eyeing Judy's clothes, 'is for me to lend you a horse. I reckon you can ride.'

'Can a duck swim?' laughed Judy. 'My father kept training stables in England, and I've ridden horses since I was four.'

'Reckon I can fix you up, then, miss. You can leave your case in the office here. I'll lock it up safe, and you can send for it when you return my horse tomorrow.'

The old man put her bag in the office, locked the door, and led her to the stable at the rear. Two horses were there, and one of them – an ancient-looking chestnut – was led out and saddled quickly.

'There you are, missie,' he said, his kindly face breaking into a grin. 'You won't win no races on him, but he'll get you there. If nothing else, he's certainly very dependable.'

'He's an old darling, anyway!' laughed Judy, stroking the chestnut's shaggy coat. 'And thank you ever so much, it is good of you.'

'I'd do that and more for a niece of Bob Carson's wife,' the railman said earnestly. 'Fate ain't been kind to her, as I guess you know, miss. But — you'd best get going before the storm breaks. Ride alongside the line until you reach the station. Maybe you'll find someone waiting for you there; but if they ain't, take the trail until you reach the fork, and turn right. You can't miss it.'

Thanking him again, Judy leapt into the saddle, and looped her handbag over the pommel. Then, with a wave to the railman, she set off at a brisk trot along the line.

She very soon reached the 'station', which, like many of the prairie halts she had seen, consisted of two or three rough cabins and a cindered track. Not a soul was to be seen anywhere, but tyre-marks in the dust told her that a vehicle had been there very recently.

'Well, what a stupid fool I am!' she groaned, smothering her disappointment with a rueful laugh. 'Daddy used to say I was too impulsive, and how right he was! What on earth will my aunt think of me?'

She set off along the winding trail, forcing her mount to break into a fast canter. Great drops of warm rain were pattering down now, and the blue sky was rapidly growing dark and threatening. A vivid flash followed almost at once by a great crack of thunder made her horse shy in terror. She had already found that he was not as docile as he seemed and it was clear that he hated thunderstorms, so now Judy had to keep him on a tight rein, talking softly to try to calm him before the storm finally burst on them both.

It came with incredible swiftness, and in a matter of seconds she was drenched to the skin, while the trail became muddy and treacherous. They had to go more slowly.

'What a start to my new life!' panted Judy, against the rain. 'It's my own fault, I suppose; I should have checked up properly before I got off the train.'

But it was useless thinking of that now. Indeed, Judy had little time for thought. It was all she could do to hold her horse, who was growing more scared as the storm increased.

The trail was rough, winding between great boulders, through thick clumps of thorny chaparral and dense scrub where prickly pear cactus grew. They passed grassy banks, vivid with blue and yellow lupins and scarlet Indian tulips, and crossed rushing streams that only an hour ago, she knew, must have been dried-up gullies.

Then suddenly she came upon a stream much deeper and broader than any she had so far encountered. Judy had to use all her will and skill to force her horse to cross, and just as he reached the middle and was battling against the fierce rush of water, a sudden flash of lightning and a crash of thunder made him rear in terror.

And as he did so her precious handbag, slung carelessly on the pommel, swung through the air in a wide arc, striking the terrified horse across his face before falling with a loud splash into the water.

This was the last straw; Judy lost all control and the horse clambered up the opposite bank, and bolted off at a wild gallop across the prairie with Judy clinging on as well as she could.

All at once, she saw a rider coming towards her. It was a boy — a little older than herself — clad in the colourful garb of a Mexican cowboy: short charro jacket, tight-fitting trousers and cone-peaked sombrero.

Judy's horse seemed to lose its blind panic on seeing the other horse and rider, for it slowed down and stopped just in front of them.

The boy swept off his wide sombrero and smiled at her. 'Good afternoon, Señorita! Can I help you in any way?'

'Oh yes, please,' gasped Judy. 'My bag has fallen into the stream and I'm afraid it will be swept away by the current.'

'Don't worry, Señorita. I will find it for you;' and without another word he cantered off in the direction she had come from, the silver ornaments on his hat and clothing glinting and flashing in the gry light.

Within five minutes he was back, holding the dripping bag triumphantly in his hand.

'See, Señorita! Here is your handbag. Now there is no problem.' She took it from him, thanking him gratefully for his help.

'It was nothing, Señorita,' he responded with a laugh. 'It is a great pleasure to be of some assistance to one as pretty as you. But you're from England?'

She nodded. Turning her head, she met his eyes and was surprised at the serious look on his face.

'Yes, I've only just come over,' she said. 'My name is Judy Rainford and I'm going to live with my aunt at the Lone Pine Ranch. Is it far?'

She broke off, suddenly aware that the boy had stiffened. His dark eyes seemed to glow.

'Ah. That — that is very good, Señorita,' he murmured, after a pause. 'Señora Carson, she is lonely since her husband died. She will, I think be so very happy to have you with her, and I feel sure that you, Señorita, will be happy there with her.' He laughed. 'Me, I am Juan Ruiz, and I work for Señor Flint at the Dos Cabezos Ranch. I will ride with you to the fork of the trails and show you the way.'

The rain had cleared, and the sun was shining again as they rode on over the steaming prairie.

'But you must come home with me,' said Judy, smiling at her companion. 'I am sure that my aunt will want to thank you. She will be grateful for all you have done for me.'

'Indeed, no, Señorita,' said Juan, chuckling. 'I am not welcome at Pine Ranch. They look on me as a thief and a rustler. If they catch me there, the Pine Ranch cowboys could be very rough!'

'Well, it doesn't seem to worry you much,' laughed Judy. 'And I certainly don't believe you are a thief or a rustler, Juan.'

'Ah, you will learn soon enough, Señorita Judy,' said Juan, and now his tone was serious. 'The Lone Pine and the Dos Cabezos ranches are enemies. Now, see!'

They had reached the fork and Juan stopped and pointed to the trail leading to the right.

'That is the Lone Pine Ranch in the valley, Señorita,' he said, pointing to a group of log-cabins in the distance. 'Again I will say that I am happy to have been of assistance to you. And now — adios!'

He turned his horse and, with a flourish of his sombrero, went galloping towards a ranch-house built in the Spanish style, that stood to the left of the valley.

Judy frowned, bewildered.

'What an odd boy he is!' she murmured. 'I — I hope I see him again. But what does he mean, pointing out those cabins as the Lone Pine Ranch. Why, there is the Lone Pine Ranch over to the left. Yes...'

Suddenly she remembered the photograph, and opened her wet handbag. Then she gave a startled gasp. Something else was in her handbag, something that had certainly not been there before. It was a small packet, wrapped in white paper. Wonderingly she pulled aside the covering — to reveal a small, beautifully carved figure of a horse! A magnificent horse, with upflung head and long, tossing mane, carved out of some white wood. Obviously it was a wild stallion — and what a stallion!

'It — it's lovely!' sighed Judy as she gazed at it.

Then she caught sight of some writing on the paper — writing in a strong, bold hand that seemed to Judy more American than Mexican.

'Follow the White Horse and bring prosperity to Whispering Valley.'

'But — but what does it mean?' wondered Judy confusedly. 'It — it can't be a joke — this model is too beautiful for that. But who can have put...'

Who else could it have been but the strange Mexican boy? He must have put it there while he was fetching her handbag from the stream. Probably he meant it as a present.

Yet that did not explain the strange message. It was extremely unlikely that a Mexican cowboy could have written such a message in that bold, grammatical style.

'Whatever can it mean?' thought Judy, puzzled. 'Anyway, I'm bound to meet him again, so I'll be able to tackle him about it.'

She remembered the photo once more, and a moment later was studying it. Yes, it was a photograph of that lovely Spanish-looking ranch.

'How strange,' thought Judy, frowning. 'Juan couldn't have made a mistake.' She shrugged her shoulders, and rode slowly towards the cluster of log cabins that the Mexican boy had pointed out as being Lone Pine Ranch.

Lone Pine Ranch

As she drew closer, she could see that the main building was a long, two-storied house, with a veranda running along the whole length.

Like the older ranch, it had red tiles, and creepers and roses grew over it in glorious profusion. It was almost surrounded by tall cottonwood trees, their leafy branches making a delicate tracery against the deep blue sky. By the entrance gate stood a single great pine-tree, which had obviously given the ranch its name.

Somehow the whole place seemed to be comfortable and homely, and Judy's heart warmed to it. Certainly it did not look over-prosperous, for many of the buildings and fences seemed badly in need of paint and repair, but Judy had already fallen in love with the place.

She rode through the gateway and dismounted. Over by the stables an old bandy-legged man was giving a couple of horses a drink. Two cowboys were attending to a sick horse in a nearby paddock. And then — the glass doors of the ranch porch burst open and a woman came flying down the steps and raced towards her joyfully.

'It is! Oh, Judy dear, I'd know you anywhere! Just like your mother was at your age!' she exclaimed delightedly. 'So — so you've really come, after all!'

'Hallo, Aunt May, how are you?' cried Judy, laughing. She flung herself into the older woman's arms, and for a moment they hugged each other affectionately.

'Gracious me, but you're wet through, Judy!' cried her aunt. 'We thought you'd missed your train or something. Zeke — that's my foreman over there — went for you in the jeep, and hasn't been back long. But, my dear, where have you been?'

'Like a fool, I got off the train before I should have done,' said Judy. 'I'm terribly sorry, Aunt May!'

'Bless you, you're here safe and sound, so why worry about that?' laughed her aunt. 'But your clothes are wet, and you really must change at once,' she added. 'Come along, dear: you can tell me everything over tea. Oh, it's lovely to see you, Judy!'

She fairly rushed Judy indoors, and, as she did so, Judy got a brief glimpse of massive old furniture, shining brass, blue china, and bright Indian rugs before she was hurried upstairs, despite her protests.

She tried in vain to explain that she had no change of clothing with her, but her aunt only laughed. And then, as they reached a pretty bedroom, with creamy walls and bright airy windows, Aunt May pointed to the bed — and Judy understood.

Laid out on the bed was everything she needed, including blue jeans, coloured shirts, a wide-brimmed stetson, riding gloves and boots, and even a shining new waterproof cape, or 'slicker.'

'There you are, my dear,' said Aunt May. 'All aired and waiting for you, and I guess they'll fit you all right. Tea will be ready when you come down, and then we can have a really good talk.'

'Oh, Aunt May, it's sweet of you,' Judy began. But Aunt May had gone, so Judy quickly set about the job of changing, after a brisk wash. To her great satisfaction, all the clothes fitted perfectly, and she began to feel her aunt must be a magician. As she looked at herself in the glass, her eyes were alight with pleasure, her happiness seemed complete.

Her aunt was just as her mother had been — sweet and good-natured, and probably just as impulsive as she was. And this bedroom, with its view over the distant mist-shrouded mountains, was sheer heaven.

With a final pat to her glossy curls, Judy hurried downstairs to the big dining-room, with its windows overloking the ranch buildings. There a tea was laid which took Judy's breath away, and certainly made her mouth water — chicken and ham sandwiches, cornbread with molasses, and thick dairy cream; home-made cakes, apricot pie, blueberry pie, and delicacies that Judy had never heard of before. And there, too, Judy was introduced to Bella, the negro cook, whose good-natured face beamed a warm welcome.

'Sure you're just like your Aunt May was when she was a girl,' she said smiling. 'You're as pretty as she was too, Miss Judy.'

'After that, you really ought to eat a good tea, Judy,' her aunt told her.

And Judy did, while Bella came in and out to hear her news. But the meal ended at last, and then Aunt May took her out on to the veranda, and they settled down in big, comfy chairs for a long talk.

'Now tell me all about your journey,' began Aunt May. 'I'm still puzzled to know how you managed to get off the train like you did.'

And Judy told her, making light of her troubles afterwards. It was lovely and peaceful out there in the golden Arizona sunset, and it seemed amusing to her now. All signs of the storm had vanished; lovely tints of orange and gold spread over the darkening blue background of sky, and the jagged mountain peaks flared like fire in the sunset.

Judy asked her aunt about the photograph of the other ranch, which looked so different from this one, and saw her face grow sad.

'You see, Judy,' she said slowly, 'when that photograph was taken and sent to you, some time ago, Dos Cabezos belonged to your grandfather, and it was our home. But — but my husband and my father quarrelled bitterly, so we left there and came here. And, afterwards, my husband was too proud to return. They — they were both hasty-tempered and obstinate, Judy. And then your grandfather was killed in a stampede.'

'Yes, you wrote and told me that, Aunt May,' said Judy carefully. 'And then...'?

'I will tell you all about it later, Judy,' went on her aunt awkwardly. 'But when the will was read it was found that Father had left the ranch and everything else to — to Wilmot

Flint, who now lives there with his daughter, Dolores.'

'Oh, Aunt May!' cried Judy, aghast. 'How unfair!'

'Many people, who knew of the quarrel between my husband and my father, were not surprised,' went on Aunt May bitterly, 'because Wilmot Flint was your grandfather's lawyer at the time, and he was on very friendly terms with my father. And in those days he seemed a kindly, good-natured man.'

She sighed.

'It was only afterwards, when he had taken over your grandfather's property and wealth, that he showed his real character,' she added grimly. 'He became greedy, arrogant and bullying. His one ambition is to be king of Whispering Valley. He's already bought out most of the ranchers, and because I refused to sell, he has become vindictive and never loses an opportunity to do me harm.'

'Oh!' gasped Judy. 'So that is why Juan warned me that the two ranches are enemies!'

'Yes. They — they have made things very, very hard for me, Judy,' said her aunt.

'I think I understand,' whispered Judy, pressing the older woman's arm affectionately. 'But you are not alone now,' she added, her eyes gleaming. 'I love being here, and I mean to take over a great deal of the burden from your shoulders. I managed Daddy's affairs after he — he died, and they'll find they have me to deal with as well as you, dear. But...'

She broke off, pausing uncertainly, and then went on gently.

'There's something I've been wanting to ask you all along, Aunt May. Mother told me many times that you had a son — Bobby — who must be a little older than I am. But you didn't mention him in your letters, and...'

Judy broke off as she saw the quick pain in her aunt's eyes.

'I knew you must ask that, Judy,' Aunt May said quietly,

her voice trembling a little. 'No. Bobby is not here, and as you are bound to learn the truth, I must tell you now. Bobby got into trouble with the sheriff at Tres Pinos: he was implicated in a rustling charge with two Mexicans on the Dos Cabezos Range. He was arrested, but escaped, and now he's a fugitive.'

'Oh, I am terribly sorry,' said Judy sincerely. 'As if you had not had trouble enough. First grandfather, then uncle, and now... But do you never hear from him?' she added.

'Yes.' Aunt May lowered her voice. 'He writes to me, secretly, of course. I think he is on a ranch in Texas. And oh, Judy, in his last letter he says he has good hopes of clearing himself and coming home.'

'Oh, how splendid if he could!' exclaimed Judy. 'He's innocent — I'm sure he must be. Aunt.'

'Yes, we know he is. That — that man Wilmot Flint was behind it! You would love Bobby, Judy, he's a dear boy. A bit wild, but then most boys of his age are. Your grandfather thought the world of him. They were great chums, and Bobby went with his grandfather on expeditions into the mountains and everywhere. That is why it was such a great shock when we learned that Flint was to inherit the ranch. Your grandfather had told Zeke Carter — who used to be his foreman before coming to us — that he intended to make Bobby his heir; not once, but many times.

'Many people,' went on Aunty May quietly, 'thought your grandfather was a bit of a crank — that he had a bee in his bonnet. But Bobby didn't think so. It wat the dream of my father's life to find a hidden valley that the Indians say exists in the mountains. Bobby and he used to go on expeditions in search of it. They've both seen the White Horse in Wild Horse Canyon, and both believe the legend that to follow the Ghost Horse will bring prosperity to Whispering Valley.'

The White Horse! She thought of the note in her bag.

In the excitement of meeting her aunt – of talking family matters – Judy had forgotten the White Horse, but now her eyes widened and she was filled with sudden excitement.

Brownie

Judy now knew that whoever had placed that model horse in her handbag had done so with an object in view.

It wasn't just a present for her, nor was it a joke. This was a model of a real wild horse, and, according to her aunt, both her grandfather and her cousin Bob had seen it, and they both believed that the wild horse was the key to a secret – a secret that lay in a hidden valley in the mountains.

And the odd manner in which the model horse had been put in her handbag seemed to be a greater mystery still. Judy could only think that Juan, the Mexican boy, must have put it there. And yet why had the strange boy done so, and what connection could he possibly have with Bobby and her grandfather?

A wild 'ghost' horse and a hidden valley! And to think that this had been her grandfather's lifelong quest – to follow the wild horse and find the secret valley.

How exciting, but how puzzling it all was!

It was on the tip of her tongue to tell her aunt about finding the model in her handbag, but just as quickly she decided against it. It had flashed into her mind that the strange way in which it had been put there proved that whoever had hidden it wanted her to keep silent – that it was for her and her alone.

So, instead, she drew a deep breath and exclaimed, 'Oh, Aunt May! A hidden valley and a ghost horse! Do tell me more about it, please! It sounds terribly exciting.'

'Oh, I'm afraid I know very little about it,' said Aunt

May, smiling. 'But it seems certain that the wild horse actually exists, though whether the Hidden Valley does is another matter. But the Indians think so, and so did your grandfather and Bobby. They went off together for days on end into the hills, searching for it. But the country there is just badlands, terribly wild and difficult.'

As she finished speaking, Aunt May pointed to the distant mountains. The red sun had vanished now behind the granite mass, its jagged edges stood out clear-cut against the darkening sky, and were tinged with a pink and orange glow. The pine forests on the slopes were deep purple, and dark shadows lay over the valley.

To Judy the whole valley and the darkening mountains seemed strangely mysterious just then – almost sinister and threatening – and she shivered a little. Aunt May noticed it.

'Yes, it's getting quite chilly,' she said, getting up from her chair. 'We'll go indoors now, and then it's supper and straight to bed for you, my dear. You must be tired out. And, oh, there's just one thing, Judy!'

She paused and her kindly face grew serious.

'It's about that Mexican boy, Juan,' she said. 'It – it was most unfortunate, in a way, that it was he who helped you, Judy. He's been found prowling round Pine Ranch many times,' she added grimly, 'but he's far too slippery to get caught. But what I mean is this, Judy dear: the boy is an enemy of ours, employed by a man who's determined to drive us from the valley. And – and though it's only natural for you to feel grateful' – she paused – 'you must not have anything more to do with him, of course. You do understand?' she ended anxiously.

'Oh, yes, Aunt May; but – but he seemed so kind and friendly!'

'So are most Mexicans – when it suits them,' said Aunt

May, wryly. 'But it makes them all the more dangerous, my dear. However, I know I can leave it to your good sense. Only I thought I would warn you that the boy is not to be trusted.'

The more Judy thought about it the more certain did she feel that Juan was, somehow, mixed up in the mysterious quest. And she was convinced that whoever actually did put the model in her handbag did so because he wanted her to follow up her grandfather's quest – to find the Hidden Valley.

'And that,' Judy told herself before she went to sleep that night, 'is just what I am going to do. I believe that whoever gave me that horse wants me to take over Grandfather's quest and find the Hidden Valley, and I'm jolly well going to have a mighty good shot at it.'

With this resolution in her mind Judy fell asleep; and the next thing she knew was that sunlight was streaming on to her face, while Aunt May was smilingly handing her a cup of coffee.

'It's really a shame to wake you,' she laughed. 'But I know you're longing to ride round the ranch.'

'Of course I am! Why, it's nearly nine o'clock!' said Judy reproachfully, as she noticed the clock on her mantelpiece. 'Oh, you shouldn't have let me sleep so long, Aunt May.'

'My dear, you had a terribly tiring day yesterday, and the sleep will do you a world of good,' said her aunt firmly. 'Breakfast will be ready just when you are, and Bella's made some specially good griddle cakes for you, so don't forget to enjoy them.'

And Aunt May laughed and departed.

But Judy had no need to be told to enjoy the griddle cakes. They proved to be delicious, and Bella smiled as she made short work of a tremendous breakfast. She was just finishing the meal when a knock came at the door and an elderly, grizzled cowpuncher entered. Aunt May looked up.

'Oh, here you are, Zeke,' she said, welcoming the old man. 'Judy, this is Zeke Carter, our foreman. He's going to take you round, aren't you, Zeke?'

'It'll be a real pleasure, I reckon,' he grinned, taking Judy's hand in a warm clasp. 'So you're old John Carson's granddaughter, eh? Right glad to see you, miss. Well, your pony's ready. He's a bit frisky, but your aunt tells me you can ride.'

'I think I rode a horse before I rode in a pram,' said Judy, chuckling. 'I can promise you I shan't fall off, anyway, Mr Carter.'

In a very few minutes – for she was longing to ride round the ranch – Judy was ready, and she accompanied the old foreman to the stables. There she met 'Curley' Gibbon and 'Fatty' Turner — who was as thin as a rail — two of the four cowboys on the Lone Pine Ranch. They greeted her with friendly smiles.

Then Judy got the surprise of her life — and a lovely surprise — as Curley led a pony from the stable.

He was a magnificent chestnut, with a proudly raised head and glossy mane and coat. His eyes were intelligent and lively, his legs were slender, and his hoofs small and clean-cut. An expert would have known instantly that he was built for speed and endurance, and Judy was an expert. In her father's racing stables in England she had never seen a horse she liked better than this one.

'Oh, he — he's lovely, Zeke!' she cried breathlessly, her eyes sparkling. 'May I ride him?'

'Well, as he's yours, I reckon you can,' grinned Zeke, enjoying the pleasure on Judy's flushed face. 'Your aunt meant this as a surprise for you, Miss Judy — a mighty fine surprise, too, eh?'

'You — you mean...'

'I mean that this pony's a present to you from your aunt,'

said Zeke. 'Now, if you're ready, Miss Judy...'

But Judy wasn't quite ready. She raced off indoors, found her aunt in the kitchen, and greatly astonished that lady by hugging and kissing her fondly. Then, having explained why, she hurried back to Zeke, eager to get into the saddle again.

And she was not disappointed in her mount. At first he was nervy and a bit troublesome, but she soon gained his confidence and respect. She learnt that her cousin Bobby had broken him in, and she had to confess that he had made a good job of it. The chestnut, high-spirited and game, was all she had judged him to be.

Brownie was his name, and before long, girl and pony were great friends. After a tour of the ranch buildings Judy and Zeke paid a visit to the corral to see the foals and calves — which was great fun — and then she got a chance to put Brownie through his paces on the open range, racing against Zeke's sturdy horse.

'He's grand!' praised Judy, as horse and pony slowed down at last. 'Zeke, he's a born racer! Haven't you ever thought of putting him in a race — at a rodeo, I mean?'

The old foreman, delighted at her keenness, nodded.

'Young Bobby's ridden him in a good few, and ain't lost a race yet,' he said. 'Yes, Miss Judy, if Bobby had been here now, he'd have been riding Brownie in the rodeo at Tres Pinos day after tomorrow. It's hard luck on your aunt too, as I happen to know she could have done with the five hundred dollar prize-money that goes with the trophy.'

Judy pulled up dead, full of her sudden plan.

'Hold on a minute, Zeke,' she said excitedly. 'Is it too late to enter for the race?'

'Why no. Entries got to be in by today, though,' he returned, staring at Judy. 'But you ain't thinking of going in for that race?'

'I certainly am,' announced Judy firmly. 'You see,' she went on, 'like Bobby, I've ridden in quite a few races, and, like Bobby, I haven't lost one yet. Yes, Zeke, I'm going to ride Brownie in that race, and I'm going to win.'

'Gosh, girl, you can't mean it!' interrupted the old man. 'If you can ride like young Bob, then I'm mighty sure you will win. Far as I know, you've only got that Flint girl to beat. She's riding another chestnut — a mighty fine pony — but he ain't as good as Brownie, and Flint knows it. He's tried to buy the pony from your aunt more than once. Wilmot Flint's a skunk, but he's a mighty good judge of horse flesh.'

'Then I'll see Aunt May as soon as I get back,' said Judy decidedly. 'How far is Tres Pinos? Can I ride there this afternoon?'

'Yeah. It's about eight miles, and I reckon that won't hurt Brownie none. In fact, a little run like that's just what he needs. If you really mean it, Miss Judy, I'll get Curley or someone to ride over with you, or maybe I'll come myself.'

The old foreman was obviously delighted. He had been watching Judy as she rode, and his shrewd eyes had missed nothing. He knew she could ride, and he did not doubt that, on Brownie, she would win.

And he was thinking, too, of Judy's Aunt May. He knew, better than Judy did, what a brave fight the widow had been making to keep Lone Pine Ranch going. He knew that even five hundred dollars would be a tremendous help to her just then.

And his heart warmed towards Judy. He was thinking that she was as brave and as persevering as her aunt.

They rode on over the sun-baked prairie, Judy enjoying every moment of the ride. They saw squirrels running up and down trees, chattering shrilly, and Judy laughed at the quaint antics of prairie chickens — the clowns of the prairie, as Zeke told her they were called.

'It's lovely country,' she cried at last, her face flushed with happiness. 'But oh, how terribly dry the ground is! How do the cattle feed on this grass?'

'Aye, that's the big trouble with Whispering Valley, lass,' said old Zeke grimly. 'Shortage of water — the constant dread of drought. We've never enough water for the cattle, just a few water-holes, and Yaqui Springs over yonder. On Flint's ranch they ain't so badly off, but us smaller ranchers have a hard time of it. And yet long ago — maybe centuries ago — there was plenty of water in this valley.'

He pointed out a deep, ravine-like depression that seemed to run right across the prairie.

'You see that, Miss Judy?' he asked. 'That's the ancient bed of a river that used to run right through this valley. It starts in Wild Horse Canyon, and I reckon it runs right down to the Rio Grande River. But there must have been an earthquake long ago, and Wild Horse Canyon was blocked up and the river was dammed.'

'But where did the water go?' asked Judy. 'The river must have gone somewhere.'

'Underground, I reckon. Leastways, the Indians say it flows through a hidden valley in the mountains, and then goes underground just beyond Wild Horse Canyon. And I reckon them Indians should know. They say their ancestors used to live in cave dwellings in this secret valley.'

'Oh, how wonderful!' cried Judy. 'Aunt May did say something about a hidden valley and a ghost horse. Tell me about it, Zeke.'

'Ain't much to tell that I know,' grinned the old foreman. 'But that horse ain't no ghost horse. He's real, and a mighty fine horse he is. I've seen him myself one night when we was out hunting strays, and your grandfather and young Bobby have seen him, too. They say he comes out of this hidden valley and rushes round crazy-like, then bolts back again, and nobody's ever found out where he gets out; but it's somewhere in Wild Horse Canyon. The Indians say there's a big herd of them in this secret valley, and if there is, then they must be worth a fortune.'

'Oh, I'd love to go there,' exclaimed Judy. 'How far is it to the canyon, Zeke?'

'Now don't you go getting such ideas into your head, Miss Judy,' said the foreman, growing serious. 'That canyon's in mighty bad country, and besides it's a hide-out for outlaws, and a happy hunting-ground for snakes and cougars and such-like. It's right in the badlands, and it's no place for a young lady like you.'

'Oh,' sighed Judy, 'am I to stay at home and do knitting and dull things like that all the time?'

'I dunno about that,' chuckled Zeke. 'But you'll get quite enough excitement out of Brownie when he's in one of his moods without looking for trouble by riding in Wild Horse Canyon...Well, Miss Judy, I reckon we'd best be getting back home, if you and Brownie are planning on riding to Tres Pinos this afternoon.'

Arriving at the ranch, Judy gave her pony a careful rub down; then fed and watered him, despite Zeke's protests and offers to do the job for her. The old rangeman had undoubtedly taken quite a fancy to Judy.

In Tres Pinos

She ran indoors to find her aunt, who was busy in the kitchen.

'Oh, Aunt May — can you make me up a few sandwiches, please? I've got to get to Tres Pinos before six o'clock at the very latest.'

'Tres Pinos?' echoed Aunt May. 'But — but whatever for, Judy?'

'To enter Brownie and me for the Gold Spurs,' said Judy

calmly. She studied her aunt's face for a reaction.

'Judy, my dear, you don't mean it,' began Aunt May, her eyes shining.

'Of course, I do,' said Judy. 'Brownie's a darling, and a real wonder horse. We're going to win, too! Then I'll take the Gold Spurs and you'll take the five hundred dollars!' she added gaily. 'Now don't start raising objections.'

But Aunt May was not likely to do that! She was so happy at Judy's proposal. She knew what Brownie could do, and she knew that Judy had not only had great experience, but was a born rider too.

Zeke was called in, and a conference held there and then. It was decided that Judy and the cowboy, Curley, should ride over to Tres Pinos that afternoon to enter for the race. On the following day, save for a brief gallop, Judy and her horse should rest, and the next day — the day of the race — she would be driven over in the jeep by Zeke while Curley and Fatty Turner took Brownie over in the horse-box.

So it was settled, and, after a quick lunch, Curley Gibson and Judy set off for Tres Pinos. Curley was terribly shy and awkward at first, but Judy's lively chatter soon put him at his ease. And Judy was glad of his company during the long ride. He was a likeable chap, and he told Judy a great deal about the country and customs as they rode — things that astonished her.

They took the route that led over the parched rangeland, and into the foothills, riding between great forests of pine and spruce, and then on into wilder country, most of which was bare of vegetation save for cactus and sage, with here and there a clump of withered mesquite. Lizards abounded, scampering away at their approach, and more than once Curley gave sharp warning of a rattlesnake in their path.

And all the time the Arizona sun slanted scorching rays from a cloudless blue sky, until Judy felt as if she was riding through a Turkish bath. She had never known such heat!

Then, topping a slope, Judy found herself gazing down on the town of Tres Pinos. She had seen many such cattle towns from the train, but now she was to see one from close quarters.

It was not a big place, she found, when they rode in, and it was mainly composed of wooden frame buildings with false fronts, and quaint brick houses, flat-topped, roofed by poles covered with sage-brush, and made secure from wind and rain by a thick layer of soil.

Most of the people she saw were cattle folk, with one or two Mexicans; though she also noticed several Indians — dark, fierce-looking men, whom she guessed must be Yaquis — with a hair fringe cut in a straight line across their foreheads.

At the sheriff's office Judy dismounted, while Curley rode on to the Cattlemen's Bank on an errand for her aunt.

A notice announcing the rodeo was in the dusty window, and after reading it through, Judy entered the office. Seated on a chair with his feet on a battered desk was an elderly man with iron-grey hair and moustache. This proved to be Sheriff Moore, and the other man in the office — a tall, lanky individual — was a deputy sheriff, Jim Cross.

The sheriff smiled as he hurriedly dropped his feet to the floor and rose, holding out a friendly hand.

'Reckon no need to ask you who you are, Miss Rainford,' he said heartily. 'You're just like your aunt. I heard as you was coming. Reckon I'm right?'

'You are — quite right,' said Judy, laughing, as she shook hands with him and then with the deputy. 'I've come, sheriff…'

'Not to give yourself up, I hope,' grinned the sheriff. 'You don't look to me like no outlaw!'

'No, I've come to enter for the Gold Spurs,' announced Judy. 'I know I'm in time.'

Judy and Curley rode together into the small town.

'Sure, sure,' chuckled the sheriff. 'Well, I'm right glad to hear that, miss. You'll be riding Brownie, I reckon. A right grand horse, and if you can ride as well as he can run, I don't reckon I'll lose my money — for it's sure all going on Brownie.'

'I'll do my best to help you win it then,' smiled Judy. 'I see there are only two entries, and mine will make three.'

'Yeah — a horse from the Sunblaze Ranch, named Cutey, and Miss Dolores Flint's Golden Glory. But I guess the race'll be between you and Miss Flint. And everybody allows as Brownie's the better pony. Your cousin, young Bobby, rode him to victory more'n once. Pity the lad weren't here now.'

He paused.

'I reckon I'm right glad to know as your aunt will have your company now, Miss Rainford,' he added quietly. 'She's a grand woman, and since her son — well, went away — I guess she's been mighty lonely.'

'It's a wicked shame,' said Judy. 'I'm absolutely sure from what I know that Bobby was innocent, sheriff.'

'Maybe so, young lady — it ain't for me to say,' returned the sheriff grimly. 'But the lad shouldn't have run like he done. He'd have had a fair trial — I'd have seen to that — and considering as the two Mex witnesses against him weren't none too reliable — I reckon there ain't no knowing what a jury would have decided. Yeah, pity he bolted like he done.'

Judy felt inclined to agree with him there, and after asking a few more questions about the rodeo, she was about to leave the office when a man and a young woman strode in. He was fat, and had a smooth face with fish-like eyes, which stared at her now with a hostile gaze. The girl was tall, with swarthy features and a mass of fluffy dark hair.

The sheriff looked somewhat embarrassed, and introduced them to Judy as — Mr Flint and Miss Dolores Flint!

Judy excused herself on the grounds that she was in a hurry, but Dolores' dark eyes were fixed on the folded rodeo notice in Judy's hand, and, as if unable to contain sudden fear, she gripped Judy's arm and detained her.

'Just a minute, Miss Rainford,' she said curtly. 'You — you've not entered for the Gold Spurs, have you?'

'Looks like it, doesn't it?' said Judy pleasantly as she pointed to the window. Jim Cross was just replacing the list of entrants for the rodeo, with Judy's name and that of her horse added to it. 'Have you any objections, Miss Flint?'

'Yes, I have,' snapped Dolores, her face crimson with rage. 'It's a shame — it oughtn't to be allowed at such short notice; upsetting everybody's arrangements.'

'Yours, I suppose, you mean,' said Judy angrily.

'Now, look here, Miss Rainford,' cut in Wilmot Flint, forcing a smile to his expressionless face. 'If you'd be prepared to sell that horse, I'd give you a good price!'

'The horse isn't for sale, Mr Flint.'

'Now listen, Miss Rainford,' said the rancher pompously. 'I'm a powerful man in this valley. It's mighty important for me to have the best horses in my string. You ain't got a chance, of course, against my daughter's Golden Glory, but...'

'Then why waste time making offers for Brownie?' said Judy abruptly. 'Good afternoon!'

She would have walked out of the office, but this time it was the rancher who detained her with a rough hand on her arm.

'Just a minute, you,' he snarled. 'What's that you've got round your neck, young woman — that model stallion, I mean?'

Judy started. She looked down and caught her breath as she saw something dangling above her shirt top, open at the neck.

It was the model of the wild horse. Judy, wanting to keep

it with her to remind herself of the quest she was determined to follow, had fastened it to a gold chain she always wore around her neck. She had kept it hidden, but during the ride it must have jumped out over her shirt neck.

Judy was astonished at the look of fury and surprise in the rancher's face.

'What are you doing with that, young woman?' he almost shouted. 'If — if you think...'

'Is it any business of yours?' asked Judy; and she would have moved on, but now Flint planted himself between her and the door.

'Just a minute, girl,' he said threateningly, his voice low and hard. 'I just want to warn you, young woman. In case you get any ideas — I want to warn you to keep away from Wild Horse Canyon! It's mighty bad country — and it's on my land. And if I catch you or any of your outfit there I'll make things warm for you. Get that!'

Kidnappers!

Judy laughed, though her heart was thumping. So Wilmot Flint was interested in Wild Horse Canyon — and the legend. He was so interested, indeed, that he wanted to keep everyone else from visiting the mysterious place.

'So it's your land, is it?' she asked. 'Do you happen to be the President of the United States by any chance?'

'I don't want your impudence,' muttered Flint with a quick glance at the sheriff. 'I'm just telling you, girl. I happen to own that land, and I ain't allowing any trespassers on it. Wild Horse Canyon's a mighty unhealthy place for strangers, Miss Rainford. Keep out — and stay healthy!'

Judy walked on, but this time, the rancher let her go and he and Dolores followed her out of the office.

'So — so someone's put her on to that game,' he said to

his daughter in an undertone. 'Her aunt ain't likely to have done it. Then who in thunder has?'

'Oh, why get all het up about it, anyway,' drawled Dolores. 'I expect she's picked up that thing somewhere and just wears it for an ornament or as a charm. You're worrying about nothing, poppa. It's — it's about the race I'm worrying.'

She paused and now her face was pale, her eyes furious.

'Poppa, she's not going to win that race,' she cried. 'You've got to stop her somehow. I — I've just set my heart on winning the Spurs. I don't care a thing about the money. She mustn't win — she *mustn't!*'

'And she ain't going to,' said Wilmot Flint. They had moved on along the street now, and Flint's eyes were shrewd, calculating. 'I tell you I shan't feel safe, Dolores, until the whole of that family's out of the valley.'

'What's that got to do with the race?' sulked Dolores.

'Just this! That five hundred dollar prize-money's going to help that Carson woman stick it out longer — that's why! And that's why that girl ain't going to win, Dolores. Say, Juan and Pablo are in town, ain't they? I sent them to the blacksmith's to get a job done. We've got to find them — pronto!'

Judy strolled along the street, leading her horse and looking for the Sunshine Restaurant, where she had arranged to meet Curley Gibson. She was uncomfortably aware that she was coated from head to foot in the dust of the trail, but she was quite unconscious of the admiring glances cast upon her trim figure.

She found the place at last — a small eating-house, but unexpectedly clean and tidy. A young girl served her with a cup of coffee, and she sat down to wait for Curley, rather surprised not to find him there. For some minutes she chatted to the girl, but new customers came in, so she waited alone, toying with her coffee. What had happened to Curley?

Ten minutes — twenty — half an hour passed, and still Curley did not turn up. But at last a young, bare-footed Mexican boy came in, looked around, and then came towards Judy.

'Are you the Señorita Rain – Rainford?' he asked.

'Yes; that's right!' Judy smiled and nodded. Then to her surprise, the boy handed her a grubby note. She opened it and found it was a message signed, 'Curley Gibson': 'Dear Miss Rainford — I'm very sory but I been caled away. My brother that is a cowboy at the Twin Forks Ranch over West has broke his leg and I've got to go and see him pronto. You know the trail and shud find yore way easy and hope you won't mind me not takking you homelike.'

That was the message, and Judy grinned hugely at it.

'Well, dear Curley isn't very strong on spelling or punctuation,' she thought. 'But — oh gosh! That means I've got to ride home by myself.'

Judy was not over pleased at the thought. On the way, she had enjoyed the company of the big, homely cowboy, and had looked forward to her ride back with him.

'Oh, gosh!' she exclaimed. 'I'm not looking forward to riding through those badlands, either — not alone, anyway. Sooner I get home the better.'

Giving the little Mexican boy a coin, Judy hurriedly paid her bill and, going outside, mounted Brownie and set off out of town.

'I hope I can remember the way,' she thought. 'On the trail I'll be all right, but I'm not at all sure of myself in the badlands.'

To be lost amid the forests lining the foothills would be no joke, but it would be worse in the desert as she well knew.

'Anyway, why worry yet,' she mused. 'Chin up, Judy! Time enough to wail when I do hit trouble. Step out, Brownie, old boy — your boss has got the jim-jams, and wants to be home.'

Brownie stepped out willingly, and soon they were in the foothills.

She had been walking Brownie along the trail for about twenty minutes when she caught sight of something red lying on the ground ahead of her. When she reached it, she saw it was a knotted neckerchief.

'That's odd,' she mused. 'How could someone fail to notice they'd dropped it?' She dismounted and picked it up. Tucked inside it was a folded piece of paper, which she hurriedly read: 'For the sake of your safety, leave the trail and hide behind the copse for one hour. Please trust me — I am your friend.' The note was unsigned.

Judy looked quickly around her. There was no one about, but sure enough, there were some trees on one side of the trail which would give very good cover to anyone wanting to hide. Her heart thumping, she dropped the neckerchief where she had found it, and led Brownie round to the far side of the copse, where she found a place between the trees which was out of sight from anyone passing along the trail. She sat down and waited.

Judy was just beginning to feel sleepy when she heard the sound of horses travelling fast in the direction of Tres Pinos. Praying that Brownie would keep quiet, she moved until she could just see two horsemen, rapidly approaching.

Both were dressed in Mexican cowboy's clothes; one looked elderly, with grey hair, dirty and untidy, showing under his sombrero, while the other was young, smooth-faced though deeply bronzed, and rode with an almost jaunty air. As they drew closer, the young man gave a shout, reined in his horse, dismounted and picked up the red neckerchief, which he waved cheerfully in the air. Judy immediately recognised Juan, the Mexican cowboy, who had come to her rescue the day before. Surely he wouldn't betray her now...

'Ah! Here's my neckerchief,' he shouted gaily, seeming to Judy to turn in her direction.

'Hurry up, can't you?' shouted the other harshly. 'Mr Flint's going to be real mad when he hears we failed to get the girl and the horse.'

But Juan had already leapt back into his saddle, and with a gay 'Yahoo!' cantered off again down the trail, with the older man close behind.

When they were out of sight, Judy led Brownie out, mounted him and rode home fast. 'Please trust me — I am your friend,' the note had said. Juan had obviously left the note for her, and had wanted her to know he had done so. But why did he go out of his way to help her, when he was part of Mr Flint's outfit? If only she could be absolutely certain he was her friend, and not her enemy! After all, he had been one of the two cowboys who were supposed to have kidnapped her. Judy was completely mystified by this strange Mexican boy. She decided that, when she told the others about her adventure, she would not mention that she had recognised Juan, as they would be sure to think he was double crossing her in some way. She wanted to make her own mind up about this.

When she got home, Zeke was the first person she met.

'You're late, Miss Judy — we was beginning to get worried. And where's Curley?'

Her aunt came out and Judy told them the whole story. Zeke exploded when she had finished.

'Them Dos Cabezos snakes,' he roared. 'Miss Judy, this here is a serious thing, girl! We got to report this to Sheriff Moore first thing in the morning.'

'But Zeke, we can't prove anything! I only heard one of them say Flint had told them to find me.'

'That's true,' admitted Zeke.

'Listen — I'm going to get even with him myself,' said Judy. 'I'm going to punish him by beating his daughter in the race for the Gold Spurs. I believe that will hurt him far more than bringing a useless charge against him.'

Just at that moment Curley rode up. 'What happened to you, Miss Judy?' he said, looking worried. 'I went to the Sunshine Restaurant, and waited for you there a long time; and then someone said they'd seen you set off alone along the trail, a while back.'

When Curley heard the story of what had happened, he was even angrier than Zeke. 'I'll pay back that... that rattlesnake, Flint, if it's the last thing I ever do!' he shouted, striding up and down, and thumping his fist on the barn door.

'Never mind, Curley,' said Judy, 'No harm's done, thanks to the mysterious person who wrote me that note! And now, let's get some rest as there's a lot to do tomorrow, and we must be fully prepared for the great day!'

Judy had suddenly discovered that she was ravenously hungry, and she did justice to the meal soon set before her.

'That — that wicked man, Flint,' said Aunt May. 'He really should be punished, Judy, my dear. I — I sometimes wonder if — it would not be best to give in to him — to sell him the ranch and make a start somewhere else.'

Judy caught her breath. She saw that her aunt, usually so brave and stout-hearted, was really upset by this affair.

'Aunt May, whatever are you saying?' she cried aghast. 'You mustn't do anything of the kind. Why, I haven't really started fighting yet. Gosh! I'm not letting that fat toad beat me, Aunt May. You don't really mean it, do you? I jolly well won't let you give in, even if you want to, Aunt May — which I know you really don't.'

'Well, perhaps you're right, Judy,' said her aunt, smiling faintly. 'Only to think what nearly happened to you!'

'Never mind me, Aunt May,' said Judy cheerfully, 'it was a jolly good adventure after all, and I'm safe home now!'

Aunt May nodded thoughtfully.

'You really must be off to bed, Judy dear. You — you're quite sure you still want to go in for the race on Thursday?'

'I'll be fit as a fiddle, and after what's happened I wouldn't miss the chance of beating Dolores Flint for anything!' laughed Judy.

And that was the thought in her mind when she did fall asleep at last. Apart from the necessity of winning the five hundred dollars, she was determined to win, if only to punish the plotters.

At the Rodeo

Judy did not wake up until late next morning. She had a good breakfast, and then busied herself about the house, visiting the young foals and calves in the paddocks. Judy had come to the ranch to work, and that's what she meant to do. She did it with a keen zest and delight which proved she really was cut out for it.

Later on in the afternoon she took Brownie out for a training run. Zeke insisted on Curley Gibson accompanying her, and made sure that he was armed; Zeke, at least, was taking no chances. They kept fairly close to the ranch, too, but Brownie got a really good try-out, and Judy was more than pleased with his performance.

After that training run her hopes became certainties. Unless anything unusual happened, she was certain of winning the Gold Spurs.

Judy spent the whole evening in a comfortable chair on the veranda. With her aunt she watched the Arizona sun disappear over the western peaks in golden grandeur. It was lovely sitting there while the whole valley filled with purple shadows, until the cool breeze sent them indoors at last. And soon after that Judy went to bed, determined to be at the top of her form the next day.

She was up and about early in the morning, however. She did not mean to neglect her work, the jobs she had set herself to do about the ranch. She knew how overworked her aunt had been, and she was determined to take some of that load on to her own shoulders. There were the chickens to feed, the horses to see to, Bella to help with breakfast and the washing-up — all the innumerable chores of a ranch.

But at last came the time to start for the rodeo at Tres Pinos.

Judy had superintended the operation of getting the spirited Brownie into the horse-box, which the pony objected to strongly; but her coaxing got him safely in at last, and the two boys, Curley and Slim, another of her aunt's cowboys, set off on the long journey with smiles on their faces — and guns in their holsters.

They had to make an earlier start, not only because they were slower than the jeep would be, but because they had to take the trail round by Cedar Creek. This was a longer route, but more suitable for a high van — indeed, the Tres Pinos trail was so overhung with the low branches of trees in places that the horse-box could never have cleared them.

Then Judy and Zeke Carter set off in the jeep by the Tres Pinos trail.

Judy was in high spirits, looking forward to the rodeo — and the race. Starting late like this, they were not likely to see many of the events, but Judy realised how shorthanded they were, and that neither Zeke nor the two cowboys could be spared for long from their work.

She knew she would get the opportunity of seeing many another rodeo, and she was not out for pleasure today. She was out to win the Gold Spurs, and the help this would bring to Lone Pine Ranch. She was determined to do it!

Judy found the jeep anything but luxurious to ride in on that rocky trail, but she enjoyed the trip to Tres Pinos for all that.

They found the cattle town packed with horses and cars and the roar of voices and ringing of bells soon guided them to the rodeo grounds.

Used to English race-courses, Judy was taken aback at the sight of the 'stadium', which was nothing but a collection of wooden buildings and a roughly constructed stand, while the race-course was a more or less circular enclosure on rough ground.

In the stand and all along the wooden rails were groups of cattle-men and their families and Judy was amazed to see such a huge crowd. Excitedly she scanned the colourful scene and heard the uproarious yells and laughter.

Judy and Zeke were in time to see one or two events — a cattle roping contest, a trick-riding event, and a wildly exciting series of attempts to ride a 'killer' horse — and then the Lone Pine horse-box arrived, and the two hurried to meet it.

The grinning faces of Curley and Slim told them that all was well, and Judy gave a deep sigh of relief. Up to the last she had feard that Wilmot Flint might attempt something but Curley laughingly reported that nothing unusual had happened on the trail.

Judy was taking no chances, however, and she did not leave her pony for a second after that. In the temporary canvas stables she rubbed him down and brushed his coat in readiness for the event. The ride in the box did not seem to have disturbed him, so she took him for a brisk trot to limber him up in readiness for the great race.

When she got back she found quite a crowd round the stables. And the first people she saw were Wilmot Flint and his daughter Dolores.

The rancher was a picture! He wore shining black riding-boots, vivid yellow cord breeches, a red and green spotted waistcoat, a grey jacket, and an enormous wide-brimmed stetson. He puffed importantly at a huge cigar, and his fat face wore a self-satisfied smile.

Dolores was already on her chestnut pony. She looked smart and purposeful in a neat-fitting riding-suit, but the glance she shot at Judy was full of malice.

Judy sighed a little. How different it would be if they could have been friends. How nice it would be to have a girl of her own age as a neighbour whose company she could enjoy. As it was, they were bitter enemies, and could never be at ease with each other.

To Judy's surprise Wilmot Flint gave her a welcoming smile.

'You look mightily fit, Miss Rainford,' he remarked affably. 'And your horse looks in fine fettle. Well, what I say is, let the best horse win and good luck to its rider!'

Judy said nothing. That the man could have the nerve to speak to her like that after his attempt to have her and Brownie kidnapped left her speechless. She turned away and rode over to where Zeke and his two cowboys were waiting.

Dolores' malice did not disturb her unduly, but somehow her father's bland, smug smiles did. It made her feel uncomfortable — suspicious. Was he still plotting treachery against her? Did his self-satisfied smiles mean that he wasn't beaten, after all?

She quickly forgot Wilmot Flint; soon it would be time for the race, and she had not weighed-in yet. At the weighing-in enclosure she met her other rival for the Gold Spurs, a dark, exuberant girl who greeted Judy with a friendly smile.

Zeke knew her and introduced her to Judy. Her name was Mary Ortez, and the English girl found her a refreshing change after the insufferable Dolores. They chatted gaily together, until, at last, the bell rang for the competitors to line up for the Gold Spurs race.

Young Bobby Carson had ridden Brownie more than once on this ground, and the crowd yelled uproariously as they recognised the pony, stepping proudly and daintily through the starting-gate.

Dolores Flint's beautiful chestnut also came in for a great cheer, and so did the big black that Mary Ortez rode. He was a bigger, more powerful horse than Brownie, but he looked as if he lacked Brownie's dash and toughness.

At last, after what seemed an eternity of waiting, the signal flag came down with a swish and the race was on.

All three horses got away to a flying start, and for a good fifty yards there was scarcely an inch between them. Mary Ortez had the inside position, and it was she who first began to edge ahead, amid a roar from the crowd of excited cowboys and ranchers. Then Judy got a sideways glimpse of Dolores' face, and she was surprised by its determined expression.

She was already using whip and spur, and now Golden Glory was edging to the front, slowly and surely. But Judy, at least, did not worry. Plenty of time yet for Brownie to show his paces.

But though Judy's face was composed and she herself was unruffled, she had never felt more determined to win a race in her life. Somehow she felt she was fighting to save the Lone Pine Ranch — to save it from the greedy clutches of the ambitious, unscrupulous Wilmot Flint.

On the horses swept, their hoofs beating like thunder on the sunbaked ground — ground that was hard as iron. Judy's face was flushed, her eyes sparkling now with battle. This was a game she loved above all others — a game she knew from A to Z. How different this was from what she had been used to in England, yet the fight and struggle were just the same, of course. It was all so tremendously exhilarating.

Bunched together near the rails, the horses thundered on, with very little between them. Mary had lost that momentary lead, though she was still racing superbly. Now Golden Glory was ahead, leading by a good two yards, and Dolores' fierce face was flushed, almost triumphant already. Judy was astonished at the dust raised by the thundering hoofs. She wasn't used to it, and it troubled her a little.

Then they were round the first bend, and Golden Glory was still leading; Mary's Cutey and Brownie were running neck and neck. The second bend, and Golden Glory remained ahead. But Brownie had edged a trifle in front of Cutey, who seemed in trouble now; his pace had slackened a little, so Judy sent Brownie tearing ahead of him.

Dolores was riding like a fiend and strive as she would, Judy could not shorten the other girl's lead. Whip and spur were goading Golden Glory to desperate efforts, and Judy's face grew anxious after a while.

'Brownie!' she gasped appealingly. 'Brownie, old boy, don't let me down! You don't need a spur or whip, do you, old boy?'

As if he understood, the gallant pony responded, tireless and still fresh as paint. Grimly, Judy settled down to ride the race of her life. She realised now that she had underestimated the chestnut's endurance and courage, and Dolores' determination to win.

In the straight now, and Golden Glory still leading... Judy had forgotten the other horse. It was well behind them. There was only herself and Dolores. From the crowds lining the rails came a thunderous roar as Brownie edged closer and closer to his rival.

A few moments later and Judy had cut out the lead. They were thundering on, galloping and straining head to head.

Two hundred yards to go — a hundred — and then they

rode neck and neck, both horses putting up a terrific fight for supremacy. Dolores was flogging her horse unmercifully and the sight did nothing to improve Judy's opinion of her.

Fifty yards! Judy was feeling desperate now. She felt she had been too cocksure – had sadly underrated the other girl's skill and ability.

But Brownie had more in him than even she knew. It was then, with the winning-post before them, that the magnificent pony really showed his paces — proved himself worthy of the trust the Lone Pine Ranch people had in him.

Abruptly, he put on a spurt that fairly hurled him in front of Golden Glory — a few inches, then a foot, then a yard.

And suddenly they were well ahead and the winning-post was only a few yards away. Judy knew that they had won through at that moment, so, thrilled with delight, she snatched off her stetson and waved it joyfully to the crowd pressing on the barriers.

One final, easy stride and Brownie's head was past the winning-post.

She had won!

Disaster for Judy

'Oh, Brownie, you darling! You — you've done it, after all!'

Choked with dust, soaked in perspiration, Judy swung almost dizzily from the saddle and hugged her pony. Immediately a swarm of excited cattle folk surrounded horse and rider, amid cheers and hearty congratulations.

Judy could scarcely believe they had won. She had been blaming herself, feeling she had lost the race, and Brownie's almost unbelievable last spurt had amazed her.

'Gee, I was just waiting for that, Miss Judy!' cried Zeke, almost dancing in his glee. 'I know that pony! I knew there was quite a packet in him, and there was — a packet o' sizzling dynamite! He always explodes like that just as you think he's licked. You rode a mighty fine race, Miss Judy.'

'I'll say she did! The best rider and the best horse won!'

Flushed and deliriously happy at all this, Judy led Brownie to the stables. She had just finished grooming him and was about to load the pony into the horse-box, when the ringing of a bell sent her hurrying with flushed cheeks to the judge's box in front of the stand.

There, amid cheers, the judge smilingly handed her a case containing two small, beautifully fashioned spurs of gold, and the prize money in an envelope. Then they shook hands, and amid another salvo of cheers Judy raced back to the stables. She found Zeke alone, waiting for her; the horse-box with Brownie, guarded by the cowboys, had already gone.

'They'll be working mighty late tonight, as it is, to make up for this lost time,' explained old Zeke. 'Pity them boys had to go, but it just can't be helped, us being so shorthanded like. Well, I reckon I'd better do a bit of shopping — I've got to get some horse-linament and a few odds and ends for your aunt. See you here in half an hour, Miss Judy.'

The old foreman went off, his weather-beaten features still wreathed in a smile of triumph, and Judy made for the nearest café for a cup of coffee and a wash-and-brush-up which she felt she badly needed. She seemed to have swallowed tons of dust, and knew she looked an awful fright.

The café was almost full of customers, but Judy found a small table by a rear window and was quickly served with cakes and coffee. She took her time, for she knew Zeke was no hustler, and she was just finishing her coffee when a hand suddenly came through the open window behind her and gripped her arm.

Never had Judy had such a shock, especially one so utterly

unexpected. At first she imagined it was someone playing a joke, but as she angrily looked out of the window, she received another shock.

It was no joking urchin who had grabbed her arm. It was a Mexican youth who stood there, his back to the wall, and as she recognised him, Judy gasped aloud.

'Juan! You?'

'Yes, señorita, it is Juan, your friend.' The answer came in a low whisper. 'Listen, Señorita Judy. Do not return by the Tres Pinos trail. Take the Cedar Creek trail. Your enemies, they lie in wait for you on the Tres Pinos. Remember, Señorita, take the Cedar Creek trail.'

Judy stared for a moment at his earnest bronzed face, his dare-devil eyes, and then he was gone — as silent as a shadow round the corner of the building.

Judy gasped, her eyes widening in sheer amazement. So quickly had Juan appeared and disappeared that she could scarcely believe her ears and eyes. Yet it was real enough.

But was it so amazing? Hadn't her enemies already tried to prevent her winning the money prize? Might they not even now make a desperate attempt to take the money from her?

She knew the money itself was nothing to Wilmot Flint. He wanted it to stop it from helping her aunt at Lone Pine. His one object was to ruin her, and this five hundred dollars would prove a delaying factor of great importance to his unscrupulous plans.

Almost unconsciously Judy's hands closed tightly on her handbag. In the bag were not only the Gold Spurs, but the envelope containing the prize-money. She realised now the vital importance of taking great care, of using the greatest caution.

Should she trust Juan's message?

She knew she just had to; dared not risk his warning not

being genuine. How could she doubt it after what had already taken place? There were no bounds to Wilmot Flint's treachery. She must find Zeke and tell him at once.

She paid her bill and hurried from the café, seething inwardly with excitement and anger. Now she understood that smug smile on the Dos Cabezos rancher's fat face. It was a knowing, secret smile that told her now that, whether she won the race or not, she would not be allowed to keep the prize-money; Wilmot Flint had obviously prepared his plans for that eventuality.

But he had not counted on Juan, her young Mexican friend. Had it been just a message, as on the previous occasion, Judy would have suspected a trick, would have ignored it.

Arriving at the stables, Judy found Zeke had not returned, so she started loading everything into the jeep. Zeke turned up just as she was finishing, and stared blankly.

'Gosh, you're in a mighty hurry all at once, Miss Judy!' he grinned. 'Them boys Curley and Slim will be home long before us, and they'll break the good news to your aunt, you bet.'

'It isn't that, Zeke,' said Judy tensely. 'Listen. I've just had a warning message.'

Hurriedly she told him of what had happened at the café, and Zeke set his square jaw as he listened.

'It's a trick, right enough,' he exploded at last, fairly bristling. 'But not the kind you mean, Miss Judy. It's that young Mex snake trying to put one over on us, of course. We ain't going to take no Cedar trail just on that tricky scamp's word!'

'Yes, we are, Zeke,' said Judy flatly, but there was steel in her voice. Somehow it made her see red when even these Pine Ranch cowboys she liked so much said things about Juan. They were prejudiced against him because of his association with Wilmot Flint's ranch. 'I say we are, Zeke. We dare not risk it, anyway. I know you're armed, but...'

'Now, listen, Miss Judy,' said Zeke almost angrily. 'We know that young snake better'n you do. Me, I wouldn't trust the coyote no further than I can see. We're sticking to the Tres Pinos trail. It's shorter by miles, and...'

'I say we're not!' persisted Judy, a spot of colour showing on both cheeks, now, and unconsciously her voice rose heatedly. 'I've had one narrow escape on that Tres Pinos road. My aunt has given me full authority in all ranch matters, Zeke, and though I respect your advice, in this case I can't take it. We'll go by the Cedar Creek route.'

There was finality in Judy's voice, and her eyes were full of resolution. She climbed into the jeep and put it purposefully into gear.

The old foreman shrugged, and then he grinned as he patted the two revolvers holstered in his belt.

'Very well, Miss Judy,' he said mildly. 'Have it your own way. I got two good friends here, and I know how to use them. Don't matter much either way to me.'

He chuckled and climbed up into the jeep. Judy had won, so the jeep moved out of town, heading for the Cedar Creek trail.

Neither of them noticed the man who was saddling a horse in the stable close to them. But he had noticed them — and he had heard the last part of their heated argument.

The jeep had scarcely moved out into the dusty street when the man swiftly led his horse out and mounted. He set his horse to a gallop, taking the opposite way to the one the jeep had taken — towards the Tres Pinos trail.

And his horse wore the brand of the Dos Cabezos ranch.

Judy drove fast, for the evening was upon them, and she knew it was a long journey to the Lone Pine. She felt regretful now that she had spoken so sharply to the old foreman. She knew his whole heart and soul were in the Lone Pine Ranch and that he had stuck to his opinions because he honestly believed in them.

Out into the open country they drove at a smart pace, and Zeke pointed out the Cedar Creek trail, winding up into the foothills.

In a way Judy was glad of the change of route. She loved this country and she wanted to be able to find her way about — to learn every road and trail in the district. The road was rocky and terribly rough, but the old jeep took it all at a spanking pace, and Judy hardly noticed the bumping discomfort. This was the life she loved, and her eyes were alight as she thought of her aunt's joy when she received the prize money.

She was returning home in triumph and she meant to enjoy every minute of it.

Now they were driving up a pine-clad slope, and Judy took in deep breaths of the sweet-scented air. How quiet and lovely everything was here. Yet — how terribly lonely. Zeke did not speak a word, only gazed about him warily, as if expecting trouble at any moment.

She could not blame him for that in the circumstances. She knew that Wilmot Flint was capable of anything. He believed himself to be the king of Whispering Valley already, and looked upon himself as above the law. He would do just as he wished, regardless of consequences. And she knew he was vindictive and ruthless — a man who would not be beaten easily.

Even now, she reflected grimly, a trap was set for them on the Tres Pinos trail. They had only escaped owing to the timely warning of Juan. What a good thing it was that she had a friend on the Dos Cabezos ranch: a friend who could warn them of Flint's plotting.

But Judy's blissful dreams were suddenly shattered as Zeke's grim voice came tersely.

'Horsemen coming through them trees, Miss Judy. Reckon

we're about to have company. Take it easy, honey.'

Judy had heard nothing above the rattling of the jeep's wheels over the hard trail. But now, through the thinning trees, she sighted moving horsemen converging on the trail.

A startled, incredulous look flashed into her eyes as she caught a full glimpse of one of the men.

He wore a cloth mask over his face, leaving only his eyes visible!

It was enough for the quick-witted Judy. In a blinding flash she knew they had been tricked. She knew that Zeke had been right and she, in her obstinacy, had been wrong — utterly wrong.

Juan had tricked — had betrayed her!

But Judy's first thoughts were not entirely of that. For she knew instantly that this was a hold-up, and what the bandits were after. They were after the envelope in her handbag — the envelope containing the five hundred dollar prize money.

Wilmot Flint had struck again!

And in that flash of realisation, Judy reacted instantly. On the seat by her side was the handbag. She grabbed it with one hand and sent it whirling into the bushes lining the trail.

She knew that it was useless to try to turn the jeep on the narrow trail and escape, so she drove on, ready for what was to happen.

A sudden twist in the track brought them out into the open. Across the trail was a pile of boulders at the entrance to a rocky gully. Four men sat on their horses there, two on either side of the barricade.

Judy was forced to pull up. She glared at the masked horsemen, whose hands were significantly resting on holstered guns.

'What's all this?' she cried sharply, though her heart was

thudding like a steam engine. 'How dare you stop us!'

One of the men rode forward and swung from the saddle.

'Take it easy, lady,' he chuckled. 'We won't bother you more than a minute if you're peaceful-like. We just want to congratulate you on your dandy win at the rodeo. It were a right good race, I'm told, and you deserved to win. So we'll let you keep them Gold Spurs if you hand over the five hundred dollars. It ain't good for a young girl like you to have as much money as that.'

From the other masked men came chuckles and laughs. Judy's eyes blazed.

'So — so this is more of that crooked Flint's work,' she cried angrily. 'You're Flint's men! Those masks won't save you!'

'Course they's Flint's men,' bellowed Zeke, his face red with rage. 'I know one of them — that red-bearded jigger! Their horses ain't branded, but that don't mean a thing. The sheriff...'

'Sheriff — nix!' was the leader's grinning retort. 'D'you reckon there's only one red-bearded gent in the State of Arizona, old man? Now, young lady, just you hand over what we wants, peaceful-like. And you,' he added, a harder note in his voice, 'take your hands off them guns, old-timer.'

Zeke was silent; he felt so helpless. He had been extremely confident with the guns in his belt, but now he realised they were useless in this situation.

He dared not use them — dared not risk a fusillade of shots by the jeep with Judy there. At another quick, harsh command, he handed over the guns to the leader, who threw them into the bushes.

The leader's eyes had scanned Judy, but she obviously had not got the envelope on her, nor the Gold Spurs. So the man clinked into the jeep and searched. He looked under the seats, in every likely and unlikely place, and then his

A pile of boulders blocked the trail.

eyes glinted angrily. He peered menacingly at Judy.

'Now, lady,' he snapped harshly. 'We mean you no harm, but we got to have the dollars. Where's that envelope?'

Judy laughed in his face, though her heart was pounding.

'I suppose it didn't occur to you,' she exclaimed, 'that we might have anticipated this. There are banks in Tres Pinos, aren't there?'

'Damn you, you're too clever by half!' said the leader savagely.

'No, she ain't — hold on a bit,' came a sudden interruption from one of the men. 'I saw that girl chuck something into the bushes higher up there. Hold your horses!'

He rode back along the trail, and Judy's heart sank like lead. It was the man she had seen first, and he must have had his eyes on her at that moment when she had thrown the handbag overboard.

'I guess you're a mighty smart girl,' said the leader, when the man rode up and handed over the bag. 'But not smart enough. Too bad this gent saw you! But never you mind — we'll let you have them spurs as we're sporting gents,' he added with a chuckle, 'and we won quite a stake on Brownie. Fine horse and a grand rider! Here you are, lady!'

He drew from the handbag the leather-covered case, opened it and revealed the Gold Spurs. With a mock bow he handed the case up to Judy. The envelope he crammed into his pocket after a glance inside. Then he leaped into the saddle, and the four men rode off through the trees at a gallop.

Judy felt the hot tears spring to her eyes.

She had fought hard to win her victory — and now she knew it was a hollow victory indeed. She had been allowed to retain the spurs — rather to her surprise — but the five hundred dollars her aunt needed so vitally were gone.

She had failed — and it was all her own fault; her own stupidity. Why hadn't she listened to Zeke — to her aunt?

Why had she gone her own blind way, heedless of advice? They had been right. Juan was a traitor, a false friend. He had tricked her!

The Indian Girl

They climbed down from the jeep. With a heavy heart Judy helped the old foreman to move the boulders from the trail.

Zeke said nothing for some moments, but now he glanced at Judy's white face, and smiled at her.

'Now, don't take on so, honey,' he said gruffly. 'Just can't be helped — and it might'a been worse. There's no blame attached to you, Miss Judy. It was your warm heart as let you down, girl. You trusted that young varmint, and it ain't your fault, honey.'

Judy felt a quick rush of tears. Had the old foreman scolded her, blamed her, she knew she would have deserved it. But he did not blame; he did not say 'I told you so!' and Judy felt quick gratitude towards him. He could easily have made her feel worse than she did; but instead he was comforting her in his kindly way.

Zeke recovered his weapons from the bushes, then they got into the jeep, and Judy drove on miserably.

What hurt her, wounded her most, was not so much the loss of the money, though that was serious enough, but the fact that Juan had betrayed her trust in him; had acted so treacherously.

'You see, Miss Judy,' said Zeke at last, 'they knowed that, 'cause of the rodeo, there'd be plenty of people using the Tres Pinos trail today. This trail ain't much used at the best of times, as it's more lonely like. That's why they tricked us into coming this way. I sees it all now, drat them!'

Judy saw it, too, and her lips tightened. Well, Juan, with all his smooth manners, would not trick her so easily again.

Zeke had been right all along, and she had been wrong, utterly wrong.

They drove on, mostly in silence. At any other time Judy would have thoroughly enjoyed that drive through the pine forest. It was shady, after the scorching sun of the prairie; the lively wildlife among trees and bushes was a constant fascination for her. But all she could think of now was this tragic ending to the expedition.

But was it the ending? Judy soon discovered that it wasn't.

Turning a leafy corner in the winding trail they abruptly came upon a scene that made her catch her breath hard in utter dismay and amazement.

Just off the trail, on a patch of green grass, stood a horse-box. And tied to the wheels of the van were two cowboys whom she recognised instantly as Curley Gibson and Slim Jim Bates.

The back doors of the horse-box were wide open, and the van itself was — empty!

Brownie, her precious pony, was gone!

She pulled up with a jerk, and Zeke let out a yell of rage.

'What the heck... Why, darn me if them galoots ain't raided the horse-box too!' he yelled. 'Curley, Slim, what in thunder's happened? You — you guys let those varmints get away with this?'

The old foreman scrambled down from the jeep, red with fury. Judy followed him, and a few moments later she and Zeke had cut the two cowboys free.

Both were seething with rage and humiliation.

'I — I'm awfully sorry, Miss Judy,' mumbled Curley Gibson, shamefacedly. 'We've kind of let you down, I reckon.'

'It were either that or seeing that dandy little pony riddled with lead,' put in Slim heatedly. 'We was all set to start a scrap soon as we saw them, but one of the guys lets out a holler, saying as they'd pour bullets into the horse-box if we got tough-like, and well, I reckon we just couldn't let that grand little feller get shot up.'

'We reckoned it was better to let them take him than that,' finished Curley grimly. 'But we feel mighty sore about it, Miss Judy.'

'You did quite right,' agreed Judy quickly. She saw how upset, how humiliated the cowboys felt about it all, and she realised what a difficult position they had been in. 'They might have killed him if you had shown fight, boys.'

Zeke was furious, but he could not help seeing that the cowboys had been forced to submit to save Brownie, just as he had been forced to submit to save Judy.

'That snake Flint's gone too far this time,' he vowed. 'Miss Judy, we've just got to get the sheriff in on this.'

'Reckon we can't prove nothing, Zeke,' said Curley glumly. 'Each of them snakes was masked, and we can't prove a thing against Flint. There was one gent with a red beard as looked mighty like Luke Deakin from the Dos Cabezos.'

'Yeah, I saw him,' said Zeke grimly. 'It were Luke right enough. But proving it ain't going to be easy. You see, boys, those guys held us up higher up the trail. They got that five-hundred dollars from Miss Judy.'

'What? The snakes!'

The news increased the anger and dismay of the cowboys.

'Well, it ain't no good talking about it now, boys,' said Zeke heavily at last. 'Let's get along to the ranch. And to-morrow, Miss Judy, I reckon we ought to report this to the sheriff.'

'We're certainly doing something about it,' snapped Judy grimly. 'We aren't letting them get away with this.'

In her own mind Judy had already determined to do something — herself! It was unlikely the money would ever be recovered now. But Brownie was a different matter. The pony was well known in the district, and it wouldn't be easy to keep him hidden; so Judy was unusually silent as they started for Lone Pine Ranch.

Juan, the Mexican boy, had betrayed her trust! The thought made Judy clench her hands. Never again would she allow herself to be tricked by his smooth talk.

There was Brownie, too. She said nothing to Zeke, but in her own mind she was planning to try and get him back — this very night.

She would visit the Dos Cabezos Ranch that evening and investigate, she decided. If it was at all possible she would search the stables for her pony, and, if she found him, immediately bring him away. It would be risky, perhaps dangerous. But she was quite prepared to risk anything to get Brownie back again.

If nothing came of that, then she herself would go over to Tres Pinos and see the sheriff.

They reached the ranch at last and, leaving Zeke to garage the jeep, Judy hurried up the veranda steps.

She met her aunt in the hall. The older woman's face was a mixture of hope and anxiety.

'Well, Judy dear,' she cried. 'So you've got back. But — how did you get on?' She broke off as she saw the distress in Judy's eyes. 'My dear! You had no luck?'

'Oh, yes, Aunt May; Brownie won,' said Judy quietly. 'But — oh, Aunt May, I hate to tell you, but — we were held up by masked, armed men on the trail. They took the five hundred dollar prize-money from me. And — and they've stolen Brownie!'

'What? Oh, Judy, how terrible. But — never mind, dear,' Aunt May went on hurriedly. 'We're no worse off — except, of course, for the pony. Oh, I'm sorry for your sake, Judy darling.'

Impulsively she slipped an arm over Judy's shoulder. She led the girl into the living-room where tea was already laid.

'Now forget about it, Judy, until you've had your tea,' she said firmly. 'You've done your best, and you did splendidly to win. I suppose this is more of Wilmot Flint's work?'

'Yes — both Zeke and I are sure of it. Zeke says he recognised one of them, and so did Curley — a man named Luke Deakin.'

And despite her aunt's protests, Judy told her there and then of their adventures on the trail. Aunt May listened quietly, but her face was troubled.

'I'm afraid it will be useless reporting it to the sheriff,' she said finally. 'He's a good man, and honest. But he'll want proof. And how can we prove that Wilmot Flint is behind these hold-ups?'

Judy realised the truth of this, and it made her all the more determined to do something herself. But she kept her idea to herself, knowing her aunt would only be alarmed if she knew of her intention.

Soon they were sitting down to tea, a tea Judy had intended to be a real victory tea. But she could not enjoy it. She had the Gold Spurs, yes — a prize well worth winning, as Aunt May pointed out — but the loss of the prize-money and Brownie were bitter blows. Better never to have won than to have lost her pony.

Judy was glad when the meal ended, and while her aunt went to help Bella in the kitchen, she saw her chance and slipped out of the house. Aunt May would wonder what had happened to her, but that could not be helped. It was vitally important to act swiftly before Flint had time to move the stolen pony out of the district.

It was just growing dark, and Judy swiftly saddled a horse and led him quietly from the stables.

In another moment she was mounted and riding hard in the direction of the Dos Cabezos Ranch. A few minutes hard riding and the sprawling outbuildings of the huge ranch loomed up ahead in the dusk. She took a deep breath.

Judy knew she was taking a great risk. There was no knowing what Wilmot Flint would do if he caught her prowling around.

In a bunch of cottonwoods behind the buildings Judy tied up her horse. Then, after a careful look around, she slipped into the shelter of a gully and crept towards the back of some buildings which she judged to be barns.

She reached them at last. Another swift survey, and then she stole round to the corner of the barn and peered cautiously round.

She could see the long lines of stables now. And as she looked her heart sank. There were at least a dozen cowboys lounging about in the stable-yard, some of them Americans, but most of them Mexicans, and all of them rough-looking men. Some were cleaning saddles and harness, others were just talking and smoking. To reach the stables without being seen would be quite impossible.

Well, it meant she would have to wait and bide her time.

She felt sure that when darkness fell they would finish and make for the bunk-houses. Then her chance would come.

But suddenly, as she crouched there, she heard voices and footsteps coming from the other direction. Glancing round swiftly, she stiffened at what she saw.

Coming towards the barn were three people — Wilmot Flint, his daughter Dolores, and a tall cow-puncher who, by his clothes, she judged to be the ranch foreman whom Zeke had once mentioned — Kurt Santer.

Just in time Judy slipped behind a pile of cottonwood logs at the side of the big barn. She crouched down, her heart thumping. If they turned to walk down the side of the barn...

But they did not. They stopped just in front of the barn doors, and she heard Wilmot Flint's harsh voice.

'Yes, Kurt, things is going my way right smart now. You done some good work today, mister, especially in grabbing her. Fetch her out, Kurt, and we'll soon know how to handle her.'

Judy held her breath. Who was Flint speaking about? It could not be Brownie, for Flint had said 'her'. Yet, judging by his tone, he was speaking of an animal.

She soon knew. The foreman put a key in the padlock of the barn and dragged open the doors. He called out roughly, 'Come on out of that! The boss wants you.'

And out from the dark interior of the barn walked a woman — an Indian woman!

Her clothes were dusty and travel-stained. Her hair, black as jet, was cut in a straight fringe on her forehead, and kept in place by a leather band. Her face was thin, and she looked half-starved. Yet she held her head proudly and fearlessly as she walked straight up to Wilmot Flint.

'What do you want?' she demanded fiercely. 'Why do you bring me here? You've kidnapped me — I shall tell the sheriff!'

The ranch-owner looked taken aback for a moment. Then he lit a cigar and watched the young woman through narrowed eyes.

'Now, don't talk like that, young woman,' he said. 'You've got us all wrong. If the boys made you come, it was against my orders. I just asked them to invite you to look me up.'

'That's not true! You have brought me here against my will! I'll tell the sheriff.'

'Now, you just listen, young woman. Your name is Maorio, ain't it, and you used to work for the Dos Cabezos?' wheezed the fat rancher.

'I worked for Boss Carson, yes,' said the girl. 'He was a good man. I used to look after young Bobby Carson when he was a boy, but when you came, I went. I don't work for you —

you're a bad man. You accused Bobby of being a rustler and got him arrested. He's no rustler, we all know that. You framed him.'

Flint's face grew purple with rage, but he held himself in check with an effort.

'Now listen here, Maorio,' he said softly. 'How'd you like your old job back at the ranch? And how'd you like to have nice clothes to wear and pretty beads and jewellery? And plenty of good food to eat?'

'What do you want? I won't work for you.'

'Well, just as you like, girl,' said Flint smoothly. 'But I reckon you'd be glad to earn money that would buy you beads and nice clothes and all the things women like.' His tone altered. 'Now, listen. You're a Yaqui, ain't you? And one of my men, Pablo, tells me that you know the secret way into this here Hidden Valley. Well, I'm asking you to lead us into that valley, or else tell us how to get there. Why don't we make a deal? Well, what d'you say?'

Maorio's Story

Wilmot Flint waited eagerly for the Yaqui woman's answer. But his eagerness was nothing to that of the listening Judy. She stood there breathlessly, lips parted in amazement and sudden excitement.

Never had she expected such a surprise as this. And now, what would the Yaqui woman's answer be?

Judy felt quick pity for the girl, and admiration for her courage. She also sensed a keen loyalty to the Carsons, and especially to Bobby.

She did not have to wait long for an answer.

'I say that I won't tell you, nor will I show you,' said the Indian woman. 'I am a Yaqui and the Hidden Valley is a sacred place. I refuse to betray my people and lead you there. Now, let me go, or I'll tell the sheriff about this.'

'Now, listen here, girl,' Wilmot Flint was beginning furiously, but his daughter nudged him.

'Leave her to me, poppa,' she said, smiling a false smile at the Indian girl. 'Now, Maorio, my dear, you've got us all wrong, you know. We only wish to help you, and see you have good food and clothes and nice, pretty jewellery like mine. It is very little my father asks of you, isn't it? Now, listen. I'll come with you, if you like, and you shall show me how to get into Hidden Valley. Then you can come back here and be my personal maid. How's that, Maorio?'

'I don't like you, either. I will not tell you or show you.'

There was firm finality in the Indian girl's voice. Judy knew she meant it, and that nothing would change that decision. Kurt, the foreman, knew it as well.

'No good, boss,' he grinned. 'You could talk till you're blue in the face and it won't make no difference. These Yaquis ain't human, and you can't shift them once they gets set. You'll have to try some other way,' he added significantly.

'And we will at that,' said Wilmot Flint. 'I ain't the man to be defied by no Indian. Now, for the last time, woman, will you do as I ask?'

'I won't tell you. I won't show you.'

'Right!' The rancher's eyes glinted. 'You can go back among the rats in that barn, then. A few nights in there without food or water should make you change your mind. I ain't allowing no Indian to frustrate my plans, girl. Shove her in again, Kurt.'

'O. K., boss.'

The foreman gave the Indian girl a rough push, sending her staggering back into the barn. He closed and padlocked the doors, pushing the key in his pocket.

'I knew as you was wasting your time on her, boss,' he

said. 'Them Yaquis is mighty funny about that Valley. I reckon we'd best stick to Wild Horse Canyon. Listen. I got an idea about that. We can't find the entrance to Wild Horse Canyon because of the brush. Why not set fire to it? All that undergrowth would go up in smoke, and then we'd easily find the entrance.'

Wilmot Flint shook head.

'Nix on that, Kurt. I thought of that long ago. Setting fire to that brush would be a mighty dangerous thing to do. Once a fire were started, there'd be no stopping it. It'd spread among the pine forests and prairie like fury. Everything's dry as tinder, and before we'd know what had happened, every ranch in the valley might be wiped out. No, too mighty risky, Kurt, I'm telling you.'

'Maybe you're right, boss, at that.'

The three schemers moved on, and Judy drew a deep, deep breath of relief — relief not only because of her own safety, but because Wilmot Flint had, so far, failed in his effort to discover the secret.

But Judy's face was set, her eyes gleaming with determination.

Brownie must wait! Despite her desperate desire to regain her stolen pony, this development almost swept him from her mind. That poor Indian girl must be rescued from Flint's clutches somehow. Admiration for her courage, and pity for her, mingled in Judy's mind. How could she help her? How could she rescue her? Yet she must!

The Dos Cabezos foreman had the key in his pocket. In any case, the doors were in full view of the men in the stable yard. No, she must find some other way.

She moved round to the back of the barn, examining every inch of the structure. The foundations were of brick, but the walls and roof were of timber, old and warped. At the back of the barn Judy paused, suddenly alert at what she saw.

Rats had been at work here. Between the brick and warped planks were rat holes here and there. If she could only get a tool to use...

A rusty spade lying on a pile of logs caught her eye. Stealthily she crept round to the back of the barn with it. Inserting a corner of the blade into one of the holes, she began to jab and prise. The wood where it joined the brick was rotten, and splintered easily. Soon she had worked the full end of the blade through, and then she levered with all her strength.

With a crack that made her heart jump, the plank was levered outwards, and she instantly set to work on the next. Soon she had made a wide opening, and suddenly a figure appeared in the improvised doorway.

It was the Indian girl and her dark eyes widened as she peered through.

'Quick, Maorio,' whispered Judy. 'I want to help you out of this. I am a friend — I'm Judy Rainford, and I live with my aunt at Lone Pine Ranch. I'm Bobby Carson's cousin, you know.'

'Cousin? How's that?'

'My mother was Mrs Carson's sister,' explained Judy, almost smiling at the puzzled look on the Yaqui girl's face.

'I see. I'm coming with you.'

A moment later the Indian girl had squeezed through the opening. Judy took her arm and led her into the little gully. Keeping low they hurried along to where Judy's horse stood among the trees, Judy feeling amazed at the ease with which she had succeeded. But they were not out of the wood yet.

'Jump up behind me, Maorio,' she breathed. 'I'm taking you to Lone Pine Ranch.'

'I'm ready!'

The horse was already untethered, and Judy sprang into the saddle, helping the other girl up behind her. The horse moved out of the cottonwoods with his double burden. Only when they were out on the trail did Judy breathe freely again.

'We're safe enough now, I think,' she said. 'You'll be safe at the Lone Pine. My aunt is very kind, and...'

'I know that. Bobby's mother knows me well. What are you doing at Dos Cabezos? Why are you saving me?'

She was evidently puzzled, and suspicious, though she smiled as Judy turned her head. She went on without waiting for an answer.

'I recognise you now. I saw you at the rodeo. You are a very fine rider, I was so glad that you won. Miss Dolores is not good; her father is a bad man. What were you doing there?'

As they rode on along the trail, Judy told her of their return from the rodeo, and how they had been held up on the trail — of the loss of Brownie and the prize-money.

The Indian girl listened to all this gravely.

'Señor Flint is a very wicked man,' she said, as Judy paused at last. 'Maybe I shall be able to help you get your Brownie back. You are good; you are helping me now and I won't forget it. I am a good tracker, and tomorrow I shall help you find out where the pony is.'

The young Indian woman was obviously grateful and she took to her at once. Judy's story had fully convinced her.

'You must have known my grandfather then, Maorio,' she said, after a slight pause. 'I overhead what was said just now — that you worked for him. I suppose you left after he died in that stampede.'

'Your grandfather was not killed in any stampede. I know, I saw him in the desert after the accident.'

'Wha-what?' Judy was thunderstruck. 'But how do you know — I mean, are you sure that you saw him?' she asked, her voice shaking.

'I am quite sure; I knew him well, Miss Judy, and he spoke to me in the desert. When I left Dos Cabezos I went in search of my father and I met Señor John Carson; he was with Señor Ben Bolt, an old prospector. They were on horse-back. I didn't see them again. But he was not killed in the stampede. Señor Flint says so, but he is lying.'

Judy drew in a deep breath of amazement. She could not doubt the Indian girl's sincerity. If she had worked at the Dos Cabezos, then she could not possibly be mistaken. She must have known her grandfather well. The whole thing seemed incredible.

'But I can't understand it, Maorio,' she said blankly. 'Everyone says my grandfather was killed in a stampede. Do you think — listen Maorio: I overheard Flint asking you to guide him to some secret valley. Did — did my grandfather know you knew the secret? Did he ever ask you about it?'

'He did not ask me. He often spoke to me about it. Maybe he did not know that I knew. If he had asked me I would have said, " I will show you".'

'You — you would have guided grandfather into the Hidden Valley, Maorio?'

'Of course, he was a good man, a friend. Señor Flint — he's an enemy, and I won't guide him. You ask me, Miss Judy, and I will guide you into the Hidden Valley. I will show you the cave-dwellings my people lived in long, long ago. I will take you and show you.'

'Oh, that would be splendid, Maorio,' burst out Judy. 'I'd love it. We could make a picnic of the trip. We'd take food and drink, you know, and have a lovely outing.'

'I would like that, too. I'll take you — tomorrow, Miss Judy, if we can't find any trace of Brownie.'

'Yes, yes — that's grand, Maorio,' cried Judy excitedly. 'We'll start early, and — hello, here we are at Lone Pine!'

As they rode towards the ranch-house Aunt May came hurrying down the steps, relief all over her face.

'My goodness, Judy, wherever have you been?' she cried. 'I was so worried — I couldn't imagine what had happened to you. But — who is that with you, my dear?

She had caught tight of Maorio standing by the horse in the gloom.

'It is the Indian girl — Maorio,' said Judy quickly. 'You — you remember her, Aunt May; she used to work at the Dos Cabezos. And, oh, Aunt May...'

'Why, of course, Judy,' exclaimed Aunt May, quickly smiling. 'Of course I remember you, Maorio. I've often wondered why we never had any news from you. You must stay with us — we're short-handed, and I'll be only too glad of your help.'

And Aunt May, in her usual impulsive manner, rushed over to the timid Indian girl and almost dragged her into the house.

'Now, you can tell us your story afterwards, Maorio,' she said firmly. 'First you must have a good meal, my dear. Come along and we'll see what Bella can rustle up. She's a marvel in an emergency!'

She led Maorio towards the kitchen, and Judy, smiling, was just about to take the horse to the stables when Curley came running across the patio in a state of great excitement.

'We got him, Miss Judy,' he yelled. 'Caught the young rattler in the act. Zeke saw him first, hanging around, and then we copped him trying to break in at the back of the ranch-house.'

'Who?' demanded Judy blankly. 'Who are you talking about, Curley?'

'That young Mexican varmint, Juan,' cried Curley, with deep satisfaction. 'Copped him in the act of breaking in, the thieving scoundrel! Slim's riding over in the morning for the sheriff. We got him at last!'

Aunt May must have heard Curley's excited voice, because she came hurrying out again a moment later.

'What's the matter, Curley?' she cried.

'Zeke saw someone hanging about acting suspicious-like,' explained Curley. 'He got me and Slim and we trailed him down — just caught him as he were about to climb the creepers at the back of the house.'

'Yes, that's right,' said Zeke Carter, joining the group just then. 'We got him this time. The young varmint's slipped up for once, and we've got something to put before the sheriff now about them hold-ups!'

'Where — where is he now, Zeke? asked Judy, trying to keep her voice steady.

'We shoved the snake in the feed store, and locked him in,' said Zeke, with great satisfaction. 'I reckon he were up to something pretty desperate. Maybe he'd had orders from that rattler Flint to burn the ranch down. I tell you, boss, that Flint's bad enough for anything. He's out to ruin you, and he won't stop at nothing, I reckon. We'll have to watch out night and day.'

'It's growing more serious every day,' said Aunt May in a troubled voice. 'Judy, whatever happened to you? I did not ask Maorio, but she looked very frightened.'

'I went on my own to scout round Dos Cabezos,' said Judy seriously. 'I wasn't going to take things lying down, Aunt May. I meant to find out if Brownie was there, and to rescue him if it was possible.'

She paused. Maorio's story would have to be told, so she went on grimly.

'I overheard Flint, his daughter and their foreman talking. They'd got poor Maorio locked up in a barn full of rats. Flint vowed he'd keep her a prisoner there unless she agreed to show him the secret way she knew into the Hidden Valley.

'I had to forget about Brownie then,' she said. 'I just had to do something to save Maorio. I managed to help her escape and brought her here.'

'Gosh, girl, you've got some courage to enter that nest of snakes all by yourself like that,' said Zeke admiringly. 'You and your aunt makes a grand pair, eh, boys?'

'I'll say they does,' said Curley, while Slimo nodded and grinned. 'And what's more they'll lick that coyote yet.'

'Then Flint must believe in the Hidden Valley legend,' said Aunt May. 'Whatever can he be after there?'

'Them horses — if they exist, and I think they do,' said Zeke. 'Them horses must be worth a fortune, and you can bet that's what Flint's after. He's greedy and grasping as they make them, the skunk!'

The foreman and cowboys drifted away, taking Judy's horse, and Judy went indoors with her aunt. But even the thrilling thoughts of the Hidden Valley took second place now in her mind. Juan was a prisoner — awaiting arrest by the Tres Pinos sheriff.

She should be pleased — relieved after the way the Mexican boy had tricked and betrayed her. She knew she ought to feel that way — to be glad he had been brought to justice at last.

But she wasn't.

He had taken a part in the theft of her pony, of the five hundred dollar prize-money. He had tricked her cruelly. Yet — at the back of her mind there was always that strange doubt. In any case she could not let him be arrested — she knew she could not.

As soon as possible, Judy escaped from her aunt, and slipped out of the house. She had made up her mind. She must see Juan somehow, to hear what he had to say. She would give him a chance to defend himself.

She was running a grave risk, she knew — a risk of antagonising Zeke Carter and the cowboys, if not of seriously offending her aunt. They would not understand how she felt, they might even think she was a traitor. But she knew she had to do it.

It was dark now — the moon had not yet risen, and Judy could hear voices from the bunkhouse as she quietly slipped by. Then she reached the feed store and halted under the small window at the side.

'Juan,' she called softly. 'Juan, it's me, Judy.'

There was a noise of movement inside the store. Then a face appeared at the small window — a dark, handsome face wearing a dare-devil grin.

'Ah! It is the Señorita. Buenas tardes, Señorita Judy. It is good to see your pretty face, little flower.'

But Judy was in no mood for his easy compliments.

'What are you doing here, Juan?' she asked. 'They tell me you were breaking into the ranch-house!'

'Not so. I was breaking out of the ranch-house, not in,' grinned Juan. Then his face grew grave. 'But never mind that now, Señorita. I must get out of here quickly. Will you get the key and help me to escape, Señorita Judy?' asked Juan.

Judy gasped. 'Well, of all the nerve,' she exclaimed. 'After the way you've tricked me and pretended to be my friend! You know, don't you, that Brownie and the prize-money have been stolen. And I know you are at the bottom of it all — you and your boss Flint!' Her eyes smarted with tears. 'You — you fooled us into taking the Cedar Creek trail, knowing there was a trap set for us there. You're no friend of mine and you deserve what you're going to get!'

'Ah! You are so beautiful when you are angry, Señorita Judy,' chuckled the Mexican boy. 'But we waste time — precious time. I did not betray you. You and Zeke betrayed yourselves. You talked of your plans in the stables at Tres Pinos. There was a man there, saddling his horse, a fat man with heavy moustaches. Pedro Cortez is his name, and he is one of the Dos Cabezos boys. He jumped on his horse and galloped off to warn the hold-up men on the Tres Pinos road. They immediately cut across country at top speed and waited for you on the Cedar Creek trail.'

He paused and went on.

'They had no orders to capture Brownie, but when the horsebox came along, Señor Kurt Santer saw a chance to pull a fast one. So they captured the five hundred dollars and the pony as well. But — it was your fault and not mine, Señorita. It ruined my plan to save you.'

'Oh!' gasped Judy. 'Yes. I remember that fat man in the stables now. Oh, I'm sorry for doubting you, Juan,' she went on in a rush of remorse. 'Of course, it was our fault. Oh, I'm so glad!'

'Then please help me to escape, Señorita Judy,' said Juan quickly, and his voice was desperate now.

'I must not fall into the hands of the sheriff; please help me! It will spoil all my plans — it will ruin me. Dear Señorita Judy — hurry!'

Judy did not hesitate after that. In her own mind, she knew she would have released him anyway. But now — now she was sure he was innocent — she did not hesitate for a moment; she was desperately anxious to save him.

Her heart was full of joy at the thought that he had proved to be her friend as she raced for the bunkhouse where all the keys were kept. In the doorway she paused cautiously. A glance inside showed her that Curley and Slim were there: they were in the far corner of the room engrossed in a game of cards.

Judy did not hesitate. She just had to take the risk of being seen, of being found out. She slipped inside, and unhooked the store-shed key. Then she slipped out again and raced back to the shed.

Another moment and the key was grating in the lock. She flung it wide open and Juan stepped out, grinning almost impudently now.

'Gracias, Señorita Judy,' he chuckled. 'I am afraid the Señor Zeke Carter will foam at the mouth when he finds I've gone and it is a great pity to disappoint him. But I must make my escape. Very soon you will find out that I'm no traitor — that I am a friend of the Lone Pine Ranch. And now — adios, Señorita Judy.'

He swept off his steeple-crowned sombrero, bowed elaborately, and then faded away into the velvety darkness of the night. She heard sudden hoof-beats but they soon died away.

Now Judy felt sudden doubts. Had she done the right thing? Juan's explanation seemed reasonable enough. She remembered the fat cowboy in the stables perfectly well. But was it just an excuse — Juan's clever story to explain away his double-crossing?

She shook her head, forcing herself to banish suspicion. She had to believe in him — she must. But she knew Zeke and the others would not believe his story.

Then suddenly she remembered Juan's last words. He had said she would soon find out he was not a traitor. What did he mean by that? Another thing: he had shamelessly admitted that he was 'breaking-out' of the ranch-house when he was caught. What had he been doing there?

Judy felt bewildered. And as she stood there Zeke Carter came across the yard towards her.

'That you, Miss Judy?' he called. 'I heard voices, and — thunder! Who opened that door? Why —'

He rushed to the store-shed door and looked inside and then he turned on Judy, his face stern and angry.

'Miss Judy, who opened the door? Who helped that young scoundrel to escape?' he cried.

There was no help for it.

'I did, Zeke,' she said quietly.

'You did? By thunder! Why?' demanded the astonished Zeke.

'Because I believe he was innocent,' said Judy firmly. 'He didn't trick us this afternoon, Zeke. One of the Dos Cabezos cowboys heard us saying we were returning by the Cedar Creek trail. He immediately warned the hold-up men on the Tres Pinos trail and the trap was switched to the Cedar Creek trail.'

'So that's his yarn, is it?' growled Zeke, eyeing her in anger. 'I don't believe him for one minute. I must say as I'm surprised at you acting like this, Miss Judy. You should have talked it over with me and your aunt first, anyway. We've lost the best chance we had of proving something against that snake Flint.'

'I'm sorry, Zeke, but — but I felt I just had to do it,' said Judy miserably.

Doubts were rushing in again. Was Zeke right? Was Juan's explanation a trick to excuse his actions? And they did not know, even yet, what the Mexican boy had been up to at the ranch. What would they find out later?

She turned slowly away and was making for the veranda steps when abruptly she paused — from one of the stables lining the yard had come a sudden whinny, a familiar whinny that sent her heart leaping. She rushed for the stable. She fumbled frantically at the fastenings in the darkness. Another moment and the door was open. And then Judy gave a cry — an incredulous shout.

'Zeke — Zeke! Brownie's here! He's come back! Brownie's safe in his stable!'

It was the truth.

A shaft of moonlight through the stable window fell full upon the pony as he munched hay at his stall. Another glad whinny greeted Judy as she dashed into the stable.

'Brownie, old boy!' she cried breathlessly. 'Oh, thank goodness! How did you get back here?'

She rushed to the pony, hugged and fondled him, tears of joy in her eyes. Yet even as she cried out Judy knew just how he had got here.

Juan had brought him. This was what he had meant when he had said that she would soon find out that he was a friend, not an enemy. This was one reason to explain why he had come secretly to the ranch.

Old Zeke appeared in the doorway and stared at the pony.

'Well, this here beats everything, Miss Judy,' he gasped. 'I — I just can't believe that young varmint brought him back, and yet — how the heck did he get here?'

'Juan did bring him — I'm certain of it,' cried Judy. 'This is proof that he's our friend. Zeke, look after Brownie for a minute.'

A final fond pat and a whispered word to Brownie, and Judy raced from the stable towards the ranch-house. A sudden startling suspicion had come into her mind. What had Juan been up to at the back of the house? They had caught him — as they had thought at the time — just climbing up the thick-tangled creepers at the back. Was it possible...

Entering the hall, Judy raced upstairs, to her own room. The windows were wide open, their curtains blowing gently in the warm breeze. Moonlight flooded her dressing-table just below the window.

And as she glanced at that dressing-table Judy drew her breath quickly.

On the top was a white packet — a large envelope. It was crumpled and soiled, but instantly she recognised it. It was the envelope handed to her by the judge at the rodeo!

With trembling fingers she opened the flap, extracted the contents.

Five slips of paper came out — five one hundred dollar bills!

Judy drew a deep breath.

So that was it! Juan had visited the ranch not to commit a crime, but to bring back her stolen pony and the stolen prize-money. She could not doubt that now.

But how had he done it? How had he managed to recover both the pony and the money? What desperate risk had he taken to manage such a task? He must have taken great, dangerous chances: it must have called upon all his courage and wits. And he had risked all this for her sake, for the sake of Lone Pine Ranch.

Judy was overjoyed — not only because of the recovery of the money and pony, but because it proved Juan's innocence and loyalty. For a long moment Judy stared with shining eyes at the money, then she tore downstairs again to find her aunt.

Aunt May was just coming out of the living-room as Judy grabbed her round the waist and fairly waltzed her back into the room, waving high the envelope.

'The money, Aunt May — the prize-money,' she panted joyfully. 'Juan has brought it back; I found it on my dressing-table. And — oh, it's wonderful! Brownie's in his stable, safe and sound.'

'Judy, whatever do you mean?' cried Aunt May, laughing in astonishment. 'You mean...'

Breathlessly Judy told her, handed her the five hundred dollars, and Mrs Carson's pleasant face flushed with joy.

'That's why he came here — why he was found here,'

she ended delightedly. 'How on earth he managed it I don't know. But it's true — Brownie's back safe in his stable, and here is the money.'

And the high-spirited Judy grabbed her aunt and waltzed her round the room again. Her victory that afternoon had now become a real victory indeed. She was completely justified in being happy and in celebrating.

There was a tap on the door and old Zeke, hat in hand, came in.

'You've told your aunt, Miss Judy,' he was beginning, but Judy interrupted him gaily.

'Yes — now don't be a wet blanket, Zeke,' she cried. 'Here's the prize-money, too — look at it! Juan's brought both the pony and the money back. I found the money on my dressing-table. That was what Juan was up to — climbing down the creepers when you caught him. Now, do you still say he's a treacherous young thief, Zeke?'

Zeke put on his spectacles and examined the notes. He was dumbfounded for the moment. Then he shook his head. 'It fair beats everything,' he admitted gruffly. 'I'm glad for your sakes, of course — mighty glad, ladies. That young varmint brought them without a doubt. But that don't prove as he ain't an enemy.'

'What?' Judy gasped.

'It don't,' insisted Zeke stubbornly. 'It proves nothing of the sort, Miss Judy. I think I see what this means. I reckon it means as Wilmot Flint's got frightened. The snake knows he's gone too far this time. That red-bearded guy I saw must'a told Flint as I'd spotted him. The snake's got the wind up, and rather than face a charge before the sheriff he's decided to send the money and pony back. Yeah, that's how I figure things, ladies.'

Judy gasped.

'Oh — oh, you're impossible, Zeke!' she cried, unable

to help laughing. 'You're prejudiced against Juan. He's a dog with a bad name and you just won't give him a fair chance. Oh, it's not like you, Zeke — it's not fair. Aunt May' — she turned to her aunt — 'you surely believe he is innocent now?'

'I — I really don't know what to think, Judy,' said Mrs Carson, shaking her head. 'It is all so puzzling: so strange. But at least I am willing to give the boy the benefit of the doubt. And we've got back the pony and the prize-money, so that is all that matters.'

At Judy's suggestion one of the ranch dogs — a powerful airedale — was put in the stable with Brownie. With the dog there on guard Judy felt perfectly safe to leave them both there.

Arm-in-arm, she and her aunt returned to the ranch-house afterwards, happy now. Judy felt she could at last take a real pride and pleasure in the Gold Spurs she had won. It had been a wildly exciting day, and though tired out, she felt brimful of happiness. And now — she was thinking of Maorio, the Indian girl.

This was another exciting thing to have happened to her that day. She talked of it to her aunt. Maorio had already told Mrs Carson of seeing Judy's grandfather in the desert country, and it was a tremendous shock to her.

'It is very strange indeed, Judy,' said Aunt May. 'Oddly enough, Zeke would never have it that the old man was killed in that stampede. He said John Carson was too fine a horseman, and too skilled a rider ever to get caught in one. Zeke doesn't say much about it, but it is my belief that he thinks something happened to your grandfather up in the hills while searching for the Hidden Valley.'

'Oh, I can't help thinking that, too,' said Judy. She frowned thoughtfully. 'Listen, Aunt May; Maorio has offered to show me the Hidden Valley, and oh! I'm just longing to go. It would be a lovely adventure, and we might find something out about grandfather. Do you mind if we go tomorrow, Aunt May? We could make a real picnic of it, and I'd really love to go.'

Aunt May looked doubtful.

'It's terrible country up in the hills,' she said slowly. 'It's outlaw country, too, Judy. Are you sure it would be safe — be wise, my dear? I know Maorio knows every inch of the country, and she would never take any unnecessary risks. She's older than you, of course. But...'

'Oh, please Aunt May,' Judy pleaded eagerly. 'We could take food and things. And we really wouldn't do anything risky. Please Aunt May — say you approve?'

'I'm afraid I would not approve but for Maorio,' smiled Aunt May. 'She's sensible and competent as you are, Judy, and you should be quite all right together. Yes, it might prove a good thing.'

'Oh, thank you, dear Aunt May!' cried Judy. 'We'll work hard to make up for the day off. I'll see Maorio right away, and fix everything up.'

In the kitchen Judy found the Indian girl, and she was surprised at the difference in her. The faint trace of suspicion in her attitude had vanished now, and she smiled happily at the English girl. A good meal and kindness had made all the difference to Maorio. Together, they planned the outing, and Maorio was just as excited and eager as Judy was.

Then bedtime came, and Judy went to bed, feeling strangely happy and contented.

It made all the difference to her that she had her beloved pony with her to make the expedition; now things would be all the more enjoyable.

She fell asleep almost at once, and it was Maorio who woke her with a cup of coffee the next morning.

After breakfast she insisted upon doing her usual morning

tasks, and then she and Maorio changed into riding things, and started out, Maorio riding a grey, and Judy riding Brownie. Their saddlebags held food and drink, and they carried a stormlantern and other odd items that might be useful.

'It's not far once we reach the caves,' explained the Indian girl as they jogged along the trail towards the mountains. 'Through the caves we come to an underground river which my people call the Lost River. This leads into the Hidden Valley. My father took me a long time ago. Only a few Yaquis know the way. They won't tell white people. I think Boss Carson went there; something must have happened to him. Perhaps we'll find out today.'

She glanced a little curiously at Judy.

Why do you want to go there, Miss Judy?' she asked. 'Why are you so anxious to see the Hidden Valley?'

Judy hesitated. She did not really know herself. It had probably been that instinctive feeling that she must carry on her grandfather's quest. She had no idea what she might find if she ever reached the Hidden Valley. It was all so secret, so mysterious. Whoever had placed that model horse in her handbag and left that puzzling message must have wanted her to do this — to carry on the strange search.

The search for what? She could scarcely guess. But Judy was adventure-loving, and the strange quest appealed to her. And now there was Maorio's amazing statement that she had seen John Carson alive — while he was supposed to have died in the stampede.

'Maorio,' she said suddenly, 'why do you think that old Mr Carson went to the Hidden Valley?'

'Because I saw him riding with Ben Bolt that way,' said the Indian girl. 'Ben Bolt, the old prospector; he is the only white man known to have entered the secret valley. Maybe he took Boss Carson there; maybe something happened to them. Ben Bolt has not been seen for a long time: Boss Carson has not been seen for a long time. Both of them vanished. Where did they go?'

'I see, Maorio,' said Judy, her eyes gleaming. 'I believe that there may be a lot in that. My grandfather was terribly keen on seeing this Hidden Valley.'

She thought a moment, then decided to trust Maorio. Showing her the model horse, she explained how she had come by it, and of the message with it.

'That is very strange, Miss Judy,' said the Indian girl, puzzled. 'There is no gold in the Hidden Valley — only horses. What is there to look for? Maybe John Carson wanted the horses, though. We shall find out presently.'

They rode on along the trail, mostly in silence. Maorio was no chatterer. But she was pleasant company, for all that. Each time Judy looked at her she met a friendly smile. On over the baked, scorched prairie, and then up into the pine forests of the foothills they went. It was a lovely morning. The sun was not high yet, and it was pleasantly cool.

They took their time, enjoying their lovely surroundings to the full — the gay flowers by the trail, the sweet-smelling pines, the warm Arizona sun, the breeze that trembled among the foliage of the pines; and, most of all, the antics of prairie chickens, of squirrels and jack-rabbits, and other fascinating wild creatures.

Presently the sun grew hot. Both horses and riders began to feel the heat and to perspire freely; but they carried on until Judy's watch told her it was time for a meal.

They stopped then in a little clearing by a tiny spring. Dismounting, they took sandwiches from saddlebags, and Maorio skilfully built a tiny fire and boiled water for coffee. Judy thoroughly enjoyed that meal under the trees, and when it was over they carefully put out the fire and rode on again.

Now the landscape was growing rougher, rockier, and trees gave place to stunted mesquite and bushes and rocks, wind-sculptured into weird formations. Judy was fascinated.

Above them on one side reared the towering mountains, their tops wreathed in mist. Judy recognised Wild Horse Canyon among the jumbled mass of peaks and ravines. But they rode past that, and Maorio led the way between great piles of rock. How she found her way Judy could not imagine, but the Indian girl never seemed at a loss. Quite suddenly she stopped.

'We leave the horses her, Miss Judy,' she said, swinging from the saddle. 'They are quite safe. We must go on foot. Remember to take the lantern because we shall soon be in the caves.'

Judy dismounted, and they plunged forward through never-ending piles of jumbled rocks, and among giant, weird-looking cacti. They moved cautiously, eyes on the alert for snakes and scorpions.

Then suddenly Maorio paused before the cliff face.

'Come,' she said.

She flattened herself against the cliff, edged to one side — and vanished.

Bewildered, Judy blinked, but then she realised what had happened.

From the front it was scarcely visible, but what she had taken for a crack in the cliff wall was a slit, or fissure. She followed the Indian girl into it, finding herself in a low cave. This in turn led into another and a larger cave.

Judy lit the lantern, and suddenly the Indian girl paused and pointed to the rock face.

Hieroglyphics, scratched deeply into the walls, showed in the lantern light, preserving the history of forgotten races of cave-dwellers. Judy gazed fascinated at the strange drawings and unknown writings.

'My people lived here long ago,' said Maorio simply. 'Come.'

They moved on, the lantern-light casting gargantuan

shapes on the walls. It was quite chilly in the caves, and the air curents made an unearthly moaning sound. Through cave after cave they went, caves formed by volcanic explosions and erosion. And suddenly Judy became aware of a strange, moaning, rushing sound.

They emerged abruptly into a great, lofty cavern, and the lantern-light glimmered on a sheet of rushing black water.

'The Lost River,' said the Indian girl softly.

Spellbound, Judy gazed at the foaming water, that seemed to come out of nowhere and vanish into nowhere.

This, then, was the underground river; the river that long ago had glided through Whispering Valley and on to the Rio Grande.

Now it ran underground and vanished — where?

'Come,' whispered Maorio. 'Give me the light — I'll go first.'

They moved on to the left, Maorio leading the way with the lantern. The water gleamed like black ebony in the lantern-glow. Judy found herself walking along a narrow pathway beside the river. She was trembling with suppressed excitement. The almost silent water seemed strange and unreal, and the vast cavern, its roof unseen, filled her with awe and wonder.

'It is not far now,' said Maorio. 'Soon we shall come out...'

She broke off with a startled cry, coming to an abrupt stop. For some minutes the roof had been getting lower — had become clearly visible to them — while the river had narrowed considerably, the water rushing like a torrent between the banks of rock. And now the light was shining on a great pile of rock and earth, completely blocking their pathway.

'What — what is it, Maorio?' whispered Judy. 'Why, the pathway's blocked. Was it...'

'It was not like this when I came before,' exclaimed Maorio, her usually stolid voice showing alarm and disappointment. 'The roof — it has fallen since I came. We can't go on. I am sorry, Miss Judy.'

Judy gazed at the black river.

'Well, we're fairly stumped, Maorio,' she agreed dismally. 'Swimming in that is out of the question.'

'We would drown,' said the Indian girl simply. 'We must go back. I'm sorry, Miss Judy.'

They stood staring at the barrier, but it was obviously useless to think of trying to proceed. The great mass of rock and earth reached to the roof, and spread far into the river; half-submerged rocks showed above the water for some distance out. And they could not tell how far that barrier went.

'More rock might fall while we are here,' said Maorio. 'We must go. What's that?'

For Judy, with a sudden cry, had stopped and picked up something white from the rocky ground.

It was an envelope, damp and dirty, and covered with figures and measurements. But the writing on it, though faint and blurred, was easily decipherable, and as she examined it in the lantern-light, Judy gave a startled cry.

'Look, Maorio,' she cried excitedly, 'this is addressed to my grandfather at an hotel in Dune Crossing — the Golden Nugget Hotel.'

'Dune Crossing — that's a small town in desert country,' said Maorio. 'I know it.'

'Yes, but the date, Maorio, look at the date,' said Judy, her voice high with excitement. 'It is June 15th, and it is only August now. He must have dropped this envelope here. This proves he did come this way, Maorio — must have done. And it proves that he did not die in that stampede! Wilmot Flint lied when he identified that poor man as John Carson!'

Judy's eyes were blazing with excitement. Even if they had failed to reach Hidden Valley, this amazing discovery had made the expedition worthwhile.

Moreover, she had seen the Lost River, and would not have missed this strange underground adventure for anything.

'Never mind, Maorio,' she explained eagerly, 'we've made this discovery, even if we have failed to reach the valley. And there is Wild Horse Canyon still to be explored. Maorio, do you know of the other secret way into the Hidden Valley, through Wild Horse Canyon?'

Maorio nodded slowly, and a look of fear and alarm came into her dark eyes.

'I have heard of it,' she said. 'But I do not know the way in. Nobody knows. Only the White Horse knows. I won't go there. Wild Horse Canyon is haunted — it's a bad place, Miss Judy. You must not ask me to go there!'

There was an anxious appeal in Maorio's voice, and Judy smiled and shook her head. She had thought of asking for the Indian girl's help to explore the canyon, but now, seeing the fear on Maorio's face, she instantly abandoned the idea.

'No, not if you don't want to, Maorio,' she said quickly. 'In any case, I don't think we've the time — we ought to be starting back.'

They retraced their steps along the rocky pathway. Judy was very disappointed. But there was still Wild Horse Canyon, and she was determined to explore it some time soon, haunted or not — even if it meant going alone.

And Judy thought of her grandfather. She could not help thinking that, perhaps, that fall of rock might have had something to do with his strange disappearance. And what did the queer figures and measurements on the envelope mean? She could only suppose the old rancher had been making

Judy examined the envelope in the light from the lantern.

measurements, and had then thrown the envelope away.

Why was he so vitally interested in the Hidden Valley? What was he looking for there? Well, his quest in the Hidden Valley was her quest now, and she would find out, if determination had anything to do with it.

Back through that eerie underground world they passed, and it was no little relief to them both when they reached the blazing sunlight of the open air at last.

Brownie and Maorio's horse were still contentedly cropping the grass, and Brownie flung up his head and whinnied a welcome as Judy reached him and fastened the lantern to his saddle.

Then Maorio led the way through the maze of undergrowth and rocks.

They rode off in silence, Judy busy with her own thoughts. Despite her disappointment she felt happy and contented, and was still enjoying to the full this exciting outing. She was thinking what a lot had happened to her since leaving England — ages ago, it seemed.

To her it had been one long, thrilling adventure. And she felt quite sure there was still more adventure ahead of her. Also...

She broke off as Maorio's voice, low and urgent, reached her ears.

'I hear horses, Miss Judy. Don't make a sound.'

They stood still, and Judy listened intently. Sure enough, she could just hear a distant thudding of hoofs, and a faint jingling of harness.

The Indian girl slipped lithely from the saddle and spoke softly and urgently to Judy, her eyes wide with fear. 'Perhaps Señor Flint has sent men to look for me, to take me prisoner again. Quick! Follow me!'

She led her horse off the trail, through the trees and bushes, while Judy followed, leading Brownie. Soon Maorio stopped, and laid a finger on her lips. Together, they looked back.

Round a bend on the trail came two horsemen, one of whom Judy recognised as the elderly man whom Flint had sent to kidnap her. But the other was not Juan. He was speaking, and Judy could just make out some of the words.

'...sure wouldn't like to be in the shoes of that young coyote, Juan Ruiz, when he's found! "Round him up, bring him in — and he'll wish he'd never been born!" — that's what the boss said, wasn't it, Pablo?'

'Si. He is a foolish man, that one. Señor Flint found the prize-money gone, and the girl's horse gone, and saw Juan coming back from the direction of Tres Pinos...now Señor Flint knows Juan is a traitor to the Dos Cabezos Ranch.'

'That's right,' agreed the other. 'But he can't last long out on the prairie with just a horse, no food and no friends...'

Judy could not hear any more of what they were saying, but she had heard enough! Juan, a fugitive now, out here on the wild prairie, with no food, no friends... Suddenly, she knew she had to help him. But what she had to do was dangerous; her aunt would probably never allow her to take such risks. So she decided to work out a plan and confide only in Maorio.

'Quick, Maorio, we must return home at once!' she said, when the horsemen were out of sight and earshot.

As they neared home, Judy outlined her plan to Maorio. At first light in the morning she would take clothes, food and water, and set off for Wild Horse Canyon to look for Juan; she felt instinctively that he would go there to hide, as the country was so wild and the cover good. If she found him she would try to get him back to Lone Pine ranch disguised in different clothes.

They returned in time for supper, and after the meal Judy pleaded a head-ache and went to bed early.

Before the sun was up next morning Judy was dressed.

She crept downstairs, took food and a bottle of water from the kitchen, found a spare set of cowboy's clothes in the barn, and was away on Brownie before anyone stirred.

On she rode, heading in the direction of the badlands, her keen eyes scanning the surrounding countryside. She knew she had a long, and probably dangerous day before her, and was determined to be alert and watchful all the time.

Judy had been riding for well over an hour, when she noticed a ravine to the right of the trail, and stopped to gaze down it, at the same time giving Brownie a well deserved rest. Her attention was caught by some faint hoof marks, just noticeable in the stony, dusty ground, leading off the trail, and down into the ravine. Who else but Juan would take such a strange route, she asked herself.

With a growing sense of excitement and certainty, she urged Brownie off the trail, and guided him down the steep rocky slope to the foot of the ravine. Here, there was no sign of the hoofmarks — the ground was too hard to show them — so she just made her way along its winding course into the badlands, continually scanning the area for signs of movement, or anything unusual.

It was difficult going, but somehow she felt safer here than out on the prairie, where she could easily be seen. And she was certain that Juan had come this way...

On they went, until they reached the frowning, sinister walls of — Wild Horse Canyon!

Judy's heart began to beat faster now. She could not help a feeling of fear and dread as she peered into the brush-choked waste facing her. No wonder the Yaqui Indians looked upon this blind canyon as being haunted, the home of evil spirits. Above her towered the beetling, frowning cliffs; high above in the blue sky an eagle hovered on wide-spread wings — seeming to add to the sinister atmosphere of the place.

Had she done right in coming here — in taking this risk? Yet this was the place of secrets — the canyon that hid the entrance to Hidden Valley — and she had vowed to find it.

Slowly she rode deeper into the canyon. Even her pony seemed uneasy and unusually restive. But suddenly Brownie pricked up his ears, and then a loud, welcoming whinny sounded from the tangled mass of foliage facing them.

Judy's nerves were on edge, and the sudden, unexpected sound made her jump, and her heart beat faster. Yet next instant followed relief. Who else could be here but — Juan?

She slid from the saddle and, holding the bridle rein, led Brownie into the jungle of bush. They had to force their way through, and it was hard going. Judy gave a gasp of relief when suddenly she saw a magnificent brown horse standing against the base of the tall canyon wall.

It was Juan's horse. But there was no sign of the Mexican boy.

Judy looked about her uneasily. She called his name once, twice, but there was no reply. The minutes passed and still he did not appear. She did not know what to do. She could fasten the saddle-bags containing the supplies to Juan's horse, and return home — the safer course, she told herself. Yet, she wanted to see Juan — to be sure that he was all right. And there was her quest as well.

She had planned to visit Wild Horse Canyon some time, and to search for the entrance to the secret valley. She had lain awake hoping to be in just such a situation as this. And never, perhaps, would she have a better chance to make the search.

Somehow, though uneasy, she was not afraid with the two horses as comrades. With them she was not alone, and could scarcely wish for better protectors.

'I'll stay and search,' she decided at last. 'Perhaps that is what Juan is doing now. He's bound to return to his horse sooner or later, anyway.' She started off into the bushes.

To search that great maze of tangled undergrowth seemed an impossible task. But she faced it with a will and began to work her way along the cliff wall, ever on the look-out for snakes. The canyon was wide, and in places the thick masses of prickly bush made it impossible to reach the cliff face. It was no wonder searchers had failed to find the secret entrance.

For fully an hour she searched, and then she returned to the horses and began to work her way along the other side. She was breathless and panting, and soaked in perspiration. Her hands and face were scratched by prickly thorns, and teaming swarms of insects made matters worse. At last sheer exhaustion forced her to give up. Standing by the horses, she glanced round her. Where was the Mexican boy? Had he found the secret entrance and entered the Hidden Valley? Did that explain why he had left his horse?

In her own mind she was convinced that Juan was as interested in the Hidden Valley as she was. Indeed, Judy was thinking strange thoughts about the Mexican boy. A suspicion was forming in her mind which would not be dismissed.

She found a wide ledge of rock in the shade, just above where the horses were tethered and, with a saddle-bag as a pillow, she stretched herself out to rest and wait...

The silence was somehow eerie. But for the company of the horses, Judy could not have stood that nerve-racking vigil. The sound of them contentedly cropping the long grass and the occasional jingle of bit-chains was strangely comforting.

How long she remained there she could not tell, but she must have dozed off, for suddenly she found herself sitting upright, every nerve tense, her heart thudding.

It must have been a sudden movement of the horses that had startled her, for now she saw them standing tense, heads upflung, like statues. And they seemed to be trembling with excited fear.

Then she heard it — a queer, muffled thud of advancing hoofs, that seemed to emanate from the canyon wall itself.

Instinctively she knew that the wild White Horse was coming!

Hidden Valley

Every nerve in Judy's body grew tense and her heart beat tumultuously.

She must keep a grip on herself, on her nerves and emotions. Never again might she get such a chance to discover the spot where he came out into the canyon.

She whispered soothing words to the two frightened horses and, rising to her feet, waited, every sense on the alert.

Strangely enough, she felt little fear; only a gripping eagerness and excitement.

Nearer and nearer came the sounds; the echoing thudding became louder and closer.

Judy stood like a statue, ears strained, eyes searching. And suddenly, abruptly, the thudding ceased, and was followed almost instantly by a wild crashing of undergrowth. She saw, some yards along the cliff face, the foliage being rent and tossed. Then, through the leaves and branches she glimpsed, just for an instant, the shape of a white horse. Then amid a crashing and thudding of hoofs, the creature vanished.

The White Horse had gone — gone on his queer pilgrimage into the open country.

'Quiet, Brownie! Steady, old boy.'

The pony had given a plaintive whinny, but her soft, soothing words quietened him. And Judy, her eyes gleaming with resolution, slid down to the ground from the ledge.

Recklessly she pushed through the thickets towards the spot where she had sighted the White Horse. She reached it, and began to force her way through towards the cliff-face.

Branches flew back and struck her, and thorns tore at her face and clothing, but she shielded her face with her hands and pushed on. And now she found herself in a kind of tunnel in the mass of brush — a tunnel probably made by the wild horse.

This tunnel led, after a few yards, into a wider tunnel in the sheer rocky face of the cliff. And suddenly, after a few more moments of walking, Judy saw the blue sky above her.

She was in a great cleft in the cliffs — a cleft that cut sheer through the canyon wall, with the open sky hundreds of feet above her. By spreading out her hands she could just touch both rocky sides of the fissure.

Judy's excitement increased, banishing all thoughts of possible danger. This was, she felt certain, the secret entrance to the Hidden Valley. She thrilled at the thought, and hurried along the cleft.

Had Juan come this way? Would she find him safe in the Hidden Valley? And what else would she find there? Would she now succeed in solving the strange mystery?

Judy broke off her thoughts. Her face suddenly went pale.

She was well into the cleft, and now, from behind her, she heard a faint crashing, followed by the menacing thud of hoofs.

The wild horse was returning!

She started to run in sheer panic. The thud of hoofs grew louder, echoing thunderously in the narrow confines of the cleft. Never in her life had Judy felt so frightened, so terrified. She was trapped — the walls were sheer, and she could never escape. She would be trampled under flying hoofs; more likely savagely attacked by the White Horse.

She suddenly stopped — her limbs refused to carry her in the horror of that moment. She felt on the point of fainting when a voice reached her from above.

'Look out! Catch the rope and hold on. Quick!'

It was a husky, frantic shout in a familiar voice. Something struck her face a sharp smack, and she clutched involuntarily. Her hands gripped a rope, and she hung on, and was swung clean off her feet into the air.

Up she went, crashing into the rocky wall of the cleft, striving desperately to hold on, and to get a grip with her feet on the rock to help the person above.

Higher she swung, hardly conscious, but holding on desperately. And then a white figure flashed beneath her — the Ghost Horse!

Amid a thunder of unshod hoofs it galloped by, its head barely missing her waving feet.

Then it was gone, and the thudding of hoofs died away along the cleft.

Judy felt herself floundering helplessly, then somehow her fingers struck a rocky ledge, and she released a hand and clung to it. Next instant a strong grasp fell on her shoulder, gripping her under the arms, and then she found herself sprawling on a narrow ledge.

She lay there for some moments panting and gasping, and almost sobbing in her utter relief. She instantly recognised the figure beside her on the ledge as Juan. He lay there, too, his chest heaving as he also gasped and panted for breath. He must have used every ounce of his strength in hauling her bodily upwards like that. He was utterly exhausted.

But at last Judy sat up, her eyes shining.

'Oh!' she panted. 'That was terrible, Juan, but it — it was just grand of you! You saved my life. I thought I was done for.'

Juan raised himself then, and she knew the old, devil-may-care smile on his face. How glad she was to see him!

'It was what you might call a close shave,' he grinned. 'It was very lucky that I was on this ledge watching for the White Horse. I was never so astonished in my life when I saw you down there below. What are you doing here, Señorita Judy?'

'I came to bring you some food and things, Juan,' returned Judy. 'But you were not there, though I waited by your horse for a long time. Then I saw the White Horse come out of the brush and gallop away. I — I hunted until I found the place, and came along the cleft. It was foolish of me — I never thought of his coming back.'

'I was hunting for the entrance to the Hidden Valley,' said Juan. 'I could not find it, so I got the lariat and climbed the cliff. I reached the top and explored. I could see the Hidden Valley but I could not climb down the far side. Then I found this cleft and climbed down from above. Then the wild horse came — and you came.'

'Thank goodness you were here, Juan,' said Judy thankfully. 'It was splendid of you.' She shuddered. 'I was panic-stricken. But what shall we do now? Can we climb down?'

'We can climb down,' said Juan. 'If you feel fit, we can go and explore the Hidden Valley.'

'So you are interested in the Hidden Valley, Juan?' asked Judy.

'Very interested indeed,' agreed Juan. 'We must explore the Hidden Valley together, Señorita. It would give me the greatest pleasure.'

Judy eyed him straightly. His words made her curious again.

'Juan, what is the secret of the Hidden Valley?' she asked. 'My grandfather was very interested in it. He was always searching for it. Is there gold or something?'

'There may be, Señorita. But your grandfather, he was

looking for water. That was his interest in the valley.'

'What?'

'Water,' repeated Juan. 'The Lost River. It was the dream of his life to irrigate Whispering Valley. You know that what the ranchers dread is drought. It has ruined many of them. Your grandfather, it was his plan to find the Lost River, and so blast through the canyon wall here, and release the Lost River into its old bed in Whispering Valley. The river would run once again right down to the Rio Grande, bringing prosperity to Whispering Valley.'

'Oh, what a splendid scheme!' gasped Judy eagerly. 'And Wilmot Flint? Was he...'

'He wanted the wild horses,' said Juan briefly. 'He would make a fortune out of their sale if he could catch them. That Señor Flint, he thinks only of his own pocket. But we must climb down now.'

He fastened the lariat to a jutting knob of rock, and helped her over the edge. Judy did not find it difficult, and hand over hand she lowered herself the few yards to the ground.

He came swarming down the rope a moment later, then shook the loop of the knob. He coiled the lariat round his waist and then turned to Judy.

'Let's go and explore now, Señorita!'

But Judy shook her head.

'No,' she said firmly. 'You're going to have something to eat first — and so am I. You need it — and I might.'

Juan hesitated. Then...

'Very well, Señorita,' he chuckled.

They made their way back to the horses in Wild Horse Canyon. There, Judy unpacked her saddle-bags and soon both were enjoying the delicious chicken sandwiches and griddle cakes which she had brought.

Judy was intensely curious about Juan, his life and background. But the Mexican boy avoided the subject, and jokingly turned her apparently careless questions aside.

When they had finished their meal, they made a start. The horses were happy and contented enough, busily cropping the grass, so, leaving them, the two entered the cleft. They walked along the rocky path until at last they reached a dense mass of bushes. Pushing through this barrier they emerged at length into the open air.

The Hidden Valley! Judy had often wondered what she would see, and now she found herself gazing at a broad, gleaming river running through a fertile valley.

It appeared to spread for miles into the hazy distance. Wooded hills and beetling cliffs hemmed the valley in on all sides, wild flowers bloomed in profusion everywhere, and the valley seemed alive with game and beautiful bird life.

'Look!' exclaimed Juan. 'It is a rancher's paradise, Señorita.'

'It is beautiful,' said Judy, her eyes shining. 'And this is what my grandfather sought for so long. Oh, look, Juan!'

She pointed down the valley. Coming towards them at a fast gallop was a herd of horses, their long manes flowing in the breeze, their glossy coats gleaming in the early morning sun. All were a pure white, and all were magnificent animals.

'The wild herd,' said Juan softly. 'They are Arab strain — maybe their ancestors were brought by the Spaniards centuries ago.'

'It would be a crying shame to rob them of their liberty,' breathed Judy. 'They are lovely — and see, there is the horse we saw this morning, their leader.'

'Si — the Ghost Horse,' said Juan. 'But they will not lose their liberty if I have anything to do with it, Señorita. And now let us explore the Indian cave-dwellings. See, Señorita.'

He pointed to one of the cliffs nearby. The whole face was pitted with holes like windows.

'It almost looks like a burned-out sky-scraper,' said Judy. 'We must explore them of course, Juan. We — we might find something.'

But Judy was thinking of her grandfather. Had he ever been here? Would they find something that would tell them what had happened to him? If Maorio was right...

Eagerly Judy followed the Mexican boy as he strode towards the nearest cave-dwelling.

A cry suddenly came from Juan.

'See Señorita Judy — smoke!'

'And I smell cooking,' cried Judy, as she followed the direction his hand was indicating. 'Juan. someone is in that cave, and he's cooking.'

They ran to the cave and paused at the roughly hewn doorway. They looked inside — and Judy gasped at what she saw.

Crouching before a tiny wood fire was a small old man with a straggling grey beard, wearing a battered hat. He was busily stirring something in a tin hung over the fire, and a savoury smell wafted over towards them.

'Ah!' exclaimed Juan in a tense voice. 'It — it is the Señor Ben Bolt, the prospector!'

The Genuine Will

'*Ben Bolt!*'

Involuntarily Judy cried the name aloud, so great was her excitement. This, then, was the old prospector who had been with her grandfather when he had last been seen alive in the desert.

The old man turned a face towards them now — a tanned, seamed face full of good nature.

'I saw you coming,' he said cheerfully. 'This here rabbit ain't quite cooked yet, but it won't be long. Get a mug each out of that rucksack, and try some of my coffee while you're waiting for the rabbit.'

The calm greeting almost took Judy's breath away. She laughed.

'Good morning!' she cried. 'I hope we aren't intruding.'

'You ain't. It ain't often I has visitors — this here place is a bit out of the way,' he went on with a chuckle. 'But how come you got in here at all, and what might you be after in this valley?'

'We followed the White Horse; we saw him enter a cleft in the cliff,' said Judy. 'We — I was hoping we might find some clue to what had happened to my grandfather, Mr Bolt. My name is Judy Rainford, and I am Mrs Carson's niece, and the grand-daughter of John Carson, who used to own the Dos Cabezos Ranch. He was supposed to have been killed in a stampede three or four months ago, but...'

'Your grandfather weren't killed in no stampede,' said Ben Bolt. 'He died in my arms in this here valley a month ago today, and he's buried yonder, under that cottonwood.'

He pointed through the doorway, and, looking in that direction, Judy saw a mound of earth under the tree.

'I guided him into this valley about three months gone,' went on the old prospector. 'We come in along the underground river — only way I know. We explored the valley, and your grandfather took a lot of measurements of the river, but when we came to go back we found the road blocked by a fall of earth. We couldn't get out and we couldn't find the way that horse takes, so we were stuck here a few weeks, living on game and fish and a supply of coffee we had. Then your grandfather took ill — his heart failed, and he ups and dies in my arms, and I buried him yonder.'

'Only a month ago,' breathed Judy and Juan almost together.

'Yeah; exactly a month ago today, Miss Rainford!'

'That — that villain, Wilmot Flint,' muttered Judy fiercely. 'Why, he swore my grandfather was killed in a stampede, and he produced a will, stating that the Dos Cabezos and everything had been left to him by John Carson. That was months ago, though.'

'Wilmot Flint's a snake!' said the old man grimly. 'I know him. That will was forged, then. Hold on a minute.'

He went to a rucksack lying in a corner of the cave dwelling. He took out some documents and handed them, not to Judy, but — to Juan!

'Read them,' said Ben Bolt, pointing. 'That there's John Carson's last will — and the only will he ever made, according to what he told me. It leaves everything — the Dos Cabezos and everything else — to his young grandson, Bobby Carson of the Lone Pine.'

'Gosh!' It was the Mexican boy speaking and his voice thrilled with excitement. 'I knew it, Ben. I was certain Flint had swindled me. My grandfather...'

He broke off abruptly, suddenly realising what he was saying; suddenly aware that Judy was staring at him with wide eyes.

'Yeah, go on, young 'un,' grinned Ben Bolt. 'Your grandfather what? You young idiot,' he went on, with a chuckle, 'I knew you weren't no Mex the moment I set eyes on you. I recognised you immediately. You're young Bobby Carson, old John Carson's grandson. That Mex outfit don't fool me none.'

'Oh,' cried Judy. 'Oh you — you're quite right, Ben — I know you are! He isn't Juan Ruiz at all; he's my cousin, Bobby Carson.'

Her eyes were shining as she stared at the boy she had known as Juan.

His bronzed face flushed.

'Yes, Cousin Judy,' he said then, with a smile. 'Ben is

quite right — I'm not afraid to own up to it now. I'm your Cousin Bobby right enough. I've got the goods on Flint now, and have nothing to fear.'

'That is simply wonderful,' cried Judy. 'All along I've felt there was something strange about you. And now — now you can come home and face everybody, Bobby. And Flint will be cleared out, and you will be the owner of the Dos Cabezos.

'But Bobby,' she went on almost reproachfully, 'why didn't you confide in your mother, or in me? You know you could have trusted us.'

'I did trust you,' said Bobby soberly, 'but I'd vowed not to reveal myself until I'd proved my innocence. I was called a rustler and a thief, remember. Lies were told about me, and I was an outcast, a fugitive. But I got that job at the Dos Cabezos not only to be near Mother, but to watch Wilmot Flint, and keep an eye on him. I had to work in secret, though. And then, again, I wanted to be near Wild Horse Canyon, to carry on grandfather's quest as I'd promised him I would.'

'Bobby, it was you, then, who put that model horse in my handbag on that first day I came?'

'I put it there,' assented Bobby with a grin. 'I did it on the spur of the moment, on the principle, I suppose, that two heads were better than one. Anyway,' he ended quietly, 'we've both carried through the quest together, Judy. As for my inheritance — yes, I'll get that, but I'm taking it only on one condition.'

'And that is...?'

'That you'll be my partner, Cousin Judy,' said Bobby, his voice shaking a little. 'You've been a grand partner, Judy — a secret partner. But now I want you to be my partner in reality, to share in my inheritance; to be my partner in the Dos Cabezos. You will...?'

'But of course I will, Bobby,' said Judy.

'Better cut your speech-making short,' interrupted old Ben Bolt with a grim chuckle. 'We got visitors.'

He jerked a thumb towards the entrance to the valley, and as she looked the colour drained from Judy's face.

Charging across the valley at a mad gallop came Wilmot Flint, forcing on his mount with whip and spur. And behind were three other horsemen, Sheriff Moore of Tres Pinos, his badge sparkling in the morning sun, and two deputies.

They came thudding up and reined in to a scudding halt, amid flying tufts of earth and turf. And Wilmot Flint, his face red and gloating, slid from the saddle with a yell.

'There he is — there's the young scoundrel, sheriff! I knew we'd find him this way. I knew he'd be here when we found them horses outside, and saw the trail they left. He ain't no Juan Ruiz at all! He's that young rustler and thief, Bobby Carson! I've been suspicious of him for some time — then I found out he was a traitor to the Dos Cabezos. After he'd bolted I searched his kitbag and found a half-written letter to his mother at Lone Pine. I order you to arrest him pronto, sheriff.'

But the eshriff seemed in no hurry to do that. He advanced slowly and rather reluctantly towards Bobby, who leaned negligently against the doorway of the cave dwelling, Judy by his side.

Just then Ben Bolt chipped in.

'Hold on, sheriff — hold your horses, gents! I got something to say about this. Sheriff, the gent you wants to arrest is that snake there — Wilmot Flint.'

'How come, Ben?'

'You know me, sheriff,' said Ben. 'You know I ain't the man to shoot off my mouth about nothing.'

'Reckon I do, Ben; I knowed you all my life and there ain't a squarer shooter in all Arizona.'

'Well, listen then,' said Ben, pointing at the staring Flint.

The rope twanged, and Wilmot Flint crashed to the ground.

'That snake is a liar, a thief, a rustler and a forger! That's the coyote you want to arrest.'

'That's a tall order, Ben,' said the sheriff mildly. 'Why?'

'He lied when he swore old man Carson were killed in that stampede. John Carson died of heart-failure in my arms just a month ago in this here valley, and he lies under that cottonwood tree yonder,' said Ben, pointing again. 'That will Flint produced was forged, and so was the evidence against young Bobby. Listen...'

And the old prospector told his story to the gaping sheriff, and then handed him the will and other documents. Sheriff Moore read them, and then looked at Wilmot Flint.

'So that's it, eh?' he drawled grimly. 'I always was suspicious over that there will, and I weren't the only one. Well, Mister Flint, I reckon your course is run, and...'

He broke off sharply. Wilmot Flint, with a wild cry of rage, had leaped forward and torn the documents from his grasp. Another second and he had made a flying leap for his horse. With amazing agility for his bulk, he gained the saddle and rammed home his spurs.

The horse reared and them leaped away in a headlong gallop.

'After him!' yelled the sheriff.

There was a rush for the horses. The thought of Flint destroying the will was enough. But the first to reach the saddle was the boy they had known as Juan Ruiz.

In a flash he was up on one of the deputies' horses, and had set off in hot pursuit at a mad, tearing gallop. And as he rode, standing in the stirrups, he swung aloft a lariat, whirling it round and round his head.

Nearer and nearer he got to the fleeing rancher. Then he made his cast.

It was a perfect throw. The whirling lariat shot out like a coiling snake. The loop settled neatly and surely over

Wilmot Flint's head and shoulders, and the cow-pony Bobby was riding, trained to such work, reared high under tightened rein. The rope twanged, and Wilmot Flint was plucked from his mount and went crashing to earth.

The chasing horsemen were about him in a flash, tumbling from their horses. In another moment Sheriff Moore had the handcuffs on the scoundrel's wrists.

'Well,' said the sheriff then, rising from his knees. 'I reckon as the party's about over now, gents. Tie this coyote on his horse, boys. Ben, we've got a spare horse as you can ride.'

He grinned as he glanced at Judy and Bobby, now standing hand-in-hand, their eyes shining.

'I reckon we can leave them two to get home themselves,' he drawled, with a chuckle. 'If I wants you, young Bobby, I'll come after you, but I don't reckon as I will. Adios!'

Taking their prisoner, Sheriff Moore, Ben and the deputies rode away through the cleft in the canyon wall and vanished. Judy and Bobby smiled happily at each other, and were about to follow when Judy gave a cry.

'The rabbit! It'll be burned to a cinder, Bobby, and I could eat an elephant. Come on.'

And, shouting with laughter, the two cousins raced back into the cave-dwelling. Luckily the rabbit was just cooked to perfection, and Judy and Bobby, ravenously hungry again now, almost ate the lot between them, and finished off the last of Ben Bolt's coffee. Then, and only then, did they leave the Hidden Valley.

Mounting their waiting horses, Judy and Bobby Carson rode homewards, stirrup to stirrup, in the warm, late afternoon sunshine, to bring great happiness and peace to Judy's Aunt May at Lone Pine.

And Sheriff Moore did not 'want' young Bobby Carson, for the two Mexicans who had framed the boy were soon made to confess, as were the two witnesses to the false will.

Then, less than a month later, Aunt May, Bobby and Judy — not forgetting Bella and Maorio — rode over to the Dos Cabezos and took formal possession of the hacienda and the vast ranch-lands, leaving Zeke Carter and Ben Bolt to run the Lone Pine Ranch together.

The Early Life of Black Beauty

by Anna Sewell

The first place that I can well remember was a large pleasant meadow with a pond of clear water in it. Some trees overshadowed the pond, and rushes and water-lilies grew at the deep end. Over the hedge on one side we looked into a ploughed field; and on the other we looked over a gate at our master's house, which stood by the roadside. At the top of the meadow was a plantation of fir trees, and at the bottom, a running brook overhung by a steep bank.

Whilst I was young I lived upon my mother's milk, as I could not eat grass. In the daytime I ran by her side, and at night I lay down close to her. When it was hot we used to stand by the pond in the shade of trees; and when it was cold, we had a nice warm shed near the plantation.

As soon as I was old enough to eat grass, my mother used to go out to work in the daytime, and to come back in the evening.

There were six young colts in the meadow besides me. They were older than I was; some were nearly as large as grown-up horses. I used to run with them, and have great fun; we used to gallop all together round and round the field, as hard as we could go. Sometimes we had rather rough play, for they would frequently bite and kick as well as gallop.

One day, when there was a good deal of kicking, my mother whinnied to me to come to her; and then she said, 'I wish you to pay attention to what I am going to say to you. The colts who live here are very good colts; but they are cart-horse colts, and, of course, they have not learned good manners.

'You have been well bred and well born; your father has a great name in these parts, and your grandfather won the Cup twice at the Newmarket races; your grandmother had the sweetest temper of any horse I ever knew, and I think you have never seen me kick or bite.

'I hope you will grow up gentle and good, and never learn bad ways. Do your work with a good will; lift your feet up well when you trot, and never bite or kick even in play.'

I have never forgotten my mother's advice; I knew she was a wise old horse, and our master thought very highly of her. Her name was Duchess, but he often called her Pet.

Our master was a good, kind man. He gave us good food, good lodging, and kind words; and he spoke as kindly to us as he did to his little children. We were all fond of him, and my mother loved him very much. When she saw him at the gate, she would neigh with joy, and trot up to him. He would pat and stroke her and say, 'Well, old Pet. How is your little Darkie?' I was a dull black, so he called me Darkie. Then he would give me a piece of bread, which was very good, and sometimes he brought a carrot for my mother. All the horses would come to him, but I think we were his favourites. My mother always took him to the town on a market day in a light gig.

There was a ploughboy, Dick, who sometimes came into our field to pluck blackberries from the hedge. When he had eaten all he wanted, he would have what he called fun with the colts, throwing stones and sticks at them to make them gallop. We did not much mind him, for we could gallop off; but sometimes a stone would hit and hurt us.

One day he was at this game, and did not know that the

master was in the next field; but he was there watching what was going on. Over the hedge he jumped in a moment, and catching Dick by his arm, gave him such a box on the ear as made him roar with pain. As soon as we saw the master, we trotted up nearer to see what was going on.

'Bad boy!' he said. 'Bad boy, to chase the colts! This is not the first time, nor the second, but it shall be the last. Take your money and go home. I shall not want you on my farm again.' So we never saw Dick again. Old Daniel, the man who looked after the horses, was just as gentle as our master, so we were well off.

The Hunt

Before I was two years old, something happened which I have never forgotten.

It was early in the spring; there had been a little frost in the night, and a light mist still hung over the plantations and meadows. The other colts and I were feeding at the lower part of the field when we heard, in the distance, what sounded like the cry of dogs.

The oldest of the colts raised his head, pricked up his ears, and said, 'There are the hounds!' and immediately cantered off, followed by the rest of us, to the upper part of the field, where we could look over the hedge and see several fields, beyond. My mother and an old riding horse belonging to our master were also standing near, and seemed to know all about it.

'They have found a hare,' said my mother; 'and if they come this way, we shall see the hunt.'

Soon the dogs were all tearing down the field of young wheat next to our meadow. I never heard such a noise as they made. They did not bark, nor howl, nor whine, but kept up a 'Yo! yo, o, o! Yo! yo, o, o!' at the top of their voices.

After them came a number of men on horseback, some of them in green coats, all galloping as fast as they could.

The old horse snorted and looked eagerly towards them; and we young colts wanted to be galloping with them, but they were soon away into the fields lower down. Here it seemed as if they had come to a halt; the dogs left off barking, and ran about in every direction with their noses to the ground.

'They have lost the scent,' said the old horse; 'perhaps the hare will get away.'

'What hare?' I said.

'Oh! I don't know *what* hare; possibly it may be one of our own hares out of the plantation. Any hare they can find will do for the dogs and men to run after;' and before long the dogs began their 'Yo! yo, o, o!' again, and back they came all together at full speed, making straight for our meadow at the part where the high bank and hedge overhang the brook.

'Now we shall see the hare,' said my mother; and just then a hare, wild with fright, rushed by, and made for the plantation. On came the dogs; they burst over the bank, leapt a stream and came dashing across the field, followed by the huntsmen. Six or eight men leaped their horses clean over, close upon the dogs. The hare tried to get through the fence; it was too thick, and she turned sharp round to make for the road, but it was too late; the dogs were upon her with their wild cries; we heard one shriek, and that was the end of her. One of the huntsmen rode up and whipped off the dogs, who would soon have torn her to pieces. He held her up by the leg, torn and bleeding, and all the gentlemen seemed well pleased.

As for me, I was so astonished that I did not at first see what was going on by the brook; but when I did look, there was a sad sight; two fine horses were down, one was struggling in the stream, and the other was groaning on the grass. One

Just then the hare, wild with fright, rushed by.

of the riders was getting out of the water, covered with mud, and the other lay still.

'His neck is broken,' said my mother.

'And serves him right, too,' said one of the colts.

I thought the same, but my mother did not join in with us.

'Well! no,' she said, 'you must not say that; but though I am an old horse, and have seen and heard a great deal, I never yet could make out why men are so fond of this sport; they often hurt themselves, often spoil good horses and tear up the fields, and all for a hare, or a fox, or a stag, that they could get more easily some other way; but we are only horses, and don't know.'

Whilst my mother was saying this we stood and looked on. Many of the riders had gone to the young man; but my master, who had been watching what was going on, was the first to raise him. His head fell back and his arms hung down, and everyone looked very serious. There was no noise now; even the dogs were quiet, and seemed to know that something was wrong. They carried him to our master's house. I heard afterwards that it was young George Gordon, the squire's only son, a fine, tall young man, and the pride of his family.

There was now riding off in all directions: to the doctor's, to the farrier's and no doubt to Squire Gordon's, to let him know about his son. When Mr Bond, the farrier, came to look at the black horse that lay groaning on the grass, he felt him all over and shook his head; one of his legs was broken. Then someone ran to our master's house and came back with a gun; presently there was a loud bang and a dreadful shriek, and then all was still; the black horse moved no more.

My mother seemed much troubled; she said she had known that horse for years, and that his name was 'Rob Roy'; he was a good bold horse, and there was no vice in him. She never would go to that part of the field afterwards.

My Breaking In

I was now beginning to grow handsome; my coat had grown fine and soft, and was bright black. I had one white foot, and a pretty white star on my forehead. I was thought very handsome; my master would not sell me till I was four years old; he said lads ought not to work like men, and colts ought not to work like horses till they were quite grown up.

When I was four years old, Squire Gordon came to look at me. He examined my eyes, my mouth, and my legs; he felt them all down; and then I had to walk and trot and gallop before him. He seemed to like me, and said, 'When he has been well broken in, he will do very well.' My master said he would break me in himself, as he should not like me to be frightened or hurt, and he lost no time about it, for the next day he began.

Everyone may not know what breaking in is, therefore I will describe it. It means to teach a horse to wear a saddle and bridle and to carry on his back a man, woman, or child; to go just the way they wish, and to go quietly. Besides this, he has to learn to wear a collar, a crupper, and a breeching, and to stand still whilst they are on; then to have a cart or a chaise fixed behind him, so that he cannot walk or trot without dragging it after him; and he must go fast or slow, just as his driver wishes. He must never start at what he sees, nor speak to other horses, nor bite, nor kick, nor have any will of his own, but always do his master's will, even though he may be very tired or hungry. But the worst of all is, when his harness is once on, he may neither jump for joy nor lie down for weariness. So you see, this breaking in is a great thing.

I had, of course, long been used to a halter and a headstall, and to be led about quietly in the fields and lanes; but now I was to have a bit and bridle. My master gave me some oats as usual, and after a good deal of coaxing, he got the bit into my mouth, and the bridle fixed, but it was a nasty thing! Those who have never had a bit in their mouths cannot think how bad it feels; a great piece of cold hard steel as thick as a man's finger is pushed into your mouth, between the teeth and over the tongue, with the ends coming out at the corner of your mouth, and held fast there by straps over your head, under your throat, round your nose, and under your chin; so that by no means in the world can you get rid of the nasty hard thing; it is very bad! Yes, very bad! At least I thought so, but I knew my mother always wore one when she went out and all horses did when they were grown up. So, what with the nice oats, and with my master's pats, kind words, and gentle ways, I got to wear my bit and bridle.

Next came the saddle, but that was not half so bad; my master put it on my back very gently, whilst old Daniel held my head; he then made the girths fast under my body, patting and talking to me all the time; then I had a few oats, then a little leading about, and this he did every day till I began to look for the oats and the saddle. Then, my master got on my back and rode me round the meadow on the soft grass. I certainly did feel queer; but I must say I felt rather proud to carry my master, and as he continued to ride me a little every day, I soon became accustomed to it.

The next unpleasant business was putting on the iron shoes; that, too, was very hard at first. My master went with me to the smith's forge, to see that I was not hurt or frightened. The blacksmith took my feet in his hand, one after the other, and cut away some of the hoof. It did not hurt me, so I stood still on three legs till he had done them all. Then he took a piece of iron the shape of my foot, and clapped it on, and drove some nails through the shoe right into my hoof, so that the shoe was firmly on. My feet felt very stiff and heavy, but in time I got used to it.

And now, having got so far, my master went on to break me to harness; there were more new things to wear. First, a stiff heavy collar just on my neck, and a bridle with great sidepieces, called blinkers, against my eyes; and blinkers indeed they were, for I could not see on either side, but only straight in front of me.

Next there was a small saddle with a nasty stiff strap that went right under my tail; that was the crupper. I hated the crupper — to have my long tail doubled up and poked through that strap was almost as bad as the bit. I never felt more like kicking, but of course I could not kick such a good master, and so in time I got used to everything, and could do my work as well as my mother.

I must not forget to mention one part of my training, which I have always considered a very great advantage. My master sent me for a fortnight to a neighbouring farmer who had a meadow which was skirted on one side by the railway. Here were some sheep and cows, and I was turned in amongst them.

I shall never forget the first train that ran by. I was feeding quietly near the fence which separated the meadow from the railway, when I heard a strange sound at a distance, and before I knew whence it came — with a rush and a clatter and a puffing out of smoke — a long black train of something flew by, and was gone almost before I could draw my breath. I turned and galloped to the farther side of the meadow as fast as I could go, and there I stood, snorting with astonishment and fear. In the course of the day many other trains went by, some more slowly; these drew up at the station close by, and sometimes made an awful shriek and groan before they stopped. I thought it very dreadful, but the cows went on eating quietly, and hardly raised their heads as the black, frightful thing came puffing and grinding past.

For the first few days I could not feed in peace; but as

I found that this terrible creature never came into the field, or did me any harm, I began to disregard it; and very soon I cared as little about the passing of a train as the cows and sheep did.

Since then I have seen horses much alarmed and restive at the sight or sound of a steam engine; but thanks to my master's care, I am as fearless at railway stations as in my own stable.

Now if anyone wants to break in a young horse well, that is the way.

My master often drove me in a double harness with my mother, because she was steady, and could teach me, better than a strange horse, how to go. She told me the better I behaved, the better I should be treated, and that it was wisest to do my best to please my master; 'but,' said she, 'there are a great many kinds of men; there are good, thoughtful men like our master, that any horse may be proud to serve; but there are bad, cruel men, who never ought to have a horse or dog to call their own. Besides, there are a great many foolish men — vain, ignorant, and careless — who never trouble themselves to think; these, more than any others, spoil horses, just for want of sense. They don't mean it, but they do it for all that. I hope you will fall into good hands, but a horse never knows who may buy him, or who may drive him. It is all a chance for us, but still I say, do your best whatever it is, and keep up your good name.'

Birtwick Park

At this time I used to stand in the stable, and my coat was brushed every day till it shone like a rook's wing. It was early in May, when there came a man from Squire Gordon's who took me away to the Hall. My master said, 'Good-bye, Darkie; be a good horse, and always do your best.' I could not say 'good-bye', so I put my nose into his hand; he patted me kindly, and I left my first home.

Squire Gordon's Park skirted the village of Birtwick. It was entered by a large iron gate, at which stood the first lodge, and then you trotted along on a smooth road between clumps of large old trees. Then came another lodge and another gate, which brought you to the house and the gardens. Beyond this lay the home paddock, the old orchard, and the stables. There was accommodation for many horses and carriages, but I need only describe the stable into which I was taken. This was very roomy, with four good stalls. A large swinging window opened into the yard, which made it pleasant and airy.

The first stall was a large square one, shut in behind with a wooden gate; the others were common stalls, good stalls, but not nearly so large. The first had a low rack for hay and a low manger for corn; it was called a loose-box, because the horse that was put into it was not tied up, but left loose, to do as he liked. It is a great thing to have a loose-box.

Into this fine box the groom put me; it was clean, sweet, and airy. I never was in a better box than that and the sides were not so high but that I could see all that went on through the iron rails that were at the top.

He gave me some very nice oats, patted me, spoke kindly, and then went away.

When I had eaten the corn, I looked round. In the stall next to mine stood a little fat grey pony, with a thick mane and tail, a very pretty head, and a pert little nose.

I put my head up to the iron rails at the top of my box, and said, 'How do you do? What is your name?'

He turned round as far as his halter would allow, held up his head, and said, 'My name is Merrylegs! I am very handsome. I carry the young ladies on my back, and some times I take our mistress out in the low chair. They think a great deal of me, and so does James. Are you going to live next door to me in this box?'

I said, 'Yes.'

'Well, then,' he said, 'I hope you are good-tempered; I do not like anyone next door who bites.'

Just then a horse's head looked over from the stall beyond; the ears were laid back, and the eyes looked rather ill-tempered. This was a tall chestnut mare, with a long handsome neck; she looked across to me and said, 'So it is you who has turned me out of my box; it is a very strange thing for a colt like you to come and turn a lady out of her own home.'

'I beg your pardon,' I said, 'I have turned no one out; the man who brought me put me here, and I had nothing to do with it; and as to my being a colt, I am turned four years old, and am a grown-up horse. I never had words yet with horse or mane, and it is my wish to live at peace.'

'Well,' she said, 'we shall see; of course I do not want to have words with a young thing like you.'

I said no more.

In the afternoon when she went out, Merrylegs told me all about it.

'The thing is this,' said Merrylegs. 'Ginger has a bad habit of biting and snapping; that is why they call her Ginger, and when she was in the loose-box, she used to snap very much. One day she bit James in the arm and made it bleed, and so Miss Flora and Miss Jessie, who are very fond of me, were afraid to come into the stable. They used to bring me nice things to eat, an apple or a carrot, or a piece of bread; but after Ginger stood in that box, they dared not come, and I missed them very much. I hope they will come again now, if you do not bite or snap.'

I told him I never bit anything but grass, hay and corn, and could not think what pleasure Ginger found in it.

'Well, I don't think she does find pleasure in it,' said Merrylegs; 'it is just a bad habit. She says no one was ever kind to her, and why should she not bite? Of course it is a very bad habit; but I am sure, if all she says is true, she must have been very ill-used before she came here. John does all he can to please her, and James does all he can, and our master never uses a whip if a horse acts right; so I think she might be good-tempered here. You see,' he said with a wise look, 'I am twelve years old; I know a great deal, and I can tell you there is not a better place for a horse all round the country than this. John is the best groom that ever was, and has been here fourteen years; and you never saw such a kind boy as James is, so that it is all Ginger's own fault that she did not stay in that box.'

A Fair Start

The name of the coachman was John Manly. He had a wife and one little child, and they lived in the coachman's cottage, very near the stables.

The next morning he took me into the yard and gave me a good grooming, and just as I was going into my box with my coat soft and bright, the Squire came to look at me, and seemed pleased. 'John,' he said, 'I meant to try the new horse this morning, but I have other business. You may as well take him for a round after breakfast. Go by the common and Highwood, and back by the watermill and the river; that will show his paces.'

'I will, sir,' said John. After breakfast he came and fitted me with a bridle. He was very particular in letting out and taking in the straps, to fit my head comfortably. Then he brought the saddle, but it was not broad enough for my back; he saw it in a minute and went for another, which fitted nicely. He rode me first slowly, then at a trot, then at a canter, and when we were on the common he gave me a light touch with his whip, and we had a splendid good long gallop.

'Ho, ho! my boy,' he said, as he pulled me up, 'you would like to follow the hounds, I think.'

As we came back through the Park, we met the Squire and Mrs Gordon walking; they stopped, and John jumped off.

'Well, John, how does he go?'

'First rate, sir,' answered John. 'He is as fleet as a deer, and has a fine spirit, too; but the lightest touch of the rein will guide him. Down at the end of the common we met one of those travelling carts hung all over with baskets, rugs, and such like. As you know, sir, many horses will not pass those carts quietly; but he just took a good look at it, and then went on as quiet and pleasant as could be. They were shooting rabbits near the Highwood, and a gun went off close by; he pulled up a little and looked, but did not stir a step to right or left. I just held the rein steady and did not hurry him, and it's my opinion he has not been frightened or ill-used while he was young.'

'That's well,' said the Squire. 'I will try him myself to-morrow.'

The next day I was brought up for my master. I remembered my mother's counsel and my good old master's, and I tried to do exactly what he wanted me to do. I found he was a very good rider, and thoughtful for his horse, too. When he came home, the lady was at the hall door as he rode up.

'Well, my dear,' she said, 'how do you like him?'

'He is exactly what John said,' he replied; 'a pleasanter creature I never wish to mount. What shall we call him?'

'Would you like "Ebony"?' said she. 'He is as black as ebony.'

'No, not Ebony.'

'Will you call him "Blackbird", like your uncle's old horse?'

'No, he is far handsomer than old Blackbird ever was.'

'Yes,' she said, 'he is really quite a beauty, and he has such a sweet good-tempered face and such a fine intelligent eye — what do you say to calling him "Black Beauty"?'

'Black Beauty — why — yes, I think that is a very good name. If you like, it shall be his name,' and so it was.

When John went into the stable, he told James that master and mistress had chosen a good sensible English name for me, that meant something; not like Marengo, or Pegasus, or Abdullah. They both laughed, and James said, 'If it was not for bringing back the past, I should have named him "Rob Roy", for I never saw two horses more alike.'

'That's no wonder,' said John; 'didn't you know that Farmer Grey's old Duchess was the mother of them both?'

I had never heard that before. So poor Rob Roy who was killed at that hunt was my brother! I did not wonder that my mother was troubled. It seems that horses have no relations; at least, they never know each other after they are sold.

John seemed very proud of me; he used to make my mane and tail almost as smooth as a lady's hair, and he would talk to me a great deal. Of course I did not understand all he said, but I learned more and more to know what he meant, and what he wanted me to do. I grew very fond of him; he was so gentle and kind, he seemed to know just how a horse feels. And when he cleaned me, he knew the tender places, and the ticklish places; when he brushed my head, he went as carefully over my eyes as if they were his own, and never stirred up any ill-temper.

James Howard, the stable boy, was just as gentle and pleasant in his way, so I thought myself well off. There was another man who helped in the yard but he had very little to do with Ginger and me.

A few days after this I had to go out with Ginger in the carriage. I wondered how we should get on together; but except for laying her ears back when I was led up to her, she

Ginger and I went out together in the carriage.

behaved very well. She did her work honestly, and did her full share; and I never wish to have a better partner in double harness. When we came to a hill, instead of slackening her pace, she would throw her weight right into the collar, and pull away straight up. We both had the same sort of courage at our work, and John had oftener to hold us in than to urge us forward. He never had to use the whip with either of us. Our paces were much the same and I found it very easy to keep step with her when trotting, which made it pleasant, and master always liked it when we kept step well, and so did John. After we had been out two or three times together we grew quite friendly and sociable, which made me feel very much at home.

As for Merrylegs, he and I soon became friends. He was such a cheerful, plucky, good-tempered little fellow, that he was a favourite with everyone — especially with Miss Jessie and Flora, who used to ride him about in the orchard, and have fine games with him and their little dog, Frisky.

Our master had two other horses that stood in another stable. One was Justice, a roan cob, used for riding, or for the luggage cart. The other was an old brown hunter, named Sir Oliver; he was past work now, but was a great favourite with the master, who gave him the run of the park. He sometimes did a little light carting on the estate, or carried one of the young ladies when they rode out with their father; for he was very gentle, and could be trusted with a child as well as Merrylegs. The cob was a strong, well-made, good-tempered horse, and we sometimes had a little chat in the paddock; but of course I could not be on such friendly terms with him as with Ginger, who stood in the same stable.

Merrylegs

Mr Blomefield, the Vicar, had a large family of boys and

girls; sometimes they used to come and play with Miss Jessie and Flora. One of the girls was as old as Miss Jessie; two of the boys were older, and there were several little ones. When they came, there was plenty of work for Merrylegs, for nothing pleased them so much as getting on him by turns and riding him all about the orchard and the home paddock, and this they would do by the hour together.

One afternoon he had been out with them a long time, and when James brought him in and put on his halter, he said, 'there, you rogue, mind how you behave yourself, or we shall get into trouble.'

'What have you been doing, Merrylegs?' I asked.

'Oh!' said he, tossing his little head, 'I have only been giving those young people a lesson. They did not know when they had had enough, nor when I had had enough, so I just pitched them off backwards; that was the only thing they could understand.'

'What?' said I, 'you threw the children off? I thought you knew better than that. Did you throw Miss Jessie or Miss Flora?'

He looked very much offended, and said, 'Of course not, I would not do such a thing for the best oats that ever came into the stable. Why, I am as careful of your young ladies as the master could be, and as for the little ones, it is I who teach them to ride. When they seem frightened or a little unsteady on my back, I go as smooth and as quiet as old pussy when she is after a bird; and when they are all right, I go on again faster, so don't you trouble yourself preaching to me; I am the best riding master those children have.

'It is not them, it is the boys. Boys,' said he, shaking his mane, 'are quite different; they must be broken in, as we were broken in when we were colts, and must be taught what's what. The other children had ridden me about for nearly two hours, and then the boys thought it was their turn, and so it was, and I was quite agreeable. They rode me by turns, and I galloped them about up and down the fields and all about the orchard for a good hour. They had each cut a great hazel stick for a riding whip, and laid on a little too hard; but I took it in good part, till at last I thought we had had enough, so I stopped two or three times by way of a hint. Boys, you see, think a horse or pony is like a steam engine or a threshing machine, and can go on as long and as fast as they please; they never think that a pony can get tired, or have any feelings. So as the one who was whipping me could not understand, I just rose up on my hind legs and let him slip off behind — that was all; he mounted me again, and I did the same.

'Then the other boy got up, and as soon as he began to use his stick I laid him on the grass, and so on, till they were able to understand, that was all. They are not bad boys; they don't wish to be cruel. I like them very much; but you see I had to give them a lesson. When they brought me to James and told him, I think he was very angry to see such big sticks. He said they were only fit for drovers or gipsies, and not for young gentlemen.'

'If I had been you,' said Ginger, 'I would have given those boys a good kick, and that would have given them a lesson.'

'No doubt you would,' said Merrylegs, 'but then I am not quite such a fool (begging your pardon) as to anger our master or make James ashamed of me; besides, those children are under my charge when they are riding; I tell you they are entrusted to me.

'Why, only the other day I heard our master say to Mrs Blomefield, "My dear madam, you need not be anxious about the children. My old Merrylegs will take as much care of them as you or I could: I assure you I would not sell that pony for any money, he is so perfectly good-tempered and trustworthy." And do you think I am such an ungrateful brute as to forget all the kind treatment I have had here for five years, and all the trust they place in me, and turn vicious because a couple of ignorant boys used me badly? No! No! You never had a good place where they were kind to you; and so you don't know, and I'm sorry for you, but I can tell you good places make good horses. I wouldn't vex our people for anything; I love them, I do,' said Merrylegs, and he gave a low 'ho, ho, ho,' through his nose, as he used to do in the morning when he heard James's footstep at the door.

'Besides,' he went on, 'if I took to kicking, where should I be? Why, sold in a jiffy, and I might find myself slaved about under a butcher's boy, or worked to death at some seaside place where no one cared for me, except to find out how fast I could go, or be flogged along in some cart with three or four great men in it going out for a Sunday spree. No,' said he, shaking his head, 'I hope I shall never come to that.'

A Stormy Day

One day late in the autumn, my master had a long journey to make on business. I was put into the dog-cart, and John went with his master. I always liked to go in the dog-cart; it was so light, and the high wheels ran along so pleasantly.

There had been a great deal of rain, and now the wind was very high, and blew the dry leaves across the road in a shower. We went along merrily till we came to the toll-bar and the low wooden bridge. The river banks were rather high, and the bridge, instead of rising, went across just level, so that in the middle, if the river was full, the water would be nearly up to the woodwork and planks; but, as there were good substantial rails on each side, people did not mind it.

The man at the gate said the river was rising fast and he feared it would be a bad night. Many of the meadows were under water, and in one low part of the road the water was half-way up to my knees; the bottom was good, and master drove gently, so it did not matter.

When we got to the town, of course, I had a good feed, but, as the master's business engaged him a long time, we did not start for home till rather late in the afternoon. The wind was then much higher, and I heard the master say to John he had never been out in such a storm; and so I thought, as we went along the outskirts of the wood, where the great branches were swaying about like twigs, and the rushing sound was terrible.

'I wish we were well out of this wood,' cried my master.

'Yes, sir,' said John, 'it would be rather awkward if one of these branches came down upon us.'

The words were scarcely out of his mouth when there was a groan, and a crack, and a splitting sound; and tearing, crashing down amongst the other trees came an oak, torn up by the roots, and it fell right across the road just before us. I will never say I was not frightened, for I was. I stopped still, and I believe I trembled; of course I did not turn round or run away; I was not brought up to do that. John jumped out and in a moment was at my head.

'That was a very near touch,' said my master. 'What's to be done now?'

'Well, sir, we can't drive over that tree nor yet get round it. There will be nothing for it but to go back to the four crossways, and that will be a good six miles before we get round to the wooden bridge again; it will make us late, but the horse is fresh.'

So back we went, and round by the crossroads; but by the time we got to the bridge it was very nearly dark. We could just see that the water was over the middle of it, but master did not stop. We were going along at a good pace, but the moment my feet touched the first part of the bridge, I felt sure there was something wrong. I dared not go forward, and stopped dead.

'Go on, Beauty,' said my master, and he gave me a touch with the whip, but I dared not stir. He gave me a sharp cut; I jumped, but I dared not go forward.

'There's something wrong, sir,' said John, and he sprang out of the dog-cart and came to my head and looked all about. He tried to lead me forward. 'Come on, Beauty, what's the matter?' Of course I could not tell him, but I knew very well that the bridge was not safe.

Just then the man at the toll-gate on the other side ran out of the house, waving a torch about like one mad.

'Hoy, hoy, hoy, halloo, stop!' he cried.

'What's the matter?' shouted my master.

'The bridge is broken in the middle, and part of it is carried away! If you come on you'll be into the river.'

'Thank God!' said my master. 'You Beauty!' said John, and took the bridle and gently turned me round to the right-hand road by the riverside. The sun had set, and the wind seemed to have lulled after that furious blast which tore up the tree. It grew darker and darker, stiller and stiller, as I trotted quietly along, the wheels hardly making a sound on the soft road.

For a good while neither master nor John spoke, and then master began in a serious voice. I could not understand all of what they said, but I found they thought, if I had gone on as the master wanted me, most likely the bridge would have given way under us, and horse, chaise, master, and John would have fallen into the river. And as the current was flowing very strongly, and there was no light and no help at hand, it was more than likely we should all have been drowned.

Master said God had given men reason by which they could find out things for themselves, but he had given animals knowledge which did not depend on reason, and which was much more prompt and perfect in its way, and by which they had often saved the lives of men.

John had many stories to tell of dogs and horses, and the wonderful things they had done; he thought people did not value their animals half enough, nor make friends of them as they ought to do. I am sure he makes friends of them if ever a man did.

At last we came to the park gates, and found the gardener looking out for us. He said that mistress had been in a dreadful state ever since dark, fearing some accident had happened, and that she had sent James off on Justice, the roan cob, towards the wooden bridge to make inquiries about us.

We saw a light at the hall door and at the upper windows, and as we came up, mistress ran out, saying, 'Are you really safe, my dear? Oh! I have been so anxious, fancying all sorts of things. Have you had an accident?'

'No my dear; but if your Black Beauty had not been wiser than we were, we should all have been carried down the river at the wooden bridge.' I heard no more, as they went into the house, and John took me to the stable. Oh, what a good supper he gave me that night, a good bran mash and some crushed beans with my oats, and such a thick bed of straw! I was glad of it, for I was tired.

Up in the Woods

by Ursula Moray Williams

We were all going to live in Canada...my mother, my father, my brother Stephen, and myself, Moira Denning.

My father is an engineer. A friend in Canada found him a job, and he went on ahead of the rest of the family to get a house for us to live in, while Mother sold our English home and packed, and Stephen finished his last term at school.

Then we found we could not get passages till May, and as the house was not yet handed over, we half unpacked again, and went on living in it...at least, Mother and Stephen did, while I went back for another term at St Margaret's, wondering what it would be like to go to school in Canada.

Stephen was going in for forestry, so while he stayed at home he toned up his muscles by working with a timber gang on a neighbouring estate. We knew the land agent, Mr Wilson, and he fixed up the job for Stephen.

When I came home for Easter he was still working there and he looked quite tall and tough.

Stephen used to leave the house early in the morning and sometimes Mother or I would get up and cut his sandwiches, while on other days I would go up to the estate later in the morning, on my bicycle, to take him something hot which we had baked.

It was fun watching Stephen working with the men. Sometimes they were planting...acres and acres of little spruce firs, while the tractor ahead turned up the earth, and the men moved down the rows so slowly that you thought the job would never be finished...but a few days later, there it was, all planted with thousands of little green trees, all bent on becoming a new forest.

One day when I brought Stephen's dinner, he and another man, whom Stephen called Dumb Dave, were working on smaller trees with axes. Dave was not really at all dumb, but I seldom heard him say a word, and he had the reputation for never speaking while he worked. This must have been quite hard on Stephen, who is a talkative kind of boy.

This morning they were going at it hard...swinging their arms like real backwoodsmen. They had made quite a clearing by the side of the path.

I sat on a stump to watch, and thought Stephen looked just like Daddy used to look, chopping away at the trees in our little plantation where he had taught us both how to use axes, long ago when we were quite young.

The trees were not big, but they were solid, and it was fine to see the axes bite into the notch Stephen and Dave had made...then the gold and silver chips of wood flying, the sway, the crackle and the toppling of the tree, till with a swish of branches another trunk thudded to earth at the feet of the conquerors.

I wasn't sorry to see Stephen and Dave had an audience besides myself.

Two people had come along the track. One was a girl on horseback.

We knew her from dances at Christmas. She was the daughter of Colonel Massey, who owned the woods. Her name was Frances.

She said 'Hullo!' at once, addressing the greeting particularly to Stephen, with whom she had danced quite a lot. 'This is my cousin, Derek!' Frances said.

'We've met, too,' Derek said, looking quickly at Stephen.

'We were at the same school,' Stephen explained. 'You left about two years before I did,' he said to Derek.

'About that,' said Derek. There was a pause, and then Frances said, 'I had no idea you lived so close...where do you live?'

'Well...about three miles away at the moment,' Stephen said, 'but we are just off to live in Canada!'

'Ah! The great Dominions debarkation!' said Derek cleverly. 'I've heard of it. What are you going to do there?'

'Lumberjack,' said Stephen briefly, turning back towards Dumb Dave, who was patiently waiting to go on with his work.

Derek went on talking to me, and it wasn't long before he let me know that he was just going up to Oxford, which he obviously thought was much better than being a lumberjack in Canada.

I explained rather quickly that Stephen was going to work at being a lumberjack in the summer, and was going to a Canadian university during the winter, where he would work for a degree in forestry.

'Oh, do they have universities in Canada?' asked Frances, who had dismounted.

I very nearly asked her if she ever read the papers, only I was wholly taken up with looking at her horse. He was one of the most handsome I have ever seen, and though I hardly ever get a chance of riding, I do love horses.

'What is his name?' I asked.

'Sir Ricco. He's heaven, isn't he?' said Frances, rubbing her cheek against his nose.

I had my slacks on, but she didn't offer me a ride.

Derek had strolled after Stephen, watching him at work. 'That looks good fun,' he said. 'Let me have a knock — I'd like to see what state my muscles are in!'

Stephen drew back and looked at Dumb Dave, who remained perfectly impassive.

They were working with long-handled axes. The blades were immensely sharp, and they were not the kind of tools to lend to a novice.

Dave took the most sensible course; he just walked away. 'We've finished here...must get back to the yard,' he muttered.

I wanted Stephen to follow him there and then. He could have done so...he was on a job! But I could see that it was awkward. He was quite close to Derek, and facing him. Though Derek was half laughing, he had put out his hand very firmly and had rested it on the axe.

It was his uncle's axe, too, and his uncle's trees, and unless Frances said something it was difficult for us to interfere.

Frances did not seem very interested.

'Do you think he ought to?' I murmured.

'He only wants to show off,' Frances said. 'It can't hurt the trees, can it? Do they have to be cut in a certain way? Surely one won't matter. Go on, then...show us how!' she called jeeringly to her cousin.

Derek took the axe, and Stephen came to stand by me. He chewed his lip a bit at first, but when Derek began to make quite a good job of it he relaxed a little.

Derek was clumsy, but he cut as he had watched the others do, and his shoulders were broad and powerful.

We all cheered as the tree bent and crashed. Sir Ricco threw his head in the air and pranced a little.

'Just trim it off!' Derek cried, swinging the axe at the sliver of wood sticking up from the torn stump.

Then it happened.

The blade of the axe slipped down the side of the chip and went into his leg.

The next few minutes were so dreadful I don't think I will ever forget them, and the worst part was when I realised that *I* had to do something — and do something quickly, too.

Frances gave a terrified gasp and seemed to freeze still, holding Sir Ricco.

Stephen and I rushed to Derek. We rolled down his sock, and turned up his trouser leg and pressed on the awful spurts of blood that kept coming out of the gash. Then Stephen pressed while I wrapped up his watch in a handkerchief as I had learned in first-aid classes, and made a tourniquet by putting it under Derek's knee, tying it very tightly with Derek's own scarf. I dared not even look till Stephen said rather shakily, 'It's stopped...nearly.'

Derek was frightfully brave. He was turning the most awful colour, and his chin looked as if his teeth were chattering, but he said, 'It's all right,' whenever we looked at him, and even tried to laugh.

Poor Frances looked nearly as bad, as I saw when I asked her for a handkerchief to clean up some of the mess. She just flung it at me, and then suddenly sat down on a stump and put her head between her knees.

'I'll be all right,' she said. 'I just can't bear looking. I'm frightfully sorry...'

I felt sorry for her. She couldn't help it, and after all, Derek was her cousin.

'Tell her to ride down to the estate office and get help,' Stephen said.

But Frances could not get on to her horse.

'I'll be all right... just leave me alone,' she kept saying. 'You go. Take Sir Ricco.'

Stephen could not ride, and Dumb Dave had long ago disappeared.

Even in that crisis I was excited at the thought of riding Sir Ricco. But I didn't like leaving Derek, because Frances could not help, and Stephen had never done first-aid.

'You must loosen the bandage round his knee every few

minutes,' I told him, 'and then tie it tightly again. And put your sweater over him...he's shivering!'

As I climbed on a stump to mount Sir Ricco, Frances and Stephen were piling their coats and jerseys on to Derek, and he was protesting feebly, looking bluer than ever.

Sir Ricco hardly gave me time to get my feet into the stirrups, which were too long for me, anyway. Frances had longer legs than I.

He whipped round in his tracks and pelted down the ride with earth scattering under his pounding hoofs.

I gathered up the reins and settled down to keep my balance and enjoy it.

We flew like the wind. I did not know the wood, but Sir Ricco did, and I believe he took every short cut there was to take.

I had to cling to the pommel every now and then as he swerved suddenly to right or left, and I was glad there was nobody there to see my style. I am far from being an expert rider at the best of times, but that day it was all I could do to stay in the saddle, and I lost my stirrups long before we got to the office.

But worse was to come. As we arrived in the yard, Sir Ricco passed under the low boughs of an old chestnut tree. I did not duck in time...and was neatly swept off, almost on the doorstep of the estate office. Mr Wilson, hearing the noise, came out and ran towards me.

'Is Frances hurt?' he asked, helping me up.

'It's Derek,' I explained, and soon telephones were ringing for the doctor and the ambulance, and messages sent to the house where Frances lived. With a great sense of relief I realised that I was not responsible any more.

Mr Wilson's secretary gave me a cup of tea, and while I was drinking it she emptied the dregs out of a thermos and filled it with tea for Derek. Mr Wilson got his Land Rover

I did not duck in time and was neatly swept off.

out of the yard and called two of the men working outside.

'Jump in,' he said to me, but I turned down his offer. 'I am going back on Sir Ricco!' I said.

Mr Wilson nodded and set off along the track, leaving me clutching the thermos which I had forgotten to give him for Derek.

I shortened the stirrups while the secretary held Sir Ricco.

Somehow I mounted and started back, quite determined to arrive and give Derek his hot tea before Mr Wilson got there in the Land Rover.

I could hear the car grinding up the wide track as Sir Ricco and I set off through the woods. This time I bent low whenever the trees seemed to overhang the path. The thermos pressed most uncomfortably against my chest and we flew like the wind.

We arrived while the Land Rover was still a rumble in the distancc and I jumped off Sir Ricco, handing the reins to Frances. 'You have been quick,' she said, smiling.

She looked all right again, and even Derek looked a little less ghastly. 'We were talking about Canada...' he said.

Then the Land Rover arrived, and after a few very busy moments Stephen and I suddenly found ourselves alone in the wood, with the noise of the Land Rover becoming fainter in the distance, and the hoofs of Sir Ricco carrying Frances home just an echo that we thought we heard. But she had said I could ride him again, and that was something I could look forward to before leaving for Canada.

I was awfully tired. The exhilaration of that wonderful ride seemed somehow to have faded, and I began to feel rather weak at the knees after all the excitement.

'Have a sandwich and some pie?' said Stephen, making room for me beside him on the fallen log. 'And then, I think, as Dumb Dave says, we've finished here!'

Princess at the Circus

by Kathleen O'Farrell

It was Sunday afternoon and Cloverlands was steeped in sunshine. The air was fragrant with the scents of autumn, and the purple and gold michaelmas daisies massed around the whitewashed farmhouse were alive with peacock butterflies. As it was fast approaching half past two, when the visitors were due to arrive, Albert Potter was busily sweeping the yard between the rows of stalls and making sure that everything was ship-shape. No hospital sister, fussing over her ward, could have been more particular than Albert.

On being asked where he worked, Albert would reply proudly, 'Cloverlands. You know, the Old Folks' Home for Horses, down Windmill Lane.'

Old Folks' home was a very apt description, because most of the residents of Cloverlands were horses or ponies who had spent all their lives working very hard and were now enjoying a pleasant retirement. Not all, however. There was a little donkey who had been rescued from a cruel owner, and a splendid shire horse in perfect health who had been saved from slaughter when his master bought a tractor.

Albert paused in front of a stall to stroke the nose of a beautiful cream-coloured pony. She had a thick mane, a smooth satiny coat, and bright intelligent eyes. 'And how is Your Royal Highness?' asked Albert, smiling at his little joke. 'I trust your leg is not hurting you today?' For the pony was called Princess. A scar on her near foreleg, and a slight limp, told of an old injury.

Over her comfortable, roomy stall her name was neatly printed, with the information that she had once been a circus pony. Opposite her was a retired racehorse called Morning Star, and beside her was old Annie, a piebald mare who had once pulled a coster's cart through the streets of London. But her best friend was Mick, the blind pit-pony. Because of his blindness Mick didn't go for a trot along the lanes each morning, so instead he was given the run of a small paddock. Princess could gaze across at him now, a pathetic little form, oddly still, like a pony carved from grey stone. All his life he had worked in the dark misery of the mines, and now that he was surrounded by flowers and trees and lovely colours he was not able to see them.

Princess loved Mick. Between the two animals was a silent understanding and affection that was touching to see. It pleased Major Pontefract very much. Major Pontefract, late of the army, was the Resident Manager of Cloverlands. He knew just about everything there was to know about horses, and lived in the picturesque half-timbered farmhouse with the thatched roof that stood in a delightfully old-fashioned garden between the stables and lake. He had a cheerful wife, always surrounded by leaping dogs, and a pretty daughter called Marion who sat in the small summer-house at visiting times, telling people all they needed to know about the horses, handing out booklets, and receiving donations.

In many ways Cloverlands reminded Princess of Beech Coppice, a farm where Princess had spent one winter several years before. Indeed, the layout of the farm had been very much like Cloverlands, except that the house had been square and Victorian, with a grey slate roof. And whereas Cloverlands had a dreamy, rather fairy-tale air about it, Beech Coppice had been business-like, noisy, and always throbbing with activity. It was, in fact, a very special sort of farm...

Princess had gone to Beech Coppice when she was four years old. She had previously belonged to a family who had one daughter, and who lived in the country. Then they had moved to the nearby town, and couldn't keep the pony any longer, so she came up for sale at the local auction.

She was just the type of pony Mr Bunting, the circus owner, was looking for: pretty, well trained and sweet tempered she would obviously be an ideal choice. It was autumn when he bought her, so Princess went straightaway with the circus to its winter quarters at Beech Coppice. Here, on this Sussex farm, she was to be trained as a liberty pony. All autumn and winter she would learn her routine so that when spring came she would be ready for the ring.

The man in charge of the ponies was called Alphonso. He was a lean, weather-beaten man in old tweeds, with startlingly blue eyes and a loud, jolly voice. Princess wasn't quite sure at first what to expect, but she found Alphonso firm but very gentle. He had spent all his life with ponies, and he loved them and had a real kinship with them. 'All you need to train a pony is kindness and an unending supply of carrots,' he would declare; and though he twirled his whip round and round his head and cracked it on the ground in the most alarming way, it was only for effect or to give the animals a signal, for he never hit any of them with it.

As a liberty pony Princess had no rider. The routine she had to learn was quite difficult, but being intelligent she picked it up fairly quickly. The ponies had to circle the ring, always anti-clockwise, obeying the signals Alphonso gave them. First they walked, then they trotted, turned round, and sometimes reared up. They even learned to pirouette, which looked extremely skilful. Every day they practised in a field near the stables, and if they did well they were rewarded with a pat and a carrot, or sometimes a juicy apple from the

Beech Coppice orchard, if they had done particularly well.

Princess soon learnt that circus folk never rested. The winter, in particular, was a very busy time for them. Being a relatively small circus Bunting's could not book great halls as some of the famous ones did, and they had learnt from bitter experience that people do not want to sit shivering under the Big Top when it is freezing hard outside, or even worse, when a gale is blowing. So winter was a time for training new animals, and for teaching the old stagers new routines or tricks. It was a time for painting caravans, inspecting and repairing the rolling-stock, making new costumes, new curtains, and catching up on a hundred and one lesser but still important tasks.

During the winter the children went to school regularly, but when the circus was on the move, they had to change schools constantly. Because of this they each carried a little card, bearing details of how advanced they were in different school subjects. Yet, strangely enough, despite this haphazard type of education, the children grew up bright and quick-witted and independent, well able to hold their own with other children from a more settled background.

It was a busy, happy, friendly atmosphere at Beech Coppice. Soon Princess got to know most of the other performers, both animal and human. There was Fritz, who was in charge of the Big Cats, as the lions were called, and fat, laughing Mitzi, his wife, who trained the chimps. There was Anne-Marie, a widow and the mother of two small girls, who did a very charming act with white doves. Then there were the famous Redskins, real live American Indians who performed amazing feats of horsemanship, Orlando the Spanish acrobat, and the Four Antonios, talented trapeze artists from Italy. There was Donovan, with his clever little terriers, and a small brown man who was in charge of the huge elephants. There was Jacko, the tall thin clown with long, gangling arms and legs. But the people Princess loved the best, apart from Alphonso, were Heidi and Joey.

They lived together in a pale green caravan with cherry-blossom on the curtains, the young girl and her elderly grandfather. Heidi's mother had been Swiss, her father English, but they had both died young and Joey had brought her up. Heidi was the bareback rider. She was not only a very polished performer for her seventeen years, she was also very pretty and extremely popular. As for Joey — he was the other clown, the little simpleton who was the butt of all Jacko's practical jokes, but it was always he who triumphed in the end.

Most circuses have one clown called Joey, in memory of the most famous clown of all times, Joseph Grimaldi, and this Joey was a very appealing man, with a half-sad, half-humorous face and a gentle, childlike voice. He was very fond of all the animals and birds, but he liked the ponies best of all, and he soon made friends with Princess. Nobody knew how old Joey was, but sometimes, when he removed his elaborate make-up, he looked very tired and surprisingly frail.

And so the wintry days passed by. Sometimes it was so cold that man and beast shivered in the frosty air. The duck-pond froze over, and the wind was as piercing as a sword; then the snow came, covering up the face of the stable clock and turning the whole farm into a magical place of shimmering white and silver. Mitzi, the lion-tamer's wife, did not laugh quite so much then. She walked about wrapped in thick clothes from top to toe. Yet Heidi glowed like a rose. She coaxed one of the men to make her a toboggan, then off she went with Anne-Marie's small daughters to have fun on the nearest hill.

Then one afternoon, almost like a miracle, the air was suddenly soft and sweet and mild, and a green haze shone on the trees. Spring had come at last, and the circus was due to take to the road again.

That was the start of even greater activity.

Next morning at four o'clock everyone was astir, children as well as grown-ups, preparing for the great adventure. Although it happened every year it was still an adventure, even to the older artists like Joey. Their first booking was at a large town on the Surrey-Sussex border, and in the preceding weeks the advance agent had been there to make all the arrangements. He had to find a site, obtain permission from the authorities, and locate firms who could supply the vast quantities of food that would be needed. And not only food — even more important than food was the supply of water. 'Just think,' Anne-Marie explained to her little girls, 'one elephant alone can drink over a hundred gallons of water in a week!' The elephant trainer had just told her this astonishing fact.

But all these preparations had been satisfactorily completed long before. In the opal light of very early morning the circus prapared to move off, knowing that all was well at the other end. Everything had been organised with the greatest of care. The heavier animals, such as the elephants, were transported by rail, while the smaller ones travelled in their living cages, mounted on trailers and towed by lorries. Behind these went the cars and caravans, the big vans filled with equipment, the mobile repair workshop, the fire-fighting unit, the band-wagon, and another one loaded with costumes and props. But Princess, to her great delight, was not to travel either by train or van. As Bunting's was a fairly small circus, and the distance to be covered was only twenty miles or so, the horses and ponies were to travel in single file behind the convoy of caravans and lorries.

It was still very early when the little cavalcade of ponies set off — Princess, Daisy, Susan, Captain and Bugle, Nicky,

The ponies set off very early in the morning.

Arabella and Windflower. Some had riders and some were on leading-reins, so they went quite slowly and all enjoyed the gentle exercise. One of Anne-Marie's daughters rode Princess, while her sister rode Nicky — though they switched to other mounts after a few miles so that none of the ponies should get tired. All the circus children rode well; even the very young ones had no fear. Close behind the ponies, though, and keeping an eye on them, came Heidi on her beloved chestnut — it was Joey who had thought of naming it Conker — with Alphonso on a great black horse called Emperor. It had rained during the night, so all the hedgerows sparkled diamond-bright; and everything smelt fresh and sweet and new. The sky was a clear silvery-blue, and little catkins swung gaily from the willows, while the birds worked themselves into transports over the dawn chorus. But Alphonso didn't like the wind.

'I hope this wind dies down,' he muttered. He looked around him anxiously, and Princess was soon to learn that circus folk fear the wind almost as much as fire. A strong wind can blow down tents, snap poles, and even destroy the Big Top.

But the wind calmed down as the day wore on, the sun shone warmly, and everyone was happy. By the time the horses and ponies reached the *tober*, as circus people call the site of the Big Top, the advance party was already there and well under way with their preparations. Never had Princess seen such activity! Everyone, regardless of age, worked his hardest. The two king poles, which were to support the Big Top, were already in position, and all around them men were swinging huge hammers as they drove hundreds of stakes into the ground. The Big Top was then laced together and hauled up by long guy ropes which were fixed firmly to the stakes. Everyone helped. Heidi, in tatty old jeans and a thick sweater, worked as hard as any man. Seeing her then, few people would have associated her with the idea of a glamorous bareback rider, wearing a pretty net tutu.

It was just as though a little town was being built up. Tents and caravans were set out neatly on all sides. There were canvas stables for the horses and ponies, each with a long row of stalls, and a canteen from which drifted a delicious smell of bacon and eggs, and coffee.

'Heavens, I'm hungry!' exclaimed Joey, and as he made for the canteen, the others dropped their tools and followed him. But they did not linger over breakfast. Soon they were out again, fixing up the lighting, and digging a circle out of the turf which they filled with sawdust for the ring. After that the seats had to be set out in the Big Top, and all the properties needed for the various acts put ready near the entrance to the ring. Princess looked on with interest until she was led to her stall, where she was fed and watered and groomed, ready for the show. Then she rested, as did all the other animals, until the great hour arrived.

The people, however, still had plenty to do, but most of them managed to fit in a short nap somewhere between lunch and tea. Then, after tea, the hustle and bustle began again. The women took out their hair-curlers and dressed themselves in rich, colourful dresses, while the men washed and shaved and put on equally gay clothes. And gradually the workaday atmosphere gave place to one of romance and sheer magic.

Outside, the people lined up to buy their tickets at the turnstile, and in no time the Big Top was full and it was time for the show to begin.

Princess, waiting in the wings with the other ponies, noticed the hush that fell over the audience as Mr Bunting, the ringmaster, made his appearance. He stood there, imposing, majestic, and incredibly dignified in his scarlet coat, top-hat, and tall shiny boots.

'My Lords, Ladies and Gentlemen,' he announced, 'we now present the grand parade!'

With those words the band struck up, and a brilliant beam of light blazed down on the ring as the gay, glittering procession began. The elephants came first, followed by the Redskins on their shiny brown steeds, then Joey and Jacko the clowns in lurid make-up and comical costumes. Heidi was next, so small and delicate in her fairy-like dress that it didn't seem possible she was the sturdy teenager who had helped erect the Big Top only a few hours earlier. Then Mitzi and Frank, gorgeously arrayed in velvet and lace, followed by the Four Antonios, all wrapped in swirling black cloaks, and Orlando, dressed in silver like some strange, slender god. Anne-Marie, queenly in a long shimmering gown, a dove resting on either shoulder, was closely followed by Donovan with his merry little dogs romping excitedly around him. Finally it was the turn of the liberty ponies to trot round the ring, each gay with scarlet feathers and glittering harness.

Princess was not in the least afraid, or nervous. She had done it all thousands of times before at Beech Coppice, and Alphonso was here, smiling and winking in the most reassuring way. All the people watching were smiling too, so she knew they were friends. Then the grand parade was over, and so quickly that Princess was back in the wings almost before she realised she had been in the famous sawdust ring. Then it was time for the ring-master to announce the first act.

This was Heidi's act and the audience loved her. In her little white ballet-dress spangled with silver she came on riding Conker bareback. Round and round she went, then, as the music grew more and more dramatic, she rose, to stand on one leg. With her arms raised gracefully in the air she looked like a fairy on a Christmas tree or a tiny dancer on a music-box. There was rosin on Conker's back, which helped her to grip, but of course the audience didn't know about that — it was a circus secret. With bated breath the crowds watched, but Heidi finished as gracefully as she had begun.

Princess, from her place in the wings, saw it all.

After Heidi came Fritz, with his Big Cats. The people gasped aloud as the trainer played with the great lions just as though they were friendly kittens. Sometimes they roared at him, as though they were angry, and now and then they dabbed at him with their large paws. But this was only part of the act, to give the audience a thrill. Fritz loved his wild beasts, and could do anything he liked with them because he was their friend.

Exciting though it was, everyone relaxed and breathed more freely when the lions were removed, and Anne-Marie with her doves took the centre of the ring.

She stood there like a lovely statue. Her dress was sapphire-blue, Grecian in style, and her long black hair was beautifully arranged, caught up in a jewelled comb on top of her head and falling down her back in a cascade of ringlets. The doves came and went at their mistress's bidding, flying to and fro around the Big Top, but always returning to perch on Anne-Marie's shoulders, arms or hands. They looked so pretty, with their snow-white wings and tiny bright eyes that the audience were enchanted. Then, immediately afterwards, everyone was on tenterhooks again, as the Four Antonios swung their perilous way high above the ring, from one trapeze to another.

There were two men and two girls, and under their swirling cloaks, they all wore brief costumes of bright red satin. Once there had been five of them and they had been billed as the Five Fabulous Antonios, but that was before the tragic accident occurred. Only a year before, young Paul Antonio had crashed to his death in the sawdust ring — at the age of seventeen. Yet his father, his uncle, and two pretty sisters still carried on in the same way, accepting the fact that in circus life tragedy and gaiety invariably go hand in hand.

Princess could hear the sighs of relief that went up as the four fearless performers reached safe ground and stood there in a row, smiling.

Then, tension gave way to laughter, as Joey and Jacko tumbled into the ring. A waterproof sheet had been stretched across the floor and on this the two clowns performed the most hilarious capers. They had a carpenter's bench, two buckets of whitewash, and some rolls of wallpaper which they somehow managed to paste all over each other. They got in the most outrageous mess, especially when they spilt the whitewash and fell headlong into it! Jacko, looking very tall and bossy, pretended to give Joey a bad time, but in the end — to the great delight of the children — the little fellow outwitted him, and Jacko finished up with the whitewash bucket upside-down over his head.

It was amazing how quickly the paint was cleared up and the sawdust raked smooth. The band played, the atmosphere changed, and on galloped the Redskins, twirling lassoes and leaping from one horse to another in a series of incredible feats while careering around the ring. Then there were the Juggling Sea-lions, who looked as if they were made of sleek black satin, and after them came the Parade of the Elephants. This was perhaps the most dignified act of all. They wore superbly embroidered cloths on their backs, fringed with golden tassels, and smaller ones on their heads. They were followed by perhaps the most popular act: Mitzi and her Cheeky Chimps.

The chimps were dressed as people, a little man and a little woman, and they pushed a pram with a doll in it. When they sat down to have their tea the little lady chimp pretended to feed the doll with a baby's bottle; and when the male chimp tried to take it away from her all the children in the audience yelled their indignation...In the end Mitzi, looking very fat and jolly, fetched two small bicycles which the chimps rode around the ring. When they bumped into each other she shook her head and scolded them as if they were naughty children.

At last the moment Princess had so long awaited arrived.

'Alphonso and his Liberty Ponies,' announced Mr Bunting.

While the band played dreamy music they all trotted on, Princess and Daisy and Susan, Captain and Bugle, Nicky, Arabella and Windflower. They looked adorable, all cream-coloured, and all decked out with shining harnesses and tossing scarlet feathers. As lovely as fairy-tale creatures, they circled the ring, anti-clockwise as always, now going fast, now slow, now turning around at a signal from Alphonso, now pausing, each with one little hoof poised on a tub. Princess had done it all so often before that it came quite naturally to her now, and when the ponies trotted off, with the sound of enthusiastic clapping in their ears, each was rewarded with a sugar lump and a pat from Alphonso.

Because she was taken back to her stall then, to be settled down for the night, Princess did not see the other acts: Orlando walking the tight-rope, graceful as a beam of silver light, or Donovan's Dogs as they played Four-Footed Football. The small terriers looked irresistible as they hurled themselves around the ring after the ball, each dressed in a gay little striped jersey.

Soon Princess was asleep in her clean, comfortable stall. The great day in her life was over. It had come and gone so quickly, but it was to be followed by many more — all colourful, all exciting. No matter what people said about circus life it could never be called boring. The show travelled from town to town, and went all over the country, each route being carefully plotted out on the map so that no time or money should be wasted. And every weekday, and twice on Saturdays, Princess appeared in the ring, and always the liberty ponies received a warm welcome from the audience. As they trotted round and round in time to the music, manes flying, little hooves pounding the sawdust, great waves of friendliness and kindness swept over them from the delighted audience. Soon Princess found herself really enjoying it. But she especially enjoyed the apple or titbit which Alphonso gave her afterwards.

'That was fine, Princess,' he would say. Or, 'Very nice, Daisy. That was a lovely pirouette.'

* * *

Towards the end of the season a new tent-hand was taken on — a young Irishman with auburn hair and a cheeky grin. He was a nephew of Donovan the dog-trainer, so Mr Bunting did not hesitate to give him a temporary job. He often took on casual labour during the summer months.

But this time he made a big mistake. Although there was no real harm in Young Finnegan, as he came to be called, he was much too happy-go-lucky, as well as being inclined to disobey time-honoured rules. More than once there were harsh words between him and his uncle, especially when Young Finnegan was caught smoking where it was strictly forbidden.

Heidi did not like Young Finnegan much, although he went out of his way to be pleasant to her, and as for the animals, they positively mistrusted him. Heidi rounded on him fiercely once when she caught him teasing Conker, but he only laughed.

Then, late one night, when everyone was settling down to sleep, he went into town to spend his wages and returned with a bottle sticking out of either pocket. As he wandered rather unstedily through the maze of tents to his uncle's caravan, he let fall a lighted cigarette.

The horses and ponies smelled the smoke first. They whinnied in high, shrill voices. Then all the other animals joined in the tumult. The chimps actually cried tears, just like frightened children. As for Princess, her heart beat madly, her nostrils flared. She stood there, in her canvas stall, shaking with terror. Then suddenly, through the open tent-flap, she saw a vivid sheet of orange flame shoot up into the air. It was the very worst moment of her life. Never had she known such fear.

Into the tented stable rushed Giulio, one of the trapeze artists, whose caravan was close by. He grabbed Princess's halter and tried to pull her out of the tent. But Princess refused to move. She had never been handled by this man, and to the terrified pony, it felt as though this near-stranger was trying to make her move closer to the brilliant flickering orange light and the fearful crackling sounds. For by now, the fire had spread to the tent at the edge of the field in which the hay was stored. A change of wind could bring tragedy to the circus.

Suddenly, out of the unnaturally bright night appeared a small hurrying figure, coughing and spluttering in the smoke, making his way to the horses' quarters. He paused at the entrance to the stable tent, and saw the well-meaning young man struggling unsuccessfully with Princess, who had backed into the far side of her stall, and was standing there snorting and wild-eyed, her head thrown up in terror.

'Leave her, Giulio,' said Joey quietly — for that is who Princess's new visitor was.

He walked slowly towards her, talking in a low, comforting voice, until he reached her, and patted her neck soothingly.

'Whoa girl! Steady now,' he said.

Gradually, the terrified pony calmed down; here was a friend she knew well and trusted. She felt less frightened now.

Giulio tried to lead Princess away to safety.

Soon, she allowed Joey to lead her out of the tent...but it was just after she'd passed through the entrance that the accident occurred.

Windflower, one of the other liberty ponies, also half crazed with fear, was plunging this way and that and broke her halter; she saw Princess being led away, and raced after her. The sight and sound of the crackling flames outside made her rear up in terror; she swerved round and galloped off, narrowly missing Joey but striking Princess's near foreleg with one of her hind hoofs.

Poor Princess winced and stumbled, and Joey led her, limping, to a place well away from the fire. Blood was running freely from an ugly-looking wound just below the knee. Joey tore the long sleeve off his shirt to bind the leg above the cut.

Meanwhile, Alphonso and Heidi and some of the other circus folk managed to catch Windflower, and to lead Arabella, Nicky and the other liberty ponies out to safety.

Fortunately the fire did not reach the animals' tents. The firefighting unit went into action so quickly that it was under control within a matter of minutes. But afterwards there was all the clearing-up to do. It was the last night of their stay in that particular town, which meant that everyone had to be up at four o'clock next morning to get ready to move off, yet they all turned out to help. Not until every single animal was settled down comfortably again for the night did the circus folk take to their own beds.

It was Joey who chose to stay behind with Princess next morning; all the others left before dawn with the animals, but someone had to stay with a horse-box and supervise the vet's visit.

When he had treated Princess's leg, the vet rubbed his chin thoughtfully and said, 'Well, I'm afraid that's a torn ligament, which will take some months to mend, and there'll be a scar there for life!'

Poor Princess! She didn't know, of course, but Joey guessed the truth: she would never be fit for circus work again.

Mr Bunting was very sorry to lose Princess. She had worked hard for him and never given him any trouble and he was determined to see that she ended her days peacefully. He therefore arranged for her to go to Cloverlands.

'You'll like it there, old lady,' he told her. 'I read about it in the paper and it sounded a real heaven for horses.'

So Princess went to Cloverlands, and it had been all that Mr Bunting had promised. She simply could not have been treated better. She was well-fed, groomed with loving care, exercised as much as her injury would allow, and more important than all that, she was given affection.

* * *

The stable clock struck half-past three, and visitors began to pour through the gates. Several cars had drawn up on the parking space outside and from these scrambled several families with young children, as well as the regulars. Princess looked out of her stall expectantly. She didn't quite know *what* she expected, but she always had a secret hope that one day someone very special would come to visit her.

The little old lady in the feathered hat had come to see Mick and bring him some titbits. The bow-legged man who looked like an ex-jockey had come to visit Morning Star, and old Annie was soon nuzzling her head against the broad, homely expanse of Mrs Parker's coat. Once a month, without fail, Mrs Parker came down from Battersea to see Annie.

'How are you, old pal?' she asked, her red, jolly face beaming with tenderness. Then she added, rather sadly, 'It still seems funny without you, Annie. They were good days, weren't they, when we had our rag-and-bone cart!'

Princess watched them both, and her face was just as

wistful. If only she had someone very special to come and visit her! These other people were all very well. They patted you and stroked you and said how lovely you were, but they were just kindly strangers. If only fat, laughing Mitzi would come along, or pretty Heidi, or Anne-Marie with her small pigtailed daughters. Or Alphonso himself... Or...

It was then that the miracle happened!

Through the gates of Cloverlands came an odd little figure. He was not much bigger than a child and wore a loud check suit and a cap that was a bit too large for him. He walked slowly, awkwardly, leaning on a stick, and as he moved he gazed about him with frank curiosity. And Princess pricked up her ears, suddenly excited. She whinnied with delight, and stamped her little hooves, because it was none other than her old friend Joey.

'Princess! My little old beauty!'

As fast as he could Joey made his way to her stall. There he dropped his stick, and his two little arms, like those of a warmhearted child, reached out to hug the pony with all their might and main. 'They said I'd find you here!' His voice was husky with emotion, his eyes unashamedly bright. 'You'll never believe it, old girl, but I've bought myself a tiny cottage almost on your doorstep. Just a hop and a skip and a jump along the lane,' cried Joey, who knew quite well he would never hop or skip or jump again. 'I've had to leave the circus, you see, on account of my having one tumble too many...' He did not tell her how he had moved out of the pretty caravan so that Heidi and Orlando, the acrobat, should have it for a wedding present — for they were to be married.

Princess listened eagerly to the familiar old voice. She tried to answer with her eyes, and with the rough tickly tongue that came out to caress the little man's hand.

'So I'll come and see you often,' went on Joey happily.

'Nice little garden I've got, full of apple trees. I'll bring you some apples next time, and when summer comes, I'll grow you some carrots. Just you wait, Princess, you and I are going to see a lot of each other from now on. Just like old times, that's what it'll be...'

He glanced down at the scar on her leg, where the hair had never grown again. Then he grinned suddenly. 'We're two of a kind now, old girl! You with your limp, and me with mine!'

He stayed there until half-past four, when visiting time was over, and by then he had shuffled his way all around the Home. He had admired the lovely old farmhouse, chatted with Albert Potter and pretty Marion, and passed the time of day with each and every horse, pony and donkey, as well as the stable cat. Then he leant on the gate leading to the oatfield, where flocks of gleaming starlings pecked hopefully among the stubble.

'Mr Bunting was right,' he mused. 'This really *is* a heaven for horses. I only hope,' and he cocked a saucy eye skywards, 'they've got something just as nice up there for poor old worn-out clowns.'

Then, after giving Princess a farewell hug, he set off on the slow, difficult journey down Windmill Lane, a journey he was to make, with unfailing regularity, every Sunday afternoon for many months to come.

Horse Sense

by Evelyn Day

In Beth's view, Simon was no ordinary horse; he was dark brown, with gentle eyes; and after a long spell of standing, looking into the distance at nothing, he would sigh as if he found life a little sad. Normally he was cheerful, and enjoyed life. He jumped with zest; he cantered gleefully; and a gallop seemed to remind him that he had, it was said, Arab blood. Of late, however, he had been down-hearted, and sighed more than usual. But whatever his worries and troubles might be, they were locked away in his heart, shared only — if with anyone at all — with the Black Cat.

Beth had just returned from riding him from the nearby farm where she had collected some eggs, and she had noticed his listlessness even on that short journey.

'Cheer up,' she urged him, and stroked his sleek velvety neck that was a delight to the touch. 'Much could be worse, Simon. What a nice stable you have! What a good friend in the Black Cat! Does she not keep you warm, sleeping on your back?'

He turned his head and looked at her solemnly with large, glossy eyes that were wordlessly eloquent: he had a way of looking thoughts, and his present dominating thought seemed to be 'If only you knew!'

Beth's brother, Cyril, said she was a fool about Simon, and he was just an ordinary nag. But Cyril was no horseman; he was more successful in the schoolroom, and was looking forward to going up to Oxford. He knew far more about Athens and ancient Rome than he did about horses — or life in the eighteenth century, their own century. He was a day-dreamer and a dolt, according to Uncle Roger, their guardian. It might be better, Uncle had said, if Cyril lifted his head out of his books, and took to hunting or shooting or something else useful and manly.

These thoughts were running through Beth's head as she put the blanket snugly over Simon's back, and he had to remind her with a nudge of his muzzle that she had forgotten something.

'Oh — sweetmeat — yes,' remembered Beth, amused, and took a small decorative box from the pocket of her thick riding coat. Simon stared into the box, as if there might be something else hidden there, although what there was suited him well. When the sweetmeat was held out on the flat of her palm, he gobbled it up. 'One is enough,' she assured him. 'A spoiled horse falters at the fence.' He sighed, and in so far as a horse can, shrugged; at least his neck twitched.

'And now, Simon, you can settle down for the night,' she told him. 'That was your last ride of the day. I'll try to keep Cyril from your back tomorrow. I know you don't like the way he rides you. I *do* wish I could have you as my very *own* horse, so that no one else could ride you *ever*. But alas, I cannot!'

Alas, indeed. She had always to remember that she was an orphan; that she and Cyril were beholden to Uncle Roger since their parents were lost at sea in a storm on their way home from India. True, they were not poor. Uncle Roger was an inn-keeper, landlord of the Red Lion Inn where the coaches stopped for a change of horses. Trade was good; for it was the first inn on the London Road, a welcome halt after a bleak journey across the lonely moors, the unfriendliness of which had been marked all too often of late by highwaymen.

It was a bright winter's afternoon, cold and crisp, and the setting sun was sending out its last red rays. Soon it would be gone, all too soon.

'Your friend the Black Cat is not here tonight, Simon?' Beth said as she turned to the door, almost as if she expected at least a clomp of hoof on the cobblestones in reply. What she did get in reply was the sound of a yawn from the hay just beyond the manger; and as the hay stirred, a yawning, stretching cat rose into view, showing its wide red mouth. The Black Cat!

'Oh, good evening Mistress Cat!' smiled Beth.

The Black Cat, it was always called; for its name was not to be mentioned, the villagers said. To think it, even, was fraught with strange peril; for the cat belonged to a witch — Old Meg. It was her familiar; it told her things that happened in the village, and she in turn told the cat where to go and what to spy on. Without that cat, Old Meg could not work half her mischief. Or so it was said; for in this part of England in the mid-eighteenth century, there were still many who believed in witchcraft and witches and feared their evil.

Beth had long ago lost all fear and superstitious dread of witches, and could laugh at the silly stories she heard about the deeds of the Black Cat. She knew from experience that it was harmless, friendly, and liked to be stroked. Also, it liked Simon; and now, after a preliminary crouch, it sprang on to his back, leaving behind quite a large hole in the hay. It was the bright red flash of the setting sun on metal that caused Beth to give more than a fleeting glance at the hay. Quite startled, she pulled the hay aside, and gasped aloud. Hidden in the hay was a pistol, double-barrelled and brass mounted, the brass chased and highly polished. Warily, for

Beth held the pistol warily, wondering why it was there.

she hated pistols, she gripped the butt and pulled it out, wondering why it was hidden there; for she had recognised it instantly. It was Uncle Roger's.

It was a show piece of her uncle's; and when he was in a boastful mood, finishing his second bottle of port, he would produce it, show it around, and brag that it had belonged to a famous English general. He would not admit that he had bought it from Old Jasper, formerly Sergeant Jasper of the Hussars, wooden-legged and, so Uncle Roger said, wooden-headed, too. Sometimes, when there were rumours that rogues were abroad, or a new highwayman prowled on the moors, the pistol would be loaded and hung in a convenient and conspicuous place behind the bar counter.

Uncle Roger was away in London; so obviously, Beth reasoned, someone had taken advantage of his absence to steal or borrow and then hide the pistol. It was heavy, and she raised it, marvelling that anyone's wrist could be strong enough to wield it with ease. But she had seen Old Jasper do so — and she had seen him blow out a candle with a single shot from it...

Unguardedly she flourished the weapon in the direction of Simon. With a sharp squeal, he reared, backed into the wall and bared his teeth. The Black Cat, hissing, leaped from his back on to a stable rafter bringing a clatter from a lantern hooked there.

'Whoa, steady!' Soothing Simon, Beth tossed the fearsome pistol back on to the hay. She had forgotten that he hated pistols, and assured him he was safe, showing him that both hands were empty.

It was in the middle of this pantomime that the sound of voices came from the cobbled yard, and the thump of Old Jasper's iron-ringed wooden leg. The door was swung open, and the old soldier stared in. At his heels was Cyril. Both halted; and both stared up at the rafter from which the Black

Cat hissed and spat venom and hatred, glaring down balefully.

‘ ’Tis the very devil himself,’ snarled Jasper. ‘If I but had me sword it’s cutting off its head I’d be doing, so I would.’

‘The pistol — look!’ cried Cyril, pointing at it.

‘Ah! So my prayer was answered,’ said Old Jasper, and thumped his wooden leg almost on to Beth’s foot. But she barred his way.

‘Oh, no. ’Tis not to be,’ she said. ‘I’ll have no cruelty here. Poor Beauty...’ A horny hand was clapped instantly over her mouth.

‘Speak not its name for the love of mercy, girl! Would you bring the powers of evil on us?’ asked Jasper, shocked. ‘Have you no sense? One shot and it will be no more trouble and like as not the witch herself will drop dead at the same moment, being familiar, as they say.’

‘You shall not have the pistol,’ said Beth fiercely, barring his way.

Having a wooden leg, it was not easy for him to dodge this way and that, so he said sullenly, ‘Be it on your own head.’

It could have been no more than mere coincidence, but as he spoke, the Black Cat jumped on to his wig, skidded, clawed a better grip on his ear, and then, scared to further effort by his yells, leaped on to Cyril’s back as he stooped, and vanished into the darkness — or, as Jasper said, changed artfully into an eagle, and flew away. For some minutes there was uproar. Simon had to be calmed — and not only Simon, but Old Jasper, too. And in the middle of it, Cyril asked a question.

‘How came you to find the pistol, Sister?’ he asked sharply.

‘I saw it when the Black Cat moved. It was sleeping there in the hay for warmth.’

A sudden hush fell. She heard then the hiss of Old Jasper’s sharp intake of breath after each had stared at the other.

'So 'twas the Black Cat revealed the hidden secret? The evil spy found the pistol? What else did it tell?'

'It cannot speak,' said Beth, but she was tempted to make up something suitable.

'But it showed you the pistol,' frowned Cyril. 'A sly trick. But nothing else?'

'What else is there? And why is Uncle's pistol hidden here anyway? He would not approve. You know well how he does admire it; it is his pride. No one must touch it. Yet there it is — and loaded!'

Old Jasper explained. There was, he said, always an explanation, as any old soldier knew.

'Does not your Uncle say many a time that this lad is of poor spirit, and should be manly? And does he not admire of all men the good shot more than other skills? Very well then; when he comes back from the wicked city, what joy shall be his when he makes the discovery that this same lad is a marksman?'

'Aye...pleased he'll be, all right,' Cyril assured her, his eyes shining. 'I'll prove I *am* manly. I'll have good proof, *sound* proof, the like he cannot deny. And what's more, no longer then can he with justice hold back that hundred guineas that's my inheritance on reaching manhood.'

Old Jasper chortled. 'He'll give it you, true enough! He'll not withhold it. And likely we'll be seeing who shall prove the brave man.' He winked mysteriously.

'Ah! That could be true!' And Cyril's eyes, Beth noticed, sparkled at the thought. 'I'll have my fees for Oxford, and there I'll go, a man at last.'

'And *me* as his loyal servant! With a hundred guineas there'll be much to see in Oxford city.' Old Jasper licked his lips at the thought of it.

Their strange manner and mysterious exchange of looks filled Beth with uneasiness. She had never trusted Old Jasper, brave soldier though he may well have been, and must have been if only half his stories held a grain of truth; but she was well assured by the evidence of her own senses that he was an evil influence on Cyril. The old braggart had filled the boy's head with wild stories and flattered him; and what he had just said made it quite obvious that he had in mind the pleasing prospect of feathering his own nest. Clever scholar though he was, Cyril had learned nothing about people and ordinary everyday life. He could easily be fooled.

'Please, please, Cyril, be careful, and think well,' she implored her brother. 'Pistols are dangerous, terrible weapons.'

'Of course...of *course*. I'm no child,' snapped Cyril.

'On the point, he is, of being made a man,' Jasper added with a gurgling chuckle. 'And I'll take hold of the pistol. I know 'em well and all their tricks 'nall. I knows at which end of the bullet to be.' He winked again.

Beth paused to stroke Simon soothingly. Then, uneasy in mind, deeply troubled about Cyril, she crossed the cobblestones in the darkness that was swiftly falling, and went into the back door of the inn.

Cyril watched her go.

'She did not guess?' he asked, looking worried.

'Not she! Unless Black Cat told her something, her innocent mind is empty of evil suspicions, me lad. The moon'll be up soon. Not long to wait.' Then he limped to a sack that was roped to a hook on the end wall and took it down, taking from it, after some groping, two objects. 'You'll feel braver wearing 'em,' he said. 'See how well you look in 'em and let that daft horse get a proper look at you.'

But Simon, when he saw what it was that Cyril had put on his head, whinnied and backed nervously. The white wig did not worry him; but the black velvet mask did.

* * *

The moon had risen but was as yet low in the sky when Simon was led out from the stables some time later, across the stable yard, and into the fields beyond. The countryside was deserted, apart from the small animals who could be heard or dimly seen every now and then scampering about their business. Horse sense told Simon that all was not well; in fact, that very little was well. He could sense evil in the air, and felt restless, uneasy and reluctant. It was Old Jasper who held the bridle, and the powerful hand and arm were difficult to resist.

'This fool horse is in a tiresome mood,' muttered Jasper. 'It's that Black Cat has been poisoning his mind. The enterprise could go ill were Old Meg against it, but I'll hope to get good money's worth for that screw of baccy I gave the old witch. I crossed her hand with silver, too, and what's more, I left the silver in her palm! Surely, even a witch is not so evil she cannot sometimes give good value for money?'

Cyril was jaunty, fired with false courage, and reckless of consequences. 'If Simon is unwilling, then I'll ride Demon instead.'

'Demon! You? Don't be a fool! That stallion is more'n a match for you. He'd throw you in the first fifty yards, or he'd bolt with you across the moor, and that would be the end of it all. For if you were not killed, then the stallion would be, at large for all to see, with pistol and holsters on the saddle. It's what hangs men. It's called evidence, and rascal lawyers use it to their advantage.'

He would have said more but Simon had stopped. He did not know where he was being led, and he did not like it. He was saddled, but he was not being ridden. He could smell the pistol, and he was afraid. Also, he could smell Old Jasper's baccy and snuff. The whole situation was bad.

'Gittup,' snarled Old Jasper. 'What's wrong with you?'

'I'll soon smarten him,' said Cyril, and fetched the horse

a sharp thwack with his riding crop. It had its immediate effect. Simon reared; the pain gave him strength and he lifted Old Jasper off balance and swung him round. The old soldier tottered, lost his footing, and fell in the mud. Free, Simon pranced, kicked his heels, cavorted, and cantered off.

Cyril helped the old soldier up.

'That Black Cat,' muttered Jasper. 'It's got into him... Remember when it made old Widow Jones' hens lay pebbles?'

'Beth says mayhap Old Meg took the eggs herself and put the pebbles there.'

'The hen lay pebbles. I know what I know,' shouted Old Jasper, enraged. 'I know magic and witchcraft at my age. What does a slip of a half-baked girl know of it? Has she seen the world? Has she fought the French?'

Ashamed, Cyril had to admit that Jasper was right. Beth was only a girl and one who had never even fired a pistol, let alone hacked men with a sword. He admitted that what they were up against now was not just a recalcitrant horse, but an evil-minded, crafty black cat. In spite of being somewhere else at the time, its influence still shadowed the horse.

'What we must do,' said Old Jasper, 'is to break the spell. When we are near the horse, we must go around it in a circle to sever the evil influence. Do you now go down on all fours, and make a mewing sound!'

'In the mud?'

'In the dry if you prefer it. You shall be the Black Cat. You shall go round the horse, hissing, while I do strike at you in the likeness of the old witch muttering spells. I know two good ones!'

Cyril had had little experience of unwitching, but he was conscious of his extreme youth, and did what he was told. On all fours, he approached the astonished horse, and went round him in a wide circle, hissing. It was enough to astonish any horse, and Simon put his head this way and that, twitching his ears when he recognised Cyril's imitation of a cat's *miaouw*. It made him all the more uneasy, and worried.

And behind Cyril went Old Jasper, mimicking Old Meg, so he supposed, and striking at the 'cat'.

'Whiskers twitch, furry witch,' he muttered. 'Tail flail and plots fail. My power end and wrongs mend. I'll cut your spell with old saws, nor can you fight with claws, paws, nor even jaws. Our plot's revealed, your fate is sealed. From out the ground with mighty bound comes Satan's hound if here you're found when midnight sound!'

Fascinated, Simon could not bolt; he could not move. There's nowt so queer as folk to most animals, and Simon had seen much that was silly and puzzling; but this beat everything. Yet the plan worked; for while Simon gaped at Cyril, who was pretending to use his claws to scrape an imaginary tree, Jasper crept up behind and seized the horse anew. A yell brought Cyril to the other side, and within seconds they had tethered Simon to a tree.

'Now, the night's work begins,' muttered Old Jasper. 'Nearby is the sack I hid; you'll be needing what's in it.' He moved away, and then appeared from behind a large bush carrying a sack. From it he brought out the pistol holsters for the saddle, and then a mass of hair. ''Tis a beard and moustachios,' he chuckled, 'from a bear! But 'tis near enough. See...' He put it on to his own face. It was a crude device; for the beard and the moustache were in one piece with a hole made for the mouth, yet so brushed out that it was quite realistic. What spoiled it was that the beard side-pieces were continued upwards, and the tape to which they were glued was tied on top of the head. However, the velvet mask had wide tying strings which concealed the limitations of the beard; and when the tricorn hat was in place the disguise was good enough, even in bright moonlight.

'For it would not do that you should be known to be a young man,' explained Jasper. He affixed the mass of hair to Cyril, who felt safe at once; the fact that Simon trotted his hoofs unevenly, and laid his ears back added to Jasper's confidence, for to Simon it seemed, doubtless, magic.

But there was something else; he had some special whitewash with which to paint a diamond blaze on Simon and some conspicuous white markings here and there. It would be enough, he assured Cyril, to fool any witnesses, all of whom would assuredly mention those white markings — which, as soon as possible, would be washed off. Then there would be nothing at all to connect the highwayman with either Cyril or Simon.

'But this is only what in the theatre is called a rehearsal, is it not?' asked Cyril when the beard was affixed, and he was ready for action.

'Yes, yes. Do not fire the pistol. Show yourself, that's all, lad! 'Tis but to prove that you are abroad, so it will not seem tomorrow night that the highwayman waits specially for your uncle, true though it is; for you must know he will not be aboard tonight's coach, eh?'

Cyril patted his chest in pride; he felt brave, and noble.

'I am no ordinary highwayman. I do not rob folk — only my uncle, and then only of the hundred guineas that he carries home from the sale of some property in London.'

'Ay! And the hundred guineas shall be rightly yours when you have proved your manhood, so the law says, by your parents' will. And what better proof, eh, than being a highwayman, robbing your own uncle, and scaring the wits out of him! But you shall take perhaps a watch, a jewel or two, or some pearls, for the show of it. Else it might seem too clear that it is your uncle who's the intended victim...'

Cyril felt some momentary doubt.

'But what must I do with what I take? 'Twould be theft

As soon as Cyril was up in the saddle, Simon reared.

and robbery to keep it.' He fingered his false beard nervously.

'Crazy lad! Did I not say that I would handle it? I'll see that 'tis found in Old Meg's cottage — all of it, to be given back to the true owners. What else?'

'So long as what I do is not evil or dishonest,' nodded Cyril, comfortably reassured. 'So now, I do but mount Simon, go to the crossroads by the bend in the road, and there await the coach, ride out, shout in a loud voice, "Stand and deliver!" so that it comes to a halt...'

'No, no...are you crazed, boy? You must do it too late! The coach must drive on; but they must see you, and hear your pistol. 'Twould be a fool's plan to stop the coach and not rob anyone, and so make it seem to be play acting. Tomorrow night you will be in the roadway. There will be a heavy log on the road to slow the coach in readiness. Then be swift! There will be a sack clipped to your saddle. Into it put your uncle's bag...but that will be tomorrow...'

Cyril put his left foot into a stirrup, and Old Jasper pushed him on to the saddle. At once, Simon reared. He was having none of this; for he had seen that horrible bearded and masked face. He had not understood the spoken words, yet he had felt the general underlying mood of evil. No sooner was he released than he sped for his own stable with Cyril fiercely reining him in. But Cyril won. A few minutes later, belted by Old Jasper, Simon sped off in the darkness towards the crossroads, where only a year ago a highwayman's horse had been shot dead, and the highwayman trapped under it, arrested, and later hanged.

Old Jasper watched him go, and was pleased — until, turning suddenly, he tripped over something that moved across his path and sent him sprawling in the road. A hiss, a growl, and the moonlit sight of yellow, fierce eyes were all the evidence he needed to prove the truth of his instant guess.

* * *

The Red Lion Inn was noisy, smoky, but cheerful; for the London coach was due, and there was always expectation of excitement on such occasions. It was as good as the theatre, some said. When the passengers alighted there were new faces — rich folk, even nobility to see. There were London fashions to admire: the ladies' dresses, the men's new-style garments. And sometimes there were big-hearted men, who spent money freely. Bottles of wine were opened but not emptied. There were snacks — roast beef, chicken, fruit, pies, not all of which could be eaten by the passengers — and what was left could be had cheaply, and sometimes, when the landlord was in good humour, for nothing.

Beth had been helping out and supervising with Aunt Florence in the large kitchen. There was much to be seen to, and many small jobs needed attention. In her quiet way, Aunt Florence was a martinet. Everything had to be done in her own way, as she wished, and many a kitchen maid had a singing head if she were negligent or lazy; for it was not thought wrong that a landlady should clout a maid to help her education, and those who had been clouted themselves in childhood passed it on when it was their turn. 'No child in my care,' Aunt Florence had remarked, 'shall suffer because of a foolishly spared rod.'

Even Beth had been clouted more than once.

The ovens were ablaze; the heat and light were almost frightening, and Beth found it quite a pleasure when she was ordered to carry a tray into the dining-room. Stealing a moment of idleness, she went to the entrance door and looked out at the starry night. The moon was up, and was spreading its wonderful silvery light on the black winter scene. There was a touch of frost. She shivered, and would have gone back to the warmth had she not heard the clatter of hoofs. Someone was riding hard, approaching the inn. She saw sparks fly; and then from the shadows came the galloping horseman.

The horseman wore a tricorn hat, a dark thick coat, a scarf round his neck, and riding boots. He was excited, almost breathless.

'The coach…held up…highwayman!' he shouted.

His yell was heard and within a minute a dozen people were outside all talking at once. Old Jasper hobbled out, and took the rider by the arm.

'Was anyone harmed, sir?' he asked.

'Not that I know. I heard a shot fired… I saw the highwayman and the coach; but I rode on to seek help.'

Someone asked why he had not stayed, since help was needed there; was it not likely that some passenger might have been wounded?

'Or the highwayman?' asked Old Jasper.

'He was safe…I tell you he fired at me…was I to stay there and be killed?' asked the rider fiercely. 'Where's the landlord?'

'In London,' Old Jasper told him. ' 'Tis pity I were not there on your horse. There'd be a dead highwayman, I'll promise. They'll not like fighting soldiers. Highwayman! Pah!'

The man strode past him into the inn, saying that he needed brandy; but there were others ready to listen to the former sergeant and learn how easy it was to kill highwaymen.

'Last time it was his horse that were killed,' said a woodman.

'Shot dead it was!' confirmed a thatcher. 'And they say it haunts the bend in the road by the spinney…you can hear it whinnying on a November night. Many's heard it.'

'And me amongst them.'

Beth shivered, and drew away, but not merely from the cold, piercing though it was; she went into the great hallway of the inn where a fire blazed, logs sparking, smoke curling up lazily. But no sooner was she warmed herself than uproar arose again. She heard the guard's horn, and the thunder of horses' hoofs. And then all bedlam was let loose, as out from the coach tumbled the frightened passengers. They were shouting and laughing; some were even crying. All were wild with excitement, talking together but to no one in particular. To have been accosted by a highwayman yet not robbed was a tale worth telling.

A fat red-faced man with hat awry was taking snuff.

' 'Twas a young bearded rascal,' he said.

'Ah, but the beard were false! 'Twere off when he were thrown himself.'

'The horse threw him?'

It was Old Jasper's voice; and Beth, with a sudden leap of her heart, turned. For there was concern in his voice — such concern as he would not have shown for a stranger. And all at once, a dread seized her; the sight of the hidden pistol came back to her mind. That, coupled with the highwayman's youth — and his being thrown — and the memory of the strange conversation between Old Jasper and Cyril... All at once, she knew the truth!

She moved away from the uproar, went to her room, seized her thickest coat, and then scurried down by the back staircase to the stable yard. Already the coach horses were being led in, but at the far end. Simon's stall was round a corner, and so could not readily be seen by anyone entering the yard. She went at once to his door, and opened it. She did not walk in, but stood there, numb; for she knew he was not inside. There was no sound; just emptiness.

'Simon!' she breathed, and at last plucked up courage to walk in, stretching out her hands. He was not there.

Time seemed to stand still. It was as if she were dreaming, or not fully awake. Yet she knew it was all real; that the coach had been held up by a highwayman, and that he was assuredly her own foolish, reckless brother. Had there been any lingering doubt, then Old Jasper's thumping step would have dispelled it. It was his alarm that had first fired her suspicion, and his arrival now was proof.

'It was Cyril?' she choked. 'On Simon?'

Old Jasper looked about him uneasily, for the consequences of Cyril's being captured could be terrible indeed. There are ears everywhere, and he snatched her arm to silence her, saying that if she loved her brother at all, she must not even hint at any possible complicity of his with this night's ill work.

'But he *is* out there on the moor, with Simon, is he not? You know quite well that a highwayman's horse was shot there a year ago! Simon might easily be shot, were he to be seen with a highwayman's pistol holsters...' Now, the horny hand was put over her mouth, and she saw fear in the old soldier's eyes.

He would find Simon, he reassured her, and unsaddle him if Cyril had failed to do so; and surely Cyril would have sense enough to rid himself of any disguise, and lie low. Even in moonlight there was the cover of shadows to be found. They must pretend he was here; they must call him by name. It was all planned. Already, he had played at Cyril's being in the inn and had artfully complained what a long time he spent bringing a hot pie.

He might have calmed Beth had there not been a sudden change of circumstances. From the inn came a potman shouting for Old Jasper.

''Tis the cavalry...your own troop! It's riding here... it'll be here in only minutes,' he yelled. 'They're on the tracks of the highwayman. An officer was here and spoke to a gentleman passenger, a friend of the Lord Lieutenant. He's gone riding off at full gallop to bring the troop here. They'll get the rascal wherever he's hiding on the moor. "Shoot at sight", the Captain said to him. "Get the horse, like last time." '

Old Jasper went to him. 'Fine fellow... I'll go too — on the stallion. I'll be there ahead of them. I'll show 'em the way. I have an old trumpet. I'll be hunting the rascal.'

'Then I'll come too,' said Beth, which brought a guffaw from the potman. Still laughing he went back into the inn to tell the news of Old Jasper's military bravery — and Beth's boastful folly.

Old Jasper did indeed go to the stallion's stall. It stamped, turning bright vicious eyes towards him, and Beth drew back, awed. The horse was powerful, strong willed, and resented being ridden. And when it was ridden, it had but one intention, which was to cover the ground with all possible speed, and if possible to throw the rider; or when that failed, to knock him off at the first low branch, or brush him off against a tree.

'You will ride — with a wooden leg?' she asked him.

Old Jasper told her to help saddle the horse. It took all their skill and patience to do so, but Old Jasper was not easily beaten. Once on the moor, he said, the stallion could run free. Rearing and bucking, Demon was even wilder out of the stall than inside, and it seemed to Beth that the old soldier would not be able to keep his seat: yet he did so.

But when the stallion smelled the night air and the grass, it cleared a fence into the fields. Old Jasper cleared it too, although when the stallion landed in the field beyond, the old soldier was more than half off. Beth hurriedly climbed the fence, tearing her long frock, and saw the old soldier flung to the ground. But, bruised though he was, and shaken, he was uninjured — though in vile temper.

'The horse will find Simon. By all that's sacred, I hope he does so afore the Hussars do,' he groaned.

Suddenly aware that Demon had stopped to taste the grass, Beth left the old man and went up to the stallion, stepping softly. She had ridden astride before now, and was undaunted. To save Cyril and to save Simon, she would take whatever riding risk there was in mounting this monster. She approached him warily as he tore greedily at the grass. He looked sideways at her for a moment, and his flanks twitched; but he liked Beth.

'Please, please be gentle,' she implored. 'It's to save Simon.' The horse looked at her solemnly, and his jaws ceased to work. He gave a start when she tried to mount; it was a nervous movement, but when she was astride him he did not rear to throw her; he merely seemed puzzled.

Off he went at a canter, and then, with neck stretched out, broke into a full gallop. Beth clung on to him, heart in mouth, more afraid than she had ever been before in her whole life. A stumble, a swerve, and she would be thrown; yet the stallion was sure-footed even on the moor, which stretched before her, brilliant in the moonlight, wild and frightening.

Half a mile away was Simon as yet unseen, remounted by Cyril. His disguise gone, his plan ruined, he was convinced that he was doomed, that nothing could now go right. That the coach would halt at the inn was certain; that the story would be told was just as certain, and he imagined vividly all the uproar and excitement. Had he been recognised? Had Simon been recognised, despite the disguise? He was so terrified and so confused that he had no knowledge in which direction they were heading except that it was away from the inn where men with guns no doubt awaited him.

He blamed Simon. He was a fool to have trusted the animal.

'Idiot horse! No wonder highwaymen's horses are shot if they are all like you, losing their nerve at the last minute and throwing their riders. Imbecile horse!'

But Simon was feeling happy again. He had somehow sensed that mischief was in the air, but now all that was behind. He would throw Cyril into the pond, and that would be the end to all this business. He would never be ridden by Cyril again, or by anyone except Beth. Things would be different.

His dreaming was interrupted by a sharp cry from Cyril, who snatched at the reins having suddenly become aware of another horse and rider. He made out a black horse, coming across the moor at full gallop, ridden by a girl whose clothes billowed out behind.

Suddenly, Cyril knew that the girl was Beth and that the horse was Demon, with the bit in his teeth, bolting. Like a mad thing, the stallion was heading for the Great Pit, that hollow that dropped down suddenly into a deep hole in the earth, guarded by bushes, where more than one wild horse had jumped to disaster. The moonlight fell upon Beth's white face and the cold clear air carried her wild cry for help. She knew she could not rein in the stallion; she knew that he was bolting with her, quite unstoppable; and worst of all she knew that in his path lay the Great Pit where the earth had fallen in a thousand years before. And down into it would go both horse and rider.

It was Simon that first sensed the danger, hearing Beth's voice. He cantered, and then he galloped, already a few hundred yards ahead of the approaching Demon. Simon rather than Cyril was trying to cut across the wild horse's path; Simon, not Cyril, measured the danger; for his horse sense was greater than Demon's. He galloped, and Cyril clung on.

But it could be said in praise of Cyril that he made no effort to rein the horse in, for all that he well knew the peril. To cut across the stallion's path was now the one hope of preventing a terrible tragedy; nothing else would stop the animal.

Hoofs thundered, and the earth shook under them. Nearer

they drew, Simon cutting right across the other's path; yet it was only when they were within yards of a crash that the stallion became aware of the danger and swerved. Round he swung, while Beth clung to rein and mane. She was shaken, banged, half dazed — but she did not let go. The two horses reared, and just brushed, the shock of this near collision clearing the stallion's head. But at last Beth was unseated, and lay sprawled on the ground. Although dazed, she was conscious enough of Simon's snorting, and his nostrils breathing hotly on her cheeks.

'All right?' asked Cyril shakily, helping her up. 'Thought you'd go down the Great Pit. That stallion's mad the way he galloped, and Simon must have known it. He ran himself right out, like a horse possessed, i' faith.'

Beth looked at him with relief, almost hysterically delighted. She looked at Simon and saw no pistol holders, nor was he disguised; for to remedy that had been Cyril's first wise act.

'The cavalry, a whole troop — in search of the highwayman,' she panted. 'I...I know the truth, Cyril...'

'Yes; and I know the truth now! I — I've been mad! Old Jasper's a fool. I should not have heeded him. I did it to prove myself a man, and proved only I am a fool...'

'You have just proved you are brave...you, and Simon too,' said Beth warmly, fondling the horse's head as it stood snorting and panting. Demon was grazing, indifferent and heedless.

Then she thanked Cyril, and Simon, too. How much happier both of them were now! Simon, with a load lifted from his mind, was a horse that would have sung — if a horse could sing.

* * *

' 'Twas a mad escapade, my girl,' said Uncle Roger the next evening, looking sternly at Beth. ' 'Pon my word, gal,

I have doubt that I should give you the present I bought in London. To ride the stallion out of wilfulness, why, 'tis as much as your brother could do! Lucky he was quick-witted — a good thing Old Jasper told him what was afoot. A hero, that lad is, and I've misjudged him cruelly!'

'You mean he can now have his hundred guineas and go to Oxford, Uncle? Oh, indeed he deserves to; for no boy could have been braver, risking death. It is I who am the dolt, and deserve nothing but reproaches.' No self-reproach seemed too great if it helped Cyril to win his Uncle's favour.

However, Uncle Roger did give her the pretty bangle he had bought; and he was sure, he said, that no one who rode a bolting stallion needed any other lesson to avoid a repeat of it. Then he looked down at the Black Cat on the hearth-rug and fondled it.

'I know not where this cat comes from, nor whose cat it is,' he said, stroking it, and bringing happy purrs. 'But 'tis a kindly creature, and welcome to make this its home if it be so minded. Many a time it has called on me — as fond of this log fire, doubtless, as it is of me. They say that black cats are lucky.'

'They are indeed, I am sure,' smiled Beth, stroking the back that was arched for her hand. Any animal that could put fear into Jasper's leather heart was good to have around. As for Jasper, since Beth had told him the horrid fate of at least three men who had killed black cats, and how they had been haunted, it seemed certain that Beauty, this black cat, would in future be safe — and where safer than in Simon's stall? And in that stall where more comfortable and cosy than on Simon's back, under his blanket? The blanket that Beth had newly embroidered with his initials, and a medal design bearing the words *For Bravery*...

Redsands Gymkhana

by Sheila Thom

Jane sat down on a bucket and looked critically at Bundle. In spite of all her efforts his mane refused to lie smoothly, and his thick, bushy tail seemed to her most unsuitable for a pony entering Redsands gymkhana the next day. Not that he was expected to win anything — Miss Clark at the local pony club had made that quite clear, although she had been very kind about it. Jane and Bundle had been entered only because it would be good experience for them. They were quite definitely not part of the proper team.

All the team ponies had beautifully pulled tails and plaited manes and they could jump proper show jumps... Without any further encouragement Jane was lost in one of her favourite daydreams: she had just cleared the triple bar with inches to spare and was leaving the ring amid storms of applause...when she was roused by an impatient nudge from Bundle, who enjoyed being groomed and was very disappointed that she had stopped so soon. Jane rubbed his nose lovingly, presented him with a carrot as a peace offering and set to work once more on his plump sides.

The next morning they made an early start. It was only about three miles to the town where the gymkhana was being held, but Jane allowed plenty of time and they jogged along quietly, enjoying the sunshine and the clean, fresh morning smells.

As they approached Redsands the roads grew more and more crowded, but Bundle paid no attention to the traffic, except to toss his head when a lorry roared past, almost pushing him in the ditch, and they arrived quite cool and unruffled at the show ground.

There were lots of ponies there already — some very smart ones being led about by grooms; some prancing and dancing, dark with sweat even before the events started; and some placid, experienced old characters, calmly eating grass.

Jane saw the other people from her pony club over in a quiet corner of the field, so she rode over to join them, and to hear the last minute instructions and encouragement from Miss Clark.

'Bundle won't be doing anything for quite a while,' said Miss Clark, patting his neck and smiling up at Jane. 'The first two classes are for the bigger ponies. Loosen his girths and slip a halter on instead of his bridle and then you can come and watch from the ringside. Pat and Barbara are going to stay here with the ponies, so Bundle will be quite all right. He's looking very smart,' she added approvingly as she moved away. Jane glowed with satisfaction as she made Bundle comfortable and then ran across to the ring just in time to see the first class enter.

'Always leave plenty of room between you and the person in front of you,' Miss Clark was saying. 'You can't expect the judge to see your pony properly if he is in a huddle with a whole lot of other ponies. Look how well Robin is showing Spotlight. He has her well away from the other ponies and walking out very freely.'

The children watched with great interest while the class in the ring walked, trotted and cantered, and then performed various evolutions one at a time, and when at last the rosettes were given out they were delighted to see that Robin had won second prize.

'Jolly well done!' He was flushed, and beaming happily. 'Congratulations!'

They all clustered round Spotlight, patting her and admiring the rosette and the ticket which Robin was proudly holding.

'Come along then, David, Susan and Jane,' called Miss Clark. 'Better start getting your ponies ready. You don't want a rush at the very last moment, do you?'

The children gave Spotlight one last pat and then started to make their way back to their ponies.

'Look!' cried Susan. 'Look at all the cups and prizes and things over there on the table.'

'Wouldn't it be wonderful to win that great silver shield,' sighed Jane. 'I wonder what it's for.'

'Show jumping, 13.2. hands to 14.2 hands,' David announced, as he read the card below the shield. 'No chance of Bundle winning that,' he added with a grin.

'He's only 13 hands, so he couldn't possibly win it,' Jane retorted.

'I'll be quite satisfied if I get round the course,' said Susan, peaceably. 'What do you think that big cup at the back is for?'

David craned his neck to read the card. 'It doesn't say. It just says "Cup presented by Lady Westhaven". She's giving out the prizes, I think.'

The three of them ran off to give their ponies a final polish and to adjust their tack.

'You are all looking very smart,' said Miss Clark, when at last they were ready to enter the ring. 'Try to remember what I said about plenty of space. Good luck!'

Bundle behaved beautifully in the ring, trotting carefully round and doing everything that he should, but he and Jane were not part of the final line-up and they left the ring without a prize. Susan had a Highly Commended, and David had been in the final line-up although he hadn't actually won a ticket, so Jane couldn't help feeling just a little disappointed as she slipped down from Bundle's back.

'Well done, Jane! You rode very steadily. No one would guess it was your very first gymkhana — and Bundle's too, as far as we know.' Miss Clark was looking very pleased, and as she obviously didn't think it at all disgraceful to come out of the ring without a ticket, Jane at once began to feel much better.

There was only one other event before lunch, and that was the potato race. Jane and Bundle had been practising this for weeks and she felt quite hopeful as they lined up with the other three in their heat.

'Are you ready? Go!'

The other ponies hurtled away as if they were running in the Derby, and it took all Jane's selfcontrol to keep Bundle to the slow canter they had practised so often.

'Don't hurry!' she told herself firmly, as they reached the first post and she seized the potato off the top. Bundle never checked his pace, and as they went steadily up and down Jane was astonished to see that she was well in the lead and was, in fact, getting further and further in front. She finished an easy winner and was at once surrounded by the other children, all congratulating her and patting Bundle.

It was so exciting that she could hardly watch the other heats, and when it was time to mount for the final she didn't really know if she was on her head or her heels.

'Do just as you did before,' said Miss Clark cheerfully, rubbing Bundle's nose. 'You had him going just like clockwork in the heat.'

'Better try changing gear,' grinned David. 'The other ponies will be in top gear — pity if Bundle stays in third!'

'Don't pay any attention to him,' laughed Miss Clark.

'Keep going steadily like last time, or you will just upset him.'

Her ears ringing with advice, Jane rode out to the start. Bundle seemed very small beside the others. One of them looked almost like a horse.

'Are you ready? Go!'

Off they went again, very evenly matched this time. First one pony drew a little ahead, then another, and they raced together for the last potato.

'Come on, Jane!'

'Come on, Bundle!'

Jane could hear the shouts, and in her excitement she kicked Bundle hard as they approached the last post. Flustered, he swung rather wide and Jane, reaching for the potato, just missed it. The crowd groaned in sympathy, and Bundle seemed to sense what had happened. Wheeling sharply, he doubled back on his track and Jane, who had nearly come off over his shoulder at the unexpected turn, just managed to keep her balance and snatch the potato as they passed. Ears flat back, Bundle hurled himself up the track, but the mistake had cost too much time, and other ponies were past the winning post before he could catch up with them.

'Bad luck, Jane!'

'Well tried!'

'I never knew Bundle could travel so fast!'

The others clustered round as Jane dismounted, biting her lip with disappointment and embarrassment.

'Very well done, both of you. A little more experience, and you will be very hard to beat,' Miss Clark said cheerfully. 'Time for lunch now. You must all be hungry, and I expect the ponies could do with something after all that hard work.'

The ponies came first, of course, but when they had been looked after the children came hurrying back for their picnic lunch, suddenly realising how hungry they were.

'Golly, that was good,' said Robin at last, sitting back com-

Bundle pushed his nose hopefully into his very own cup.

fortably. 'Hullo! I think our Bundle's got some admirers.'

Jane, having drained the very last drop of her lemonade, turned to look, and saw two very little boys happily engaged in patting and stroking such parts of Bundle as they could reach.

'Aren't they sweet!' said Susan. 'Do give them a ride, Jane. I'll hold them on while you lead Bundle.'

Jane looked enquiringly at Miss Clark. She laughed and said, 'Well, you aren't entered for the bending competition, and I expect they would love it. I think that's their mother over there. Run over and ask her.'

As Jane ran off to ask, the other children packed up the remains of the picnic, and started to prepare their ponies for the bending competition which was just about to begin.

Susan went over to Bundle, and had his bridle on by the time Jane came back to say that the boys might have a ride if they wanted one. Needless to say they did want one, and Bundle paced solemnly up and down with first one little boy and then the other on his back until it was time for the jumping, and Jane and Bundle had to get ready to go into the ring.

As she watched the others jumping Jane grew more and more nervous, and more and more certain that she would make a complete fool of herself.

'Come on, Bundle, please!' she urged as they trotted into the ring and turned to face the first jump.

Bundle, with his short little legs, bushy mane and tail, and bright eyes, was by this time a favourite with the crowd, and there was a murmur of amused encouragement as he cantered sedately up to the first fence, which was a nice small one, made of brushwood, and hopped neatly over.

He went methodically round the course, knocking off several poles but never hesitating until he found himself facing the last fence, the dreaded triple bar.

Never in his life had he been asked to jump such an imposing looking obstacle, and his canter became slower and slower as he approached it, ears twitching apprehensively. He was trotting now, and Jane felt sure that he was going to refuse.

'Come on, Bundle!' She dug her heels in hopefully but without any result. Bundle slowed down to a walk, and the onlookers almost held their breath in anticipation.

'Bundle, please!' Jane sounded desperate, and Bundle suddenly hesitated no longer. Swishing his tail, he marched firmly up to the fence and straight through it, pushing off the poles with his chest.

The crowd was delighted, clapping loudly, and even Jane, mortified though she was, had to laugh.

'It's the prize giving now,' said David. 'You were the last to jump, Jane — if you can call it jumping,' he added with a grin. 'That must be Lady Westhaven giving the prizes.'

Jane looked up to see the mother of the two little boys standing beside the table with all the cups and trophies on it, and watched with interest as the various prizes were handed out. At last there was only the silver cup left, and there was a sudden silence.

Lady Westhaven picked up the cup, smiled, and said, 'There are so many prizes for achievement — for jumping and bending and all that sort thing of — that I decided to present this cup, not for achievement but for character. I decided to give it to the kindest pony I saw. I have watched all the ponies very carefully, and I have no doubt at all that I am doing the right thing in presenting this cup to Bundle.'

Hardly able to believe her ears, Jane was pushed forward to the table and was just shaking hands with Lady Westhaven when there was a roar of laughter from the crowd.

Bundle, twitching his reins out of Susan's hand, had followed his mistress up to the table and now, reaching over her shoulder, he pushed his nose hopefully into his very own cup.